AF506272

IMPERIALISMS

IMPERIALISMS

HISTORICAL AND LITERARY INVESTIGATIONS, 1500–1900

Edited by
Balachandra Rajan and Elizabeth Sauer

From Empire to Federation

by
Anthony Pagden

First published 2004 by
PALGRAVE MACMILLAN™
175 Fifth Avenue, New York, N.Y. 10010 and
Houndmills, Basingstoke, Hampshire, England RG21 6XS
Companies and representatives throughout the world

PALGRAVE MACMILLAN is the global academic imprint of the Palgrave Macmillan division of St. Martin's Press, LLC and of Palgrave Macmillan Ltd. Macmillan® is a registered trademark in the United States, United Kingdom and other countries. Palgrave is a registered trademark in the European Union and other countries.

ISBN 1–4039–6520–X

Library of Congress Cataloging-in-Publication Data
Imperialisms: historical and literary investigations, 1500–1900 / edited by Balachandra Rajan and Elizabeth Sauer.
    p. cm.
    "From empire to freedom by Anthony Pagden" included as afterword.
    Includes bibliographical references and index.
    ISBN 1–4039–6520–X (alk. paper)
    1. World politics—16th century. 2. World politics—17th century.
3. World politics—18th century. 4. Imperialism—History—16th century.
5. Imperialism—History—17th century. 6. Imperialism—History—18th century. 7. Imperialism in literature. I. Rajan, Balachandra. II. Sauer, Elizabeth, 1964– III. Pagden, Anthony.

D32.I48 2004
325'.32'09—dc22   2004044432

A catalogue record for this book is available from the British Library.

Design by Newgen Imaging Systems (P) Ltd., Chennai, India.

First edition: October 2004
10   9   8   7   6   5   4   3   2   1

Printed in the United States of America.

CONTENTS

Part III
Early Imperialisms: East and West — 127

Part IV
English and French Imperialisms: Eighteenth and Nineteenth Centuries — 185

Part V
German Imperial Philosophies and Practices — 217

CONTENTS

INTRODUCTION:
IMPERIALISMS: EARLY MODERN TO PREMODERNIST

*Balachandra Rajan and
Elizabeth Sauer*

I

In researching imperialisms, postcolonial critics and historians have concentrated on retrieving subjected cultures from the stereotypes in which they were embedded. Scholarship on empire has been much less engaged with characterizing cultures of dominance, in part because the sheer weight of dominance has precluded consideration of its varieties. Moreover, postcolonialists tend to nourish the proposition that the nuances of exploitation matter little to the exploited. In the words of V. K. Krishna Menon, defence minister for India in the early 1960s, asking a subject people what imperialism it prefers is like asking a fish whether it would rather be fried in margarine or butter. There is enough in this quip to make distinctions between imperialisms seem a matter of scholarly rather than real importance. Yet, notwithstanding their similarities, imperialisms do differ, often substantially, and have their individual ways of articulating these differences. Each imperial nation devises its own characteristic propaganda and separates itself emphatically from other nations and empires if only to advertise its special entitlement to power. Even today the propaganda for benevolent liberal imperialisms (by scholars such as Niall Ferguson)[1] demonstrates that imperialist fictions of self-justification are still alive and still being invented.

Imperialisms are formed and written in relation to specific cultural histories. Moreover, imperial powers construct not only subjected sites but competing imperialisms in order to arrive at images of themselves.

Scholars have yet to examine these complexities adequately. The purpose of this cross-disciplinary book is to explore various early imperialisms, their practices, their convergences and differences, and their attitudes to coexisting or competing imperialisms, thus bringing out the varieties and nuances of dominance.

Theories of Empire, 1450–1800,[2] an important collection of reprinted essays that provides an overview of the field of early imperialisms, has shown us that the field is anything but overworked. Anthony Pagden's *Lords of all the World*[3] remains the best scholarly work on this topic, but its primary concern is with ideologies rather than discourses and the enmeshing of culture with those discourses. Professor Pagden himself has acknowledged the need for further study by generously providing this volume with its closing essay. *Lords of all the World* focuses on the Atlantic theater and on English, French, and Spanish imperialisms within that theater. A recently published volume on multiple imperialisms, *Empires: Perspectives from Archaeology and History,*[4] concentrates mainly on ancient imperialisms. Neither book examines the relationship between Asia and early modern empires.[5]

A book characterizing imperial ideologies and practices in relation to their different cultural histories and in terms of their changing narratives of nationhood is too large in scope for any single scholar to produce. Such a book is inherently a multiauthor work but one that is badly needed. The difficulties of compiling a study of this nature and of identifying and analysing the main sites of imperialism are obvious and can be formidable; but there has never been a more propitious time for such an undertaking.

Consisting of literary analyses, contextual studies, historical essays, and case studies, *Imperialisms* is divided into five chronologically arranged sections, which encourage cross-examinations of conversant and competing imperialisms over a period of four centuries. As the imperialisms with which audiences are most likely to be familiar, European and particularly British imperialisms generally serve as points of reference throughout the volume. The contributors to *Imperialisms* demonstrate that imperialist powers fashion themselves in relation to ideas about nationhood, in relation to rival empires from which they discriminate themselves, and in relation to territories for which they compete.

One of the many challenges faced by the contributors to this volume is to annotate the terms "empire" and "imperialism," the meanings of which remain in flux throughout the centuries. "Empire" in an early modern context originally referred to a territorial and legal formation held together by structures of differentiation and containment. The significance of the term was inextricably entangled with the language of theology, colonialism, nationalism, republicanism (classical and Christian), economics, Orientalism, geopolitics, and even anti-imperialism, as the essays in this collection demonstrate.[6] Identifying the realm of England as an empire in the *Act of Appeals* of 1533, Henry VIII founded an English nation in which imperial politics were implicitly internalized.[7] The nation-empire was also a child of the Protestant Reformation and of a chain of events that, in the case of England, led to its theological independence from the Holy Roman Empire, a secession crucial to the process of its own self-formation.[8] The event was double-edged, obliging imperial discourse in early modern England to pit its unifying compulsions against its separatist origins. The empire was thus precariously built on recognitions of difference, domination, and, paradoxically, even of the need for toleration by writers who nevertheless sought to provide these unstable foundations with a sacred authorizing force.

The collusion between commerce and imperialism further complicated this already vexed notion of empire. As Klaus E. Knorr demonstrates, mercantilism arose from propositions suggesting that entrenched patterns of trade were needed to safeguard national identities.[9] Yet, while commerce was presented rhetorically as an alternative to empire, it was in fact often preliminary to territorial possession. Also informing the development of national, imperial identities was an international context within which nations tended to define their claims to distinctiveness by underlining their differences from each other. The English who seceded from the Catholic church did not have the same view of their imperial mission as the Spanish who perceived themselves as the military arm of that church. Nations vying for new territories did not have the same perceptions of those territories, and did not take the same view of the responsibilities that accompanied dominance. During the course of these encounters, imperial nations differentiated themselves from each other in ideology and in rhetoric and in the interweaving of both into their construction of an imperial mission for which each nation regarded itself as singularly qualified. As imperial powers competed with each other, distinctive-nesses became submerged to some extent in common perceptions of the sites for which they were competing. Despite that submerging, they were still able and eager to write texts of dominance that maintained an individual authorship.

II

This volume offers various points of entry into the subject of comparative imperialisms. The first group of essays, titled "Early Modern European Imperialisms" (part I), investigates several sites of imperialist contestation within the European political theater, a theater that includes Portugal, Spain, and England. Contributors to this section offer case studies of literary texts, which they examine in relation to colonial histories and the political and religious ideologies of rival imperialist powers. The opening essay by Shankar Raman (chapter 1) offers an analysis of *Auto da Índia*, a sixteenth-century play by the renowned court dramatist, Gil Vicente, in relation to the Portuguese voyages of discovery. Tristão da Cunha's 1506 journey to India became the occasion for this somewhat ribald domestic comedy that was enacted for the royal court in 1509, and which sought to expose some of the social and political tensions that complicated Portugal's colonial involvement with India.

Examining the relationship between colonial events and their literary representation for early modern Portugal also sheds light on the variations among different European colonial projects. The contrast with England and in turn with England's own rivalry with an imperialist Spain is particularly instructive. As Barbara Fuchs demonstrates in the second essay (chapter 2), Edmund Spenser's *A View of the Present State of Ireland* and *The Faerie Queene* figure significantly in a comparative study of England and Spain as colonial actors. The insistence by the English on their *difference* from the Spanish—despite their replication of Spain's colonial exploits—begs the question about the nature of the distinction between these rival nations and about their representation of those differences. The third essay (chapter 3) relocates such tensions in an early eighteenth-century framework. Robert Markley draws on the revisionist work of Andre Gunder Frank and Kenneth Pomeranz in establishing a context for a postcolonial rereading of Jonathan Swift's *Gulliver's Travels* as a literary text that registers profound anxieties about European power, identity, and religion in a world invulnerable to European claims. Even as Swift satirizes the imperial excesses of England, he has no "realistic" vocabulary to describe Asian kingdoms that are contemptuous of Western theology, trade, and technology; rather Swift converts the Far East into a fantasy realm where challenges to British nationalism and Protestant triumphalism are evaded instead of being confronted.

As Raman's and Markley's essays remind us, the European imperial vision extended beyond the Americas. While it had never been a threat to Europe, India in particular became a major site of intra-European competition,[10] especially for the Netherlands, Portugal, and France. Part II, "Early Modern Europeans on India," examines the conflicts among European nations and trade rivals in India, a nation that nevertheless managed to encounter the West as an equal for three centuries and to maintain its culture under imperial subjection into the era of its independence. Dorothy Figueria's essay (chapter 4) on Italian and Portuguese accounts of Southern India analyzes the influential classical and religious constructions of the Indian as the racial "Other," a construction underwritten by the classical binary of the civilized/barbarian and its Christian reconfiguration *polis/ecclesia*. These polarities feature prominently in works by Italians, including Nicolo de'Conti (1448) and Ludovico de Varthema (1510), as well as in those of Portuguese writers like Tome Pires (1515) whose emphasis on racial indicators reinforces the Portuguese obsession with purity of blood and fears of sexual chaos.

Britain, the most important of imperial actors, defined its role through a prolonged and complex involvement with India that gave it a character distinct from other imperialisms.[11] In chapter 5 (part II), Paul Stevens explores the coinciding emergence of the modern English nation state and India's Moghul empire in a study of travel literature, factors of the East India Company, and contemporary political theoretical perspectives. Thereafter, "The British and the Dutch in India, 1751–99" presents a comparative investigation of the British and Dutch presence in India in the eighteenth century, particularly in terms off the collusion between commerce and empire. Interrelated yet different, the various trade practices of the two nations examined by Florence D'Souza resulted by the early nineteenth century, in England's virtually complete supremacy in India at the expense of Dutch imperial and commercial influence. The greater autonomy exercised by and sometimes rampant in the East India Company's ranks may have contributed to this result. Also important was the "education" of the East India Company's operatives at institutions such as Fort William and Haileybury. By the early nineteenth century, other foreign competitors for India had withdrawn, leaving the British claim unchallenged. Nevertheless India remained a significant site for articulations by the imperial imagination of European expansion and imperialism, as shown by select essays in parts IV and V.

Nearly all studies of imperialism in the West seem to assume that imperialism is a Western invention. Influential studies on imperialism have tended as a result to be restricted to the Atlantic theater. But most empires before Columbus were not of Western origin. Even in the five centuries after Columbus, simplifyingly perceived as an era of Western dominance, the Ottoman empire abutted on Western imperialisms, rivaling or surpassing them in its duration and reach. In these circumstances, a comparative study of imperialisms should include Eastern as well as Western imperialisms, and should scrutinize postcolonial protocols in examining imperialisms, protocols that seem to be based exclusively on Western examples. At this stage in scholarship, we should be concerned with differentiating imperialisms, as well as with assembling them under unifying tropes. As shown by contributions to part III, which includes studies of Islamic empires and Europeans in the Far East, a comparative examination of imperialisms in the East and West is an important step in this direction.[12] Daniel Goffman and Christopher Stroop's "Empire as Composite: The Ottoman Polity and the Typology of Dominion" (chapter 7) provocatively reveals how the Ottomans fit into and modify theoretical models of empire, and how Ottoman imperialism influenced the development of the European concept of empire and shaped attitudes toward the multiple others that they encountered in these worlds. Nabil I. Matar's "The Maliki Imperialism of Ahmad al-Mansur" (chapter 8) exposes another aspect of Eastern empires. Matar discusses the invasion of Sudan by Morocco in 1591 as an act of "imperialism" that historians of Islam have largely neglected. The justifications for the action, this essay demonstrates, resemble those used to condone Western imperialisms: race and religion.

"The British and the Dutch in India, 1751–99," to which we have already referred, also provides material on Dutch commercial practices in the East Indies. The Dutch believed that conquest assisted trade. But trade was their paramount interest, as is evident in Robert Markley's account of their abjection before the Japanese. By way of difference, France construed its mission in the Far East as civilizing rather than commercial. Conversion, as Patricia M. Pelley shows, was the first step in a process that was cultural as well as religious. Commerce was the natural accompaniment to strengthening cultural links between distant peoples.

The brief essay that follows, "A Note on Further India" by Balachandra Rajan, lies outside the chronological boundaries of this book. We include this account because "further India" prefigures some of the issues this book raises and because the Indian presence in South East Asia differs instructively from later French, Dutch, and Portuguese presences. The essay also bears on current discussions of empires that avoid being imperialist and looks forward to Anthony Pagden's concluding study in this volume on the legacy of empires through to our own time.

French and English contributions to the rhetoric of imperialism are featured in the comparative studies in part IV (chapters 10 and 11).[13] The first study offers a textual framework for the English (later British) and French expansion into the New World. Jonathan Hart focuses on Canadian history, but extends his investigation to include the Americas and European countries examined earlier in this book, such as Portugal, the Netherlands, and Spain. Taking this collection into the Victorian period, the second contribution to part IV, Linda Hutcheon and Michael Hutcheon's "Empire and Opera: Displacement and Anxiety: Empire and Opera," assesses the role of opera in the construction of stereotypes of imperial rivals both on the European stage and in the political theater. This chapter considers in particular Giacomo Meyerbeer's opera *L'Africaine* (1865) and Clément Philibert Léo Delibes's *Lakmé* (1883) in which the imperial arena is the world of Hindu India. The imperial forces, however, are not French at all, but rather France's imperial competitors—both historical (Portugal) and contemporary (Britain), suggesting that such rivals also served as defining entities for empires like France.

The chronological limits for this volume tighten the book but also provide sufficient space for the identity statements of the world's major imperialisms—British, Spanish, Portuguese, Dutch, and French—to be adequately displayed and considered in more than one theater of competition. German imperial thought remains to be studied. It is extraordinarily in advance of the event: France and Britain were contending for empires when Germany was still short of becoming a nation state. German imaginings of otherness are uniquely in the theater of the mind. One trend in this theater is discussed by Sabine Wilke in part V, "German Imperial Philosophies and Practices." In chapter 13, "The Colonial Pedagogy of Imperial Germany," Wilke attends to German precolonial fantasy literature exemplified by the educational practices in the colonies that Germany was to acquire much later. The strongly paternalistic strain in these fantasies encourages a masochistic self-indulgence, masking imperialism's deep-seated exploitativeness, so that the guardian can see himself as suffering for the benefit of the ward. The White Man's Burden is a familiar version of this fantasy.

Another interesting trend in German imperial thought is the philosophic one, which, in accordance with the dialectical pursuit, calls not for the repudiation of the other but for its translation into the self. The discovery that the European language tree had many of its deepest roots in Sanskrit led to an intense effort to incorporate the Indian other into the evolving Germanic identity. Hegel opposes this effort by his insistence that India represents an obsolete stage in the Idea's realization, one that is to be left behind rather than taken in.

Historicizing the other as Hegel does is a familiar imperialist strategy, and one that Kamakashi P. Murti explores in "Germany's 'Orient' " (chapter 12), a study of the German contribution to an emerging Orientalist discourse about the "other" that would underwrite imperialism in the East. She suggests that there is an argumentative coherence in German thinking about India notwithstanding its apparent diversity. The Sleeping Beauty view of a classical India that can be awakened only by the Germanic kiss is implicitly dismissive. It suggests an India that is unable to make use of its own past, leaving that use to higher civilizations. The Hegelian "turn" takes the dismissiveness further by arguing that the beauty is not worth awakening. German thinking about India presents itself as driven by a passion to revitalize ancient roots; it also deploys itself so as to reinforce the supremacy of the advanced West over the "primitive," "degenerate" East. Germany thus supplied other European nations, particularly Britain, with a justification for their existing colonial rule and future colonial activity in India.

Paul Stevens in chapter 5 finds the imperialist historicizing of otherness by Hegel at work in British perceptions of the Mughals. Vasco da Gama's voyage to India, which the Old Man bewails in *The Lusiads*, can be treated as expressing deep-seated doubts about the imperial mission (see Raman, chapter 1 in this volume). Alternatively, it can be regarded as reducing those doubts to unimportance when Da Gama's voyage is seen as a journey, not so much from Lisbon to Calicut as from a medieval to an early modern world order. In German thought the idea of India can be treated as an origin crucial to any vision of the Germanic future, or as a beginning to be absorbed by the narrative it generates. German thinking about India veers between these possibilities. It cannot be regarded as homogeneous though, as already noted, its overall effect and even its internal controversies strengthen the dismissive constructions for which James Mill's *History of British India* provides a foundation.

In investigating and interrogating imperialisms, contributors throughout this volume are attentive to the rhetoric of imperialism as well as to imperial ideologies and cultural and territorial histories of imperial nations. Historians and literary scholars bring their specific strengths into this overall awareness, and in keeping with the aims of the book, have made connections among the various imperialisms where possible. *Imperialisms* seeks to be distinctive in the attention it gives to the intersecting discourses of imperialism as well as to the characteristic inflections with which each imperialism marks its discourse. The personality of each imperial power discussed here exhibits an interplay—distinctive both in its initiating drives and its subsequent development—among religion, conquest, commerce, conversion, settlement, and representations of difference. Far from being exhaustive, this list merely indicates some of the parameters that connect the various imperialisms in this project and ultimately justify the use of the plural number in the title of the volume.

Finally, all the imperialisms studied in this volume are territorially based. If we proceed to consider non-territorial imperialisms, our ways of grappling with them may have to be reinvented to cope with fluidities that evade conventional analysis. Empires that are not imperialist are the subject of an increasing number of discussions that exist side by side with calls for a higher imperialism that will be both unchallengeable and benevolent. Anthony Pagden's concluding essay examines the legacy of and connections among the various incarnations of empire—European and non-European—through to the rise of the nation-state and federation. But the narrative also turns back on itself, Padgen judges, as we confront the "liberal imperialism" of the current day and address the need for a revisionary turn in the comparative study of empire. In analyzing imperialisms from the early modern era on, then, this volume seeks to provide approaches and guidelines for a conversation that is timely and vigorous.

NOTES

We gratefully acknowledge our indebtedness to the contributors for making possible this broad-ranging study of early imperialisms; to Farideh Koohi-Kamali, Editor at Palgrave-Macmillan, for her support in seeing this work go to press; to the anonymous reader of the press for an astute assessment of the manuscript; to the Social Sciences and Humanities Research Council of Canada and the Office of the Vice President of Research at Brock University for financial assistance and release time to conduct research on early modernisms; and to Barbara MacDonald Buetter for valuable assistance in preparing this book for publication.

1. Professor Niall C. Ferguson's latest book, *Empire: The Rise and Demise of the British World Order and Its Lessons for Global Power* (New York: Basic Books, 2003), is a comprehensive history of how the British came to rule the world. Ferguson credits the British empire for serving as the chief promoter of progressive thought around the globe for much of the past two centuries, and he suggests that the United States has now assumed that responsibility.

2. David Armitage, *Theories of Empire, 1450–1800* (Aldershot: Ashgate, 1998). The collection consists of 15 essays originally published between 1949 and 1995.

3. Anthony Pagden, *Lords of all the World: Ideologies of Empire in Spain, Britain and France c. 1500–c. 1800* (New Haven: Yale University Press, 1995).

4. *Empires: Perspectives from Archaeology and History*, ed. Susan E. Alcock et al. (Cambridge: Cambridge University Press, 2001).

5. Important opening studies in this context are K. M. Panikkar's *Asia and Western Dominance: A Survey of the Vasco da Gama Epoch of Asian History, 1498–1945*, new ed. (London, Allen & Unwin, 1965; New York: Collier Books, 1969); K. N. Chaudhari, *Asia before Europe: Economy and Civilisation of the Indian Ocean from the Rise of Islam to 1750* (Cambridge: Cambridge University Press, 1990); and Richard Seymour Hall, *Empires of the Monsoon: A History of the Indian Ocean and its Invaders* (London: Harper Collins, 1996).

6. On the distinction between empire as "untrammeled authoritarian dominion" and the non-imperial republic, which allowed for the increase of empire, see David Armitage, "The Cromwellian Protectorate and the Languages of Empire," *The Historical Journal* 35.3 (1992): 550–51. On the various components of early imperialisms, see Balachandra Rajan and Elizabeth Sauer, "Introduction," *Milton and the Imperial Vision* (Pittsburgh: Duquesne University Press, 1999), 1–22.

7. Act of Appeals of 1533 (24 Henry VIII c. 12) qtd. in OED (Oxford, 1933; rpt. 1961), 5:85.

8. Klaus E. Knorr, *British Colonial Theories, 1570–1850* (Toronto: University of Toronto Press, 1944).

9. Linda Gregerson challenges Benedict Anderson's distinction between the "inherently limited and sovereign" nation and the colonial expansionary empire (*The Reformation of the Subject: Spenser, Milton, and the English Protestant Epic* [Cambridge: Cambridge University Press, 1995], 228). See Anderson, *Imagined Communities: Reflections on the Origin and Spread of Nationalism* (London: Verso, 1983), 15. On the relationship between imperialism and nationalism, most often regarded as a nineteenth-century development, see Timothy Bennan, "The National Longing for Form," *Nation and Narration*, ed. Homi K. Bhabha (New York: Routledge, 1990), esp. 58–59.

10. Edward Said, *Orientalism* (New York: Pantheon Books, 1978), 75.

11. Scholarship on this engagement is profuse but consists largely of closely contextualized case studies which resist the proposition that the engagement yields a history. Balachandra Rajan's *Under Western Eyes: India from Milton to Macaulay* (Durham: Duke University Press, 1999) offers a canon-centered view of this history. Kate Teltscher's *India Inscribed: European and British Writing on India, 1600–1800*

(New Delhi: Oxford University Press, 1995) is non-canonical and covers a similar chronological span. Sara Suleri's *The Rhetoric of English India* (Chicago: University of Chicago Press, 1992) is important for its cautionary guidances. Also see Srinivas Aravamudan, *Tropicopolitans: Colonialism and Agency, 1688–1804* (Durham: Duke University Press, 1999); and Shankar Raman, *Framing "India": The Colonial Imaginary in Early Modern Culture* (Stanford: Stanford University Press, 2001).

12. Among the best scholarly studies on this subject are Nabil Matar, *Islam in Britain, 1558–1685* (Cambridge: Cambridge University Press, 1998); Barbara Fuchs, *Mimesis and Empire: The New World, Islam and European Identities* (Cambridge: Cambridge University Press, 2001); and Daniel Goffman, *The Ottoman Empire and Early Modern Europe* (Cambridge: Cambridge University Press, 2002). Also important is John Michael Archer's *Old Worlds: Egypt, Southwest Asia, India, and Russia in Early Modern English Writing* (Stanford: Stanford University Press, 2001); for a list of recent criticism of the figure of the Jew and the Moor in the early modern world, see the Introduction: "Para-Colonial Studies," in *Old Worlds* 197, n. 54.

13. On the development of a related imperial culture in Britain and France during the Romantic period, see Saree Makdisi, *Romantic Imperialism: Universal Empire and the Culture of Modernity* (Cambridge: Cambridge University Press, 1998).

PART I

EARLY MODERN EUROPEAN IMPERIALISMS: LITERARY REPRESENTATIONS

"THE SHIP COMES WELL-LADEN": COURT POLITICS, COLONIALISM, AND CUCKOLDRY IN GIL VICENTE'S AUTO DA ÍNDIA

Shankar Raman

I

Wherein of antres vast and deserts idle,
Rough quarries, rocks, hills whose heads touch heaven,
It was my hint to speak—such was the process:
And of the cannibals that each other eat,
The Anthropophagi, and men whose heads
Do grow beneath their shoulders. This to hear
Would Desdemona seriously incline;
But still the house affairs would draw her thence,
Which ever as she could with haste dispatch,
She'd come again, and with a greedy ear
Devour up my discourse...

—William Shakespeare, *Othello* (1.3.139–49)[1]

Through such stories does Othello, famously, "beguile" Desdemona "of herself" (1.3.66). While editions of the play usually note that Othello's "travels' history" borrows from Pliny's *Naturalis Historia* and Mandeville's *Travels*—both regularly reprinted through the seventeenth century—what has been perhaps insufficiently stressed is just how antiquarian these details are, even in 1604. Arguably, Othello's "conjuration and ... mighty magic" (1.3.92) is self-consciously outdated, especially when contrasted with the play's reliance on contemporary texts such as Richard Knowles's *General History of the Turks* (1603) for its depiction of the Turco-Venetian conflict that frames its action. The quotidian realities of discovery and conquest often lacked, after all, the wonder and magic so central to medieval and classical accounts of unseen worlds. No surprise, then, that even contemporaneous adventurers such as Sir Walter Ralegh felt compelled to confirm the marvels of the past.[2] The theatrical debunking of Mandeville and Pliny would have to await the appearance of Richard Brome's *The Antipodes* (1636), a play that nonetheless shares *Othello*'s belief in the power of such stories—, precisely, *as* stories, for only as dramatic fictions capable of shaping reality do they retain their efficacy.

One might add, too, that such fictions were necessary if English adventuring abroad was to be sustained in its early phases. For the wondrous tales play a compensatory role, filling in for the relative paucity of real achievement in a field opened up and still dominated by England's Iberian precursors. In this domain, the English still seemed not much more than interlopers. It was thus with some justification that Bartolemé Leonardo de Argensola belittled Ralegh's illustrious predecessor, Sir Francis Drake, after the latter's famous circumnavigation of the globe in 1579–80: according to the Spanish historiographer, Drake's "Cruelties and Robberies might well gain him the Title of the greatest of the Pyrates, in those remotest parts, as he had in *Europe*."[3] Indeed, a dominant mode of English participation in the proto-colonial voyages was piracy, albeit tacitly backed both by the Crown and individuals of note in court and City. Not only had the queen profited greatly from Drake's plundering of Spanish shipping, but the ultimately successful East India Company voyages of the early seventeenth century had been preceded by earlier independent attempts to follow Drake's model and reach the fabled Spice Islands. Edward Fenton's 1582–83 voyage was backed by such luminaries as the earl of Leicester and Sir Francis Walsingham, while James Lancaster's 1591–94 voyage was promoted by London merchants, both groups hoping for privateering gains akin to those achieved by Drake.[4] When *Shakespeare in Love* has the eponymous hero provisionally name his newest creation *Romeo and Ethel the Pirate's Daughter*, it hits close to the ways in which the English were actually making their mark in the emerging world order.

In retrospect, of course, English (and Dutch) colonial belatedness would most radically determine the shape of the new world order. A global mercantile empire—not a monarchical one—would be the legacy of delayed entry. As Sanjay Subrahmanyam succinctly states: "When, in the late sixteenth-century, a London-based venture attempted to enter Euro-Asian trade, it was a Company, a quasi-private entity with state sanction and some diplomatic privileges, that did so—and not the state itself. Similarly, Dutch trade to Asia—although sanctioned by the States General—was conducted after 1602 by an ostensibly autonomous body, the Verenigde Oost-Indische Compagnie."[5] In contrast, trade for the Portuguese was subject from the outset to royal control. As early as 1373, there is evidence of the Portuguese Crown's direct interest in trade. Not only were trading voyages led by individuals and groups deriving their authority from the Crown, but they also involved a number of royal ships (*naus del-Rei*). According to the testimony of Fernão Lopes's *Crónica de Dom Fernando*, the Portuguese ruler (r. 1367–83) included a number of his own vessels in a commercial company in the last year of his reign. Thus, as Subrahmanyam further notes, "the epithet used by the French King François to describe Dom Manuel (r. 1495–1521) in the early sixteenth century—the 'grocer king' (*le roi épicier*)—had its roots going back to the early fifteenth century, and can perhaps even be traced as far back as Dom Fernando.... ."[6]

That *Imperialisms* should take English imperialism as, so to speak, its yardstick underscores the fact of England's dominance in later centuries. But it is salutary to remind ourselves not only of England's relative insignificance but of different conditions of discovery and conquest in the early modern colonial domain. Just as England's subsequent rise often overshadows the histories of its colonial competitors, so too does Shakespeare's status in the literary world relegate to the shadows not only his own contemporaries in England, but even more so those whose work emanated from other European centers of power. Among the neglected is Portugal's greatest dramatist, Gil Vicente.

Hard though it may seem for us today to credit the extravagant praise of the nineteenth-century Portuguese historian Alexandre Herculiano—who asserted that there was nothing before Vicente that would "foreshadow the sovereign genius, the Plautus, the Shakespeare of Portugal that was Gil Vicente"[7]—the sixteenth-century dramatist nonetheless ranks with Luís de Camões and Fernando Pessoa as one of the shining stars of Portugal's national canon—not least because he was the first playwright to write in Portuguese rather than Castilian. And it is through one of Vicente's plays, *Auto da Índia*, this essay suggests, that we can glimpse the complex tensions and struggles in the royal court that constituted the crucible of Portuguese imperialism.

II

Given Vicente's exalted place in Portuguese literary history, it is surprising that we are not even sure who he was. Scholarly consensus identifies the dramatist with the eponymous goldsmith employed at the royal court, whose most famous work is the beautiful Belem monstrance (wrought—Aubrey Bell tells us—from the first tribute of gold from the East). His plays survive in written form thanks to his son who produced and edited a *Compilação* some twenty years after his death—though even this collection does not appear to contain the totality of his dramatic output. Thought to have been born around 1465, Vicente came to prominence in Dom João II's reign (whose wife Leonor remained his main patroness after the king's death), but produced his major work for the courts of Manuel and João III between 1505 and 1531, a period generally considered the culmination of both the Portuguese Renaissance and Portuguese colonialism. He died around 1536 or 1537. His oeuvre consists of short plays staged at court, ranging from the twelve major *Farsas* (farces or comedies)— of which *Auto da Índia* is an early example—to religious autos and tragicomedies.[8]

As this brief biography suggests, Vicente's life and work were closely bound to the Portuguese court and its vicissitudes. Yet we should not make the mistake of assuming that this arena was a unified one. Just as European colonial presence in the early modern era was fragmented and uneven, so too were the individual European proto-national formations themselves internally divided. Far from representing a monolithic nationalist outlook, Portuguese colonial endeavours— much like those of its competitors—emerged from a force-field of competing interests and pressures. The conflicts were not primarily between the lower and upper classes; rather, they appear largely to be struggles among elements in the upper classes. Between 1300 and 1500 "Portugal witnessed a complex struggle," Subrahmanyam points out, "between centralising tendencies inherent in the monarchy, and the resistance of other privileged groups: the Church, the Military Orders, and the nobility."[9] Even as the voyages of discovery received their primary direction from the Portuguese court, the court itself expressed an often precarious balance among a number of different factions, of which the king and his immediate retinue was just one.

To these internal divisions need to be added the complicated relationships between Portugal and its Mediterranean neighbors. For one, the memory of Spanish interference in questions of Portuguese succession remained fresh. The bitter struggles between adherents of the so-called Castilian party—the territorial nobility and clergy that attempted to proclaim Juan I of Castile king of Portugal upon the death of Pedro I in 1367—and the future João I (Pedro's bastard son and Master of the Order of Avis, who garnered the support of the urban aristocracy and artisanal classes) continued to exert influence on court politics. For another, the conflict with the North African Moorish powers, who had been ousted from the Iberian peninsula through the long *Reconquista*, was ongoing. Indeed, Portuguese obsession with neighboring Moslem powers would result, ironically, in Portugal's ceding its sovereignty in 1580 to Spain's Philip II, after King Sebiastian's disastrous defeat (and demise) at the hands of the Moors in the battle of El-Ksar-el-Kaber. To these diverse struggles in the Portuguese court—both those emerging out of the past and those to come—Gil Vicente's *Auto da Índia* bears witness.

And yet, at first glance, this slender farce, not much more than 500 lines long, seems an unlikely text to bear the burdens of sixteenth-century Portuguese history. Ostensibly performed for his patroness—"a muyta catholica Rayna dona Lianor"—in 1509, Vicente's deceptively simple courtly entertainment concerns the domestic goings-on that ensue upon a Portuguese merchant's departure to India in 1506, as part of a fleet commanded by Tristão da Cunha. Eager for her husband's departure, his wife—ironically named Constança—immediately begins to dally with two lovers, an impoverished "escudeiro" or squire named Lemos and a bombastic Spanish soldier, Juan de Zamora, successfully playing off one against the other. The mouse play abruptly ends when the cat returns in 1509—the year of both the performance and the fleet's homecoming after an apparently successful and profitable voyage to the East. Vicente's farce ends with the cuckolded husband and his irrepressible wife going down together to the port to see the "well-laden ship," "a nao… bem carregada" (513).[10]

This brief summary may well make Vicente's farce seem rather a slight object. But the festive and playful exterior nevertheless raises the specter of a threatened domestic space and its potential violation. The merchant's wife, identified at one point as "luz de todo Portogal" [light of all Portugal, 124], functions as the site upon which a class-based and proto-national competition is enacted. For instance, the "threadbare squire" [escudeyro… çafado, 211–12] Lemos seems to stand for a declined, perhaps once landed, Portuguese nobility whose position has been partly usurped by a rising, mercantile class, of whom the husband is representative. The return of her "namorado perdido" [lost lover, 209], as the wife calls Lemos, thus marks a comic *ressentiment*, whereby the displaced squirearchy gains a measure of revenge by invading the bed possessed by the departed merchant Master. The reversal certainly echoes the resurgence of the traditional nobility in Dom Manuel's reign after its rough treatment at the hands of Manuel's predecessor, João II. Upon accession to the throne, the king "at once pardoned the nobles who had been exiled ten years before—for conspiring treasonously against João II—returning fifty properties to the new duke of Bragança. He made the nobility into a court circle, recognising seventy-two families.... Many of these were established in Lisbon or the neighbourhood, receiving grants or pensions from the royal household or the military Orders."[11]

The already complex relationship between a reinvigorated territorial nobility closely associated with the new monarch and the urban bourgeoisie and artisanal classes, who had been the beneficiaries of João II's drive to consolidate royal power, was further modulated by the long shadow of Spain. Thus, the presence in *Auto da Índia* of a Spanish courtly lover, Juan de Zamora, encodes an intra-Iberian tussle for control both over Portugal itself and over the newly discovered lands east and west. This struggle marked every succession crisis in Portugal from the fifteenth through the seventeenth centuries. But it was less a national struggle in the modern sense than a complicated series of responses by different noble houses to a monarchy bent upon asserting its authority.[12] The correspondence between the Braganças and the Spanish royal couple, Ferdinand and Isabella—"clearly pointing," as Livermore tells us, "to an intention to strengthen the Castilian grip on the Portuguese succession"[13]—led finally to the downfall of the former, the most powerful of territorial nobles. And the need to deal carefully with Portugal's dangerous and rich Iberian neighbor left its mark on tricky negotiations such as those that led to the famous 1494 Treaty of Tordesillas, as well, finally and most obviously, to the provisional absorption of Portugal into the Spanish realm in the wake of the El-Ksar-el-Kaber disaster.

In *Auto da Índia*, the debased courtly hero, Juan da Zamora, stands for both the Spanish threat and its limits. Indeed, the threat is even more specific: while the Spaniard names himself in the play, the printed text attributes his lines to the "Castelhano," thereby emphasizing the particular importance of Castile to early modern Portugal. If, as Anthony Lappin shrewdly observes, Vicente's Castilian doesn't quite succeed in gaining entry into the desired space of the wife's bedroom, he does nonetheless, in mock-epic and mock-biblical terms, threaten entry from the street below her window, barely stopping himself (or so he claims) from "pulling down the house" and "raging war" like Samson. He bombastically swears to "burn down the house" [quemar la casa, 331] and "destroy the world" [destruyr el mundo, 332] even if his defeat means being "drawn through the town" [arrastado . . . por la cuidad, 323–24] like Hector by Achilles.[14] Thus, on at least two dimensions, the domestic spaces of the play—the house and the bedroom—invoke the tensions constitutive of public spaces surrounding the play-world: the shifting balance of power between different class-factions within the Portuguese court; and the complex game of thrones Portugal was engaged in throughout the period with its more powerful Iberian neighbor.

I will return shortly to the intricacies of the Manueline court. But in order to establish the persistence of an anxiety over Portugal and its identity let us jump ahead to a point at some historical remove from Gil Vicente's *Auto da Índia* and consider briefly the unsettling place of Vasco da Gama's inaugural voyage to India in Luís de Camões' great epic, the 1572 *Os Lusíadas*. Embraced by the Portuguese, to cite Richard Helgerson, as "the prime literary representation of who they have been, who they are, and who they should be,"[15] Camões's poem is celebrated even today through street signs and monuments in Lisbon. The relevant moment concerns a point at which the epic celebration of Portuguese expansion Eastward receives an unexpected check: the much-discussed episode at the end of the fourth Canto, in which the Old Man of Restelo appears at the very moment of Vasco da Gama's departure to deliver a long harangue against the "glória de mandar" or the vainglory of command. In a characteristically syncretist manner the Old Man coordinates the worlds of Bible and epic to assault voyage and voyagers:

> O, but you [are] the true heir of that madman whose sin and disobedi-ence not only put you in this exile and sad absence from the supreme realm, but deprived you entirely of that other more than human state of tranquillity and simple innocence, the Golden Age, giving you over to the age of iron and arms. (IV.98.1–8)[16]

The episode tends to be read as a moment of imperial doubt, although opinion remains divided as to whether it actually presents a thoroughgoing and sustained imperial self-critique. The echo of the opening of Virgil's *Aeneid* in the word "armas" suggests that the Old

Man's critique extends to those human deeds that the classical epic was designed to extol. As I have argued elsewhere, even the stability of the ancient world, so much the focus of Camões's epic, comes under threat here precisely because of man's self-assertion, the restlessness that leads him to instrumentalize nature by producing "armas," instruments of destruction.[17]

Now, the logical consequence of the Old Man's admonitions would be the condemnation of not only of this voyage but all attempts to transgress the historical and geographical bounds within which the Portuguese find themselves. However, his argument is really directed elsewhere:

> Have you not near you the Ismaelite with whom you will always have wars left to pursue? If it be only for Christ's faith that you fight, does he not continue to follow the false Arabian creed? Does he not hold thousand cities, infinite territories, if lands and treasure be your desire? And is he not still dedicated to warfare [armas], if praise for victories is what you want? You leave the enemy to flourish at the gates while you go seek another so far away, through which you depopulate this ancient realm, weaken it greatly and let it decay. (IV.100 ff.; translation mine.)

For it is *this* voyage to India that must be condemned. While not explicitly mentioning spices, the Old Man of Restelo in fact accedes to each of the primary motives used repeatedly to justify the voyages of discovery: territorial expansion for cultivatable land, the extension of the Church's spiritual realm, the desire for wealth, the search for honor. In other words, the Old Man does not direct his ire at the ends of the colonial voyages as such, but rather at what the voyage to a distant East entails: the difficulty of maintaining a "wealth of titles, lords of India, Persia, Arabia and Ethiopia" without damaging the integrity of the Portuguese kingdom. At stake is the weakening and depopulation of this "Reino antigo," the problem precisely of upholding the stability of an "ancient kingdom" and a "golden age" against the putative depredations of Moslem powers.

Doubtless, Camões's palpable—and in retrospect far from unfounded—anxiety regarding Portugal's integrity is a long way from the farcical energies of Vicente's playlet. But that tonal difference alerts us to the gap between the status of the India ventures in Vicente's day and their place in Camões's Portugal. The *Estado da Índia* had only been established in 1505, and Tristão da Cunha's 1506 voyage, around which Vicente's play is constructed, was only the third assay to the East in the decade following da Gama's historic journey.

Indeed, the consolidation of Portuguese power in the East would later be traced to the achievements of da Cunha's fleet: the convoy included approximately five ships under the command of Afonso de Albuquerque, whose territorial conquest of key seaports in the Indian Ocean littoral laid the basis for Portuguese dominion over Eastern trading routes. At the same time, what the Old Man of Restelo's outburst and Vicente's farce share is equally significant: the voyage to India as a potential threat to the domestic world in that it creates an absence of authority—which in turn provokes the desire to fill that absence.

But in *Auto da Índia* such absence provides the occasion for a comedy seemingly free of any deep-rooted anxiety regarding the journey to India. The comedic treatment here contrasts with Vicente's own celebration of Portugal's North African campaigns in such theatrical pieces as *A Exhortação da Guerra* and *Auto da Barca do Inferno.* In 1513, when the current duke of Bragança was about to leave with the military expedition against the North African town of Azamor, Vicente composed the eloquent *Exhortação* in which a necromancer priest delivers a rousing call to war (in terms not dissimilar to those of Camões's Old Man): "Arise, Arise, Lords/because with its grand favours/all of heaven graces you,/the King of Fez loses heart/and the Moroccans clamour." As Maria Castelo-Branco remarks, the contrast in Vicente's attitudes could not be more striking: "the expansion in North Africa is exalted and arises as an entirely justifiable crusade, whereas India does not provide anything more than the primary material for a farce, the pretext for risible situations."[18] Likewise, for Adrien Roig the voyage to India in Vicente's play provides no more than the pretext for a satiric attack on Portuguese court culture: "Gil Vicente indicates the abuses, reveals the errors, denounces the culpable parties in a violent satire. The comic nature . . . permits the bold denunciation, in front of the Court, perhaps with a didactic intention."[19]

But a bold denunciation of whom? And for whom? We can take a pointer from Castelo-Branco's distinction between the two directions that Portuguese expansion initiated by João I took: broadly speaking, the North Africa campaigns were supported by the nobility, while the Atlantic expansion (leading finally to India and Brazil) grew out of the impulses of merchants and the urban bourgeoisie. While this description simplifies a more complex distribution of interests, it usefully locates a standing tension between two class fractions, both of whom were represented in the Portuguese court (even as their relative strength shifted from reign to reign). As I have suggested earlier, with Dom João II's accession, the balance of power shifted to the commercial factions; their support was necessary for a monarch intent upon asserting royal supremacy and concomitantly limiting the influence of a landed nobility that had conspired with dominant Spanish ruling houses against his rise to power. By contrast, Vicente's farcical denigration of the India enterprise would seem to be a historical reflex of the complicated situation of the Manueline era, which continued to pursue the centralizing aims of Manuel's predecessor but changed the alliances upon which royal supremacy rested. This shift in emphasis affected, too, the impulse behind the voyages of discovery. As Luís Thomaz has argued, for Dom Manuel, the notion of becoming emperor of the East remained largely couched in terms of suzerainty rather than sovereignty, and the push toward India was as much driven by a messianic dream of finding potential allies in a crusade against the Moorish powers, as by commercial interest in Indian Ocean trade.[20]

The waxing and waning of royal support for Afonso de Albuquerque echoes, for example, the fault lines constitutive of Manuel's court. The *Commentaries of the Great Afonso Dalboquerque* (compiled by his son) indicate that Manuel was partly persuaded by his court circle that Goa should be given up since it was "very unhealthy, and was the cause of unnecessary expense, of no use except to give trouble to soldiers." As the historiographer João de Barros tells us in his *Decadas da Asia* (ca. 1552), Manuel reconvoked a *Conselho* or council in 1502 to decide whether the voyages to the East should continue. Responding to such reservations, Albuquerque argued that Manuel needed to be "Lord of the Land, as at Goa" if the Portuguese were to maintain their seaborne empire: without an important fortress on land, "if once Portugal should suffer a reverse at sea your Indian possessions have not power to hold out a day longer than the kings of the land choose to suffer it." Moreover, defending bureaucratic and military expansion in the East, he informed Manuel that "the mere dross of India is so great, that if the Portuguese possessions be properly farmed by your officers, the revenue from them alone would suffice to repay a great part of these expenses to which we are put."[21] Convinced, Manuel decided—against the wishes of the majority of his council—to retain Goa and pursue the India enterprises.

In light of this overdetermined context, Vicente's attitude to the India voyage in his earlier *Auto da Índia*—written just prior to the heyday of Portuguese colonial domination in the Indian Ocean—would seem to indicate the playwright's dependence upon, and alliance with, those very groups once threatened by João II. (Castelo-Branco suggests that Gil Vicente followed here the footsteps of his patroness Queen Leonor, João II's widow, who remained strongly connected to the landed aristocracy despite her husband's machinations.) Through the departure for India, the female body of Constança—who stands for Portugal—becomes available for appropriation. But the struggle over her is less about Portugal's very identity (as it is in the Old Man's outburst) than about ownership. And in so far as the squire Lemos successfully (if temporarily) takes possession of the merchant's bedroom, we might see the voyage to India as fulfilling a class-inflected desire, whereby the nobility regains the land/woman at the expense of the upwardly mobile mercantile bourgeoisie. The play's mockery of the Indian venture subtly enunciates the political positions of one faction at the Portuguese court, echoing anxiety regarding the consequences of investment Eastward in inverted form, as farce.

III

What complicates Vicente's denigration of the India voyage, however, is the emergence in the play of a transverse identification: Constança, the figure of the domestic space, also stands for the extra-domestic, colonial space of India. Thus, the "Castelhano" attempts to seduce her by underscoring her husband's mistaken priorities: "what more India could there be than you" he apostrophizes, "what more precious stones,/what more things of beauty/than both of you to be together?"[22] Further, insisting on his own colonial rights, he exclaims that "God has made India/only so that we two/could go through this together;/and, solely for my happiness,/to partake of this joy/God had India discovered."[23]

That the domestic drama of desire echoes the drama of Eastern conquest becomes even clearer in the way that Juan de Zamora's courtly rhetoric of seduction prefigures the husband's description of his colonial travails. In expressing superiority to the absent husband, the Spaniard's self-interested and debased courtly language employs, for instance, the image of storms and contrary winds: "Juan de Zamora he was not;/drawn through the streets be my lot/if... I'd leave you even half an hour./And, even if the sea be humbled/and the sea storm [tormenta] cease,/and the wind obey me ... I'd not leave you for a moment."[24] Likewise, upon his return the husband evokes the memory of a three-day storm, thereby indexing the way in which he and de Zamora function in *Auto da Índia* as mimetic doubles competing for the riches of India/woman: "I underwent many dangers," he tells his wife, "a hundred leagues from here,/there rose up such southwesterlies/southwest and west-southerlies/such that I'd never seen such storms [tormenta]."[25] As with the Spaniard's journey to Constança, the husband's journey to Calicut is beset with difficulties.

He may have successfully "fought and robbed" [pelejamos &
roubamos, 465] his share of India's riches, but his journey was by
no means a smooth one: "We went out into the ocean/almost,
almost changing direction,/Our Garça flew along,/and the sea split
asunder."[26] And Constança, too, merges Zamora's futile voyage to
conquer her affections with her merchant husband's search for Eastern
riches. "May yours be a bad voyage," she intones dismissively, "on the
road to Calicut" [Má viagem faces tu,/caminho de Calecu, 343–44].

But identifying Constança with India significantly shifts the valence
of the voyage Eastward. If, as we saw above, the play mocks the
journey to India in order to reencode domestic anxiety as farce, that
voyage—as a sign of national investment in the colonial adventure—
nonetheless becomes the organizing metaphor for all the interactions
in *Auto da Índia*. Qua India, Constança also stands for the return
anticipated by the anxious investors competing for her charms.[27] The
poverty-stricken Portuguese squire Lemos invests his pittance in a loaf
of bread and pitchers of wine in the hope of her favors; whereas the
Castelhano repeatedly insists from the street that she "open up to
him" [¡Abrame..!, 251 and 314] and "fulfil" what she has promised
[Pues prometeis, mantened, 254], anticipating a corporeal return on
the courtly discourse he has expended on her. The wife's response
to Zamora makes clear her attitude to his advances: she refers to
him as "the vinagery Spaniard," wanting "to be paid for the vinegar
he gave me."[28] Even the lower classes in the play seem caught up
with a mercantilist ethos of investing in the hope of magnified—if
deferred—profit: the maid, Constança's feisty accomplice, turns down
the immediate gain afforded by her mistress's offer of a silk cap, and
opts instead for a future share in Eastern wealth. "Or, when [your
husband] gets back," she tells the wife, "give me something he's
brought you" [Ou quando elle vier/day-me do que vos trouxer, 50–
51]. Indeed, the very formal mechanisms of the *Auto da Índia* as a
theatrical piece rely on the logic of departure and return that characterizes the mercantile voyages to India. Not only does the play begin
by invoking both the incipient departure of the master, and the threat
of his not leaving, but the ensuing action is itself structured around
the arrivals and departures of the competing lovers; it ends with the
return of the husband from India and the departure of the married
couple to see the boat bearing the riches of the East.

Written at a time when the decline of Portugal's Eastern dominion was already visible, Camões's epic valiantly tries to turn history
into myth by seeing in Vasco da Gama's voyage to India the historical inauguration of an empire that his antique predecessors—Aeneas

and Alexander, in particular—had failed to achieve. History turns into myth precisely to the extent that it realizes myth in history. By contrast, Vicente's courtly drama engages history as a living event, one whose shape, indeed whose status *as* event, is still uncertain. It chooses as its occasion thus, not the momentous inaugural voyage—whose direct consequences Vicente unlike Camões has experienced—but one of its far less flashy successors, Tristão da Cunha's 1506–09 trip to the East. In its historical consequences, da Cunha's voyage would indirectly have far-reaching implications for the actual demarcation of Portugal's colonial dominions. But these effects the playwright could not, at the time of writing, know: the history of Albuquerque's achievements was yet to be composed.

A later play by Vicente, *Auto da Fama*, testifies to shifting perceptions of the ventures Eastward in the wake of Albuquerque's expansionist successes. The play, Bell writes, seems "written in a glow of pride and patriotism at Portugal's vast, increasing empire and the victories of Albuquerque."[29] To this end, *Auto da Fama* turns a litany of exotic place names into poetry: "Ormuz, Quiloa, Mombaça,/Sofala, Cochin, Melinde." Thus, in a few short years, uncertainty regarding the India voyages turned into, to cite Vitorino Godinho, "a confidence in man and his capacity to rule over the entire globe."[30] And yet, despite Albuquerque's remarkable achievements, his own success would be short-lived. By about 1515 the pressure in the Portuguese court to dismiss Albuquerque, led by the baron de Alvito, became too strong, and this time D. Manuel yielded, replacing him with Lopo Soares de Albergaria, a cousin of the baron. The colonization of "India," though, continued apace.

Probably written in the time between da Cunha's departure and his return, *Auto da Índia* seems remarkably aware of not only the lived historical conditions in which Vicente's theater thrives but also the extent to which historical and theatrical events share a mode of being or a structure. In this sense, the two competing and often opposed frames that intersect in the figure of the farce's protagonist—the wife Constança who is present in every scene—seem linked in specific ways to the split nature of the theatrical event itself and its relationship to history. On the one hand, the frame positioning the wife as a figure for Portugal evokes history in the shape of a subtext (partially recreated above) that Vicente's interlude projects and alludes to: an overdetermined context that spans the distinction between the Indian and North African ventures; between an emergent merchant bourgeoisie and a courtly aristocratic faction; between Portugal and Spain.

But, on the other hand, upon this complex *Auto da Índia* overlays another dimension: an understanding of history's openness, as a series of performances or actions whose status as events depends upon their theatrical re-creation. To cite Jacques Lezra, "it is in the form of a theatrical event that 'history' appears—that is, a referential moment presented as such, and understandable only by means of an overdetermined cultural 'context' to which the play inescapably alludes, but also a moment that doubles as purely theatrical, a moment 'about' theatricality, and 'about' the resistance of matter to theatrical appropriation."[31] To the extent that the India voyage serves *both* as "mere" occasion or pretext for the play *and* as its central metaphor, it functions as an absent cause that is present everywhere only in its effects. Thus, India appears in the text, but inscribed as the site of an absence: the missing ship we never get to see, the wife standing in for the space of the East, the repeatedly deferred riches that the play refers to but never reveals. In so doing, the play repeatedly draws attention to itself as theater, and, particularly, as a figure for the historical event—da Cunha's voyage—which it writes within itself and simultaneously displaces.

Theater, we might say, makes history eventful: the *Auto* self-consciously represents the historical event of colonial return as a theatrical event, albeit played out on a different stage. By engaging the colonial language of investment and return, the play transforms that language into a theatrical principle, indeed into its very motor. And, yet, at the same time, the voyage itself remains outside the play, resisting the theatrical appropriation it enables. From this perspective, "India" stands as the uncertain promise of a history to be fulfilled, one not yet given the shape it will take on. Even as the play makes use of different forms of temporal closure—ritual, secular, and theological—over the course of its unfolding, it nonetheless holds open the space of the possible, of that which has not been and cannot yet be written. And this openness distinguishes the proto-modern theater of Gil Vicente from Camões's epic in which history appears always conceived under the sign of completion. Just as the wife's inconstancy is constantly evoked but never quite confirmed, suspended via the ironic disjunction between the theatrical events and her name, so too are the riches of the East always projected but never fully attained, even when the well-laden ship returns.

And it is here perhaps that generic form and historical location become doubly significant. For the *Auto* is tied as theater to the singularity of the performative event. This singularity is not only that of the play's performance at court, but also marks a connection to the singularity of the historical event upon which its ending depends, the homecoming of Tristão da Cunha's fleet. The play-text's concluding direction tells us that the husband and wife "go to see the ship" and "so ends this first farce" [Vam-se a ver a Nao & fenece esta primeyra farsa]. Anthony Lappin speculates that the *Auto*'s conclusion might be the signal for the entire courtly audience to walk down to the dock and greet the returned ship, thereby participating in a social ritual, a public theater of colonial homecoming. Should this suggestion hold, the ending marks the moment at which text, subtext, and context fold into one another. Though we do not see the ship in the play, *Auto da Índia* nonetheless projects the walking-down as fulfilling the desire or dream it represents—but the action only completes the play offstage, for only there does theatrical performance merge with the domestic and colonial theater that makes it possible. For Shakespeare, by contrast, the colonial theater would always remain foreign: an imaginary island from where one only plots the return home.

NOTES

1. William Shakespeare, *Othello*, ed. Norman Sanders (Cambridge: Cambridge University Press, 1984).
2. Ralegh reports the existence of the Anthropophagi in his 1595 *The Discovery of Guiana*, as does Laurence Keymis in *A Relation of the Second Voyage to Guiana* (1596). One should note, though, that *Othello* does deviate from contemporary historical reality by making Cypress a Venetian possession.
3. See Argensola's *Conquista de las Islas Malucas* (Madrid, 1609). I cite from the translation by John Stevens: *The Discovery and Conquest of the Maluco and Philipine Islands* (London, 1708), 107.
4. Both attempts were dismal failures. The importance of piracy to the English imperial project has been thoroughly investigated by Kenneth R. Andrews in *Trade, Plunder and Settlement: Maritime Enterprise and the Genesis of the British Empire 1480–1630* (Cambridge: Cambridge University Press, 1984) and *Elizabethan Privateering: English Privateering during the Spanish Civil War* (Cambridge: Cambridge University Press, 1964).
5. Sanjay Subrahmanyam, *The Portuguese Empire in Asia 1500–1700: A Political and Economic History* (London: Longman, 1993), 45.
6. Ibid., 47.
7. Cited in Aubrey F. G. Bell, *Portuguese Literature* (Oxford: Clarendon Press, 1922), 108.
8. Ibid., 117.
9. Subrahmanyam, *Portuguese Asia*, 33.

10. Throughout, I cite by line number from the parallel text edition of *Auto da Índia* included in *Three Discovery Plays by Gil Vicente*, ed. and trans. Antony Lappin (Warminster, UK: Aris and Phillips, 1997). I occasionally modify Lappin's translation.

11. H. V. Livermore, *A New History of Portugal*, 2nd ed. (Cambridge: Cambridge University Press, 1976), 132.

12. João II insisted, for example, on a new form of oath from his subjects, requiring nobles to give a written promise and subsequently swear on their knees to deliver immediately upon demand any castle or town they held from the crown.

13. Livermore, *History of Portugal*, 124. The politics of this period are complex. The main obstacle to João's plans came from the powerful Bragança family, whose present magnate was the Queen Leonor's brother. Through a series of devious manoeuvres—which included the alleged discovery of an alliance between Bragança and the Spanish monarchs—João not only had the duke publicly executed for treason but also stabbed to death with his own hand the duke's brother and co-conspirator, the duke of Viseu. Viseu's remaining brother, Manuel, gave his allegiance to the Crown and subsequently succeeded João II to the throne. But Manuel's accession depended in part upon the intercession of Queen Leonor, his sister, who was only reconciled to João II upon his deathbed when he recognized Manuel's claim. It was she who was Gil Vicente's main patroness.

14. "Oh, my heart, be at peace!," apostrophizes the Spaniard, "Do not pull down the house,/do not wage such cruel war/that you die like Sam's son" (316 ff.) [Assosiega coraçon,/ ... no heches la casa en tierra,/ni hagas tan cruda guerra/que mueras como san Son].

15. Richard Helgerson, *Forms of Nationhood: The Elizabethan Writing of England* (Chicago: University of Chicago Press, 1992), 162.

16. Luís Vaz de Camões, *Os Lusíadas* (Lisbon: Porto Editora, 1980); The translations are mine.

17. See *Framing India: The Colonial Imaginary in Early Modern Culture* (Stanford: Stanford University Press, 2002), ch. 2 passim. For a different perspective, see Balachandra Rajan's discussion in "Milton and Camões: Reinventing the Old Man," *Portuguese Literary and Cultural Studies* 9 (2003): 177–87; and Rajan, "*The Lusiads* and the Asian Reader," *Under Western Eyes: India from Milton to Macaulay* (Durham: Duke University Press, 1999), 31–49.

18. Maria dos Remédios Castelo-Branco, "Significado do cómico do *Auto da Índia*," *Ocidente* LXX (1966): 133; the translation is mine.

19. Adrien Roig, "Le Théâtre de Gil Vicente et le Voyage aux Indes," *Quadrant* 7 (1990): 15; the translation is mine.

20. Luís Filipe F. R. Thomaz, "Factions, Interests, and Messianism: The Politics of Portuguese Expansion in the East, 1500–21," *The Indian Economic and Social History Review* 28 (1991): 98–109. On Dom

Manuel's messianism, see Sanjay Subrahmanyam, *The Legend and Career of Vasco da Gama* (Cambridge: Cambridge University Press, 1997), 54–57.

21. See Walter de Gray Birch ed., *The Commentaries of the Great Afonso Dalboquerque*, 4 vols. (New York: Burt Franklin, 1970), 1: 259–60.

22. "Que más India que vos,/que más piedras preciosas/que más alindidas cosas/que estardes juntos los dos?" (131–34)

23. "…la India hizo Dios/solo porque yo con vos/pudiesse passar aquesto./Y solo por dicha mia,/por gozar esta alegria,/la hizo Dios descobrir" (145–50).

24. "No fue el Juan de Çamora/–¡que arrastrado muera yo!–/si…/os dexara media hora./Y aunque la mar se humillara,/y la tormenta cessara,/y el viento me obedeciera,/… un momiento no os dexara" (135 ff.).

25. "Muyta fortuna passey./… cem legoas d'aqui,/saltou tanto sudueste,/sudueste & oest-sudueste/que nunca tal tormenta vi" (430 ff.).

26. "Fomos na volta do mar,/quasi, quasi, a quartelar;/a nossa Garça voava/que o mar se espedeçava" (460–63).

27. Ana Paula Ferreira notes that "each character hopes to bank on still absent profits without risking either a trip at sea or too much in advance." See "Intersecting Historical Performances: Gil Vicente's *Auto da Índia*," *Gestos* 17 (1994): 106.

28. "O castelhano vinageyro…/Vem polo dinheyro/do vinagre que me dava" (261 ff.).

29. Bell, *Portuguese Literature*, 127.

30. See Vitorino Magalhães Godinho, *Mito e Mercadoria, Utopia e Prática de Navegar, seculos XIII–XVIII* (Lisbon: Difel, 1990), 58.

31. Jacques Lezra, *Unspeakable Subjects: The Genealogy of the Event in Early Modern Culture* (Stanford: Stanford University Press, 1997), 12.

CHAPTER 2

LEARNING FROM SPAIN: THE CASE OF THE IRISH MORISCOS

Barbara Fuchs

MODEL EMPIRES

Early modern England's general disavowal—via the widely disseminated Black Legend of Spanish cruelty—of any resemblance between itself and Spain has led critics to overlook the many connections between the two nations as imperial actors.[1] Recent scholarship on Ireland's key role in Elizabethan and Jacobean literature and culture has greatly contributed to our understanding of England's—and later Great Britain's—colonial project, but has generally overlooked the larger European, and, indeed, transatlantic context.[2] Ireland functions as a key site for analyzing England's tortuous relationship to Spain as both model and rival: while the conquest of Bacon's "second island of the ocean Atlantic" provided more land for England in the period than any New World expedition, it remained for colonialists a source of great anxiety about Catholic rebellion and Spanish penetration. Representations of ideological and military encounters over Ireland reveal the resemblances hidden beneath England's insistence on the differences between itself and Spain as colonial powers. An exploration of these problematic resemblances elucidates the discursive apparatus of the Elizabethan conquest of Ireland, and, more generally, England's multiple westward ventures. As I argue here, the similarities that can only be acknowledged in the political realm once James makes peace with Spain surface during Elizabeth's reign in the peculiar genealogies and political allegories of Spenser's writings on Ireland.

Elsewhere, I have described how the rhetorical strategy of "colonial quotation" undergirds colonialist discourse: equating one colonial scenario with the last naturalizes expansion by bringing newly "discovered" lands and people under the conceptual domain of the already-known and already-digested.[3] Prior and ongoing colonial encounters may be assimilated by literally quoting "authorities" on non-European peoples, by referring to the colonists' previous experiences elsewhere, or by interpreting a new culture as another manifestation of one already othered. In analyzing England's rhetoric about Ireland, however, it becomes clear that the mechanics of colonial quotation can apply not only to the *colonized*, but also to the colonizer. Yet whereas there is little disadvantage for the European colonizer in suggesting that all "primitive" peoples are essentially equivalent, the suggestion of a similar equation between two European empires, each intent on colonial superiority, presents certain rhetorical challenges. How can England insist on its *difference* from Spain if it chooses to replicate its colonial methods, and negotiate its admiration of Spain's colonial successes with its loud denunciations of Spain's excesses? Can its own colonial exploits and colonized subjects in fact be distinguished from those of Spain?[4]

The problem becomes especially interesting when one considers how sudden the turn is from a generalized admiration of Spanish empire in England during the reign of Mary and Philip II—that odd interlude when Spain and England were to a certain extent one and the same—to the generalized condemnation of Spain following the ascent of Elizabeth to the throne.[5] The mobilization of the Black Legend in the Netherlands, France, and England in the last decades of the sixteenth century involved a large-scale rhetorical assault on Spain, with countless pamphlets published, translated, and circulated widely trumpeting the evils of Philip II's universalizing Catholicism. In this literature, Spain was portrayed as uniquely cruel, uniquely greedy. Paradoxically, one of the founding documents of the Black Legend was Bartolomé de las Casas's *Brevísima historia de la destrucción de las Indias* (1552)—a *Spanish* condemnation of Spanish behavior in the New World. While proponents of the Black Legend took this internal evidence as consummate proof of the Spaniards' culpability, it also reflects the lively debate within Spain about the ethics and proper procedures of conquest. Meanwhile, Spain excoriated England for its "heresy" in departing from the true Church, and for its depredations on Spain's established imperial possessions.

During the decades of war with Spain—declared or undeclared—English propaganda loudly proclaimed the difference between the two rivals. Yet even as relations between England and Spain soured, their colonial exploits and efforts to consolidate as nations remained intimately entwined, with competing claims often locating the two in a chiasmatic relationship of vulnerability and aggression. Thus whereas England claimed its right to Ireland based on Pope Adrian IV's grant to Henry II in the *Laudabiliter* bull, it nonetheless refused to countenance the 1493 bulls by which Alexander VI had "given" Spain the New World. Paradoxically, although the Reformation complicated the English claim to Ireland via papal donation, it also afforded a conceptual space from which to argue that Spain's claim to the New World was fundamentally suspect, and did not apply to Protestants.[6] There are strange mirrorings, also, in the two nations' attacks on one another's territorial integrity: under Elizabeth, the English employed privateers—glorified state pirates, such as Francis Drake—to despoil Spanish possessions in the New World, and to attack the coasts of Spain. When Spain protested, Elizabeth issued numerous proclamations against "unauthorized" privateering, without any intention of curtailing the activities of Drake and his kind. Conversely, England found itself vulnerable to Spanish infiltrators into Ireland, whom English authorities there labeled as "onely adventurers"—irregulars rather than proper agents of the king of Spain—the better to neutralize them.[7]

Spain in Ireland?

English propaganda during the war with Spain specifically addresses the threat posed to, and by, Ireland. As Christopher Highley has pointed out, throughout the sixteenth century Ireland was identified as a potential base for invading Britain: "Ireland was England's 'postern'—a narrow but vulnerable rear entry."[8] The anxieties over Ireland became particularly acute after the Armada, as England feared repeated attempts at invasion. One satiric pamphlet "concerning the Newes out of Ireland" (1601) makes light of Spanish attacks, defusing geopolitical threat through anticlerical satire, as the Spaniards are diverted from their penetration of Britain by the perverse pleasures of holy brothels.[9] The pamphlet invokes stereotypes of the lying, thieving Irish to suggest that any military operation that relies on their help is doomed: "some wilde Kerne sold [the Spaniards] thirty such Cowes in the day, and very honestly stole them again at night." There is no evidence that, as the author claims, Ireland does "stand all for the Queene," but the broad satire emphasizes the futility of Spanish attempts, given the wayward nature of the contested colony.

Robert Payne's *A Brief Description of Ireland* (1589) negates the Spanish threat in a more serious tone. The author asserts that the Irish would never join forces with the Spaniards because of the latter's "monstrous cruelties in the West Indies where they most tyrannously have murdered many millions more of those simple creatures than now live in Ireland."[10] Payne's certainty presupposes, first, that the Irish accepted the Black Legend that England was at such pains to circulate and, second, that they would prefer the English cruelties, which they knew, to the unknown dangers that a Spanish ally might represent.[11] Both the actual similarities between the two colonial masters—as well as those desired and those pointedly ignored—suggest the instability of claims of national difference among such real and rhetorical interchangeability.

Despite the loud protestations of difference, England had much to learn from Spain where imperial expansion was concerned. Part of Richard Hakluyt's goal in his *Principal Navigations* (first published in 1589; expanded and republished 1598–1600) was to make available to the English the secret expertise of their Spanish rivals, acquired through spying or shady diplomatic exchanges.[12] Yet the Spanish could function as a model, too, for the consolidation of *imperium*—in its early modern sense of sovereignty or state control—in territories closer to home.[13] As England attempted to extend effective control throughout Ireland, partly in order to protect its own borders, Spain was embarked upon a similar project in the Kingdom of Granada, which had fallen to the Catholic Kings in 1492 but was considered a threat to the territorial integrity of the emerging nation. Whereas the English aimed their cultural—as well as military—repression at the "mere" Irish, the Spaniards targeted the Moriscos, or "little Moors," who had remained in Spain after the fall of Granada and were perceived as potential allies of an encroaching Islam.

The two scenarios present fascinating similarities: in both cases, the territory to be subdued is populated not only by clearly identifiable "others" but by a large class of indeterminate, hybrid subjects, who call into question the stability of religious, ethnic, or national categories. Despite attempts to legislate cultural separation, such as the fourteenth-century Kilkenny Statutes, the Old English population in Ireland (descendants of the original Norman conquerors) had so adopted Irish ways by the sixteenth century that it became increasingly difficult to find cultural differences between the two groups. Similarly, the Moorish culture of Granada had not only left its mark on Spain as a whole, but produced Morisco subjects who accepted the rudiments of Christianity in order to remain within Spain, thus challenging the notion of an irreducible Moorish difference.[14] In both cases the vicious legal attacks on the culture colonized reflect a fundamental anxiety about the colonizers going native, or, worse yet, not being that different from the natives in the first place.

For Ireland, the situation is further complicated by authors such as William Camden, or Spenser himself, who offer the argument that the English have a right to the island because its early inhabitants were Britons.[15] In order to advance colonization, this claim erases any essential difference between colonizing self and colonized other. Despite the English outrage at the savagery of Irish ways, then, English subjects were willing to recognize themselves in their neighbors when it suited their purposes. The mythical claims propounded by Elizabethan colonists such as Humphrey Gilbert—that they were merely restoring King Arthur's old empire in Ireland rather than embarking upon a new one—suggest another parallel with Spain.[16] The powerful myth of Arthurian restoration, derived from Geoffrey of Monmouth's *Historia Regum Britanniae* (1138), transforms the English exploits in Ireland into an odd version of the Spanish *Reconquista* of peninsular territory from the Moors. In these instrumental narratives, territory is never conquered, but instead *reconquered* from usurpers or interlopers.[17]

The legislation targeting the Moriscos on the one hand and the Irish on the other—both ostracized cultures that threaten culturally to absorb the colonizers—follows a similar progression. Initially, the laws focus on keeping native and conqueror apart. Where England passes the Kilkenny Statutes to prevent the Old English from adopting Irish customs, the Spanish pass laws in 1513 (more than twenty years, that is, after the fall of the city to the Catholic Kings) forbidding the adoption of veils and *almalafas* (mantles) by Old Christian women living in Granada.[18] Soon, the restrictive legislation turns from the conquerors to the conquered, in a wholesale attempt to destroy native cultural forms. The Spanish laws, passed repeatedly but enforced sporadically, become more and more repressive over the course of the sixteenth century. In its most virulent form, in 1567, the law states, "that the Moors of Granada and its Kingdom (for they were baptized and Christians), the better to serve God our Lord, should change their clothing and not speak their language, or have their songs and instruments, nor perform their weddings as is their custom, nor have their traditional dishes on Christmas or the New Year, which are called 'mezuamas.' "[19] Compare this to the equivalent legislation passed for Ireland by

Henry VIII, soon after he declared himself king of Ireland and transformed the Irish into his subjects, *de iure*:

> Wherefore be it enacted...that no person or persons, the King's subjects within this land being...shall be shorn or shaven above the ears, or use the wearing of hair upon their heads, like unto long locks called "glibes"...or use or wear any shirt, smock, kerchief, "bendel," neck handkerchief, "mocket" or linen cap, coloured or dyed with saffron, nor yet use or wear in any their shirts or smocks above seven yards of cloth, to be measured according to the King's standard...and that no person or persons...shall use or wear any mantles, coat or hood made after the Irish fashion...
>
> And be it enacted that every person or persons, the King's true subjects, inhabiting this land of Ireland, of what estate, condition or degree he or they be, or shall be, to the uttermost of their power, cunning and knowledge, shall use and speak commonly the English tongue and language...and shall bring up his children in such places, where they shall or may have occasion to learn the English tongue, language, order and condition.[20]

In both cases, the consolidation of *imperium* by the new masters requires a concerted legal attack on older customs, from language to dress to clan structures. Only by legally erasing the signs of native culture can the colonizing power assert its own customs and supply the missing "civility" that the colony lacks.

Both in Ireland and in Granada, the repression of native peoples became more vicious as the imperial powers encountered increasing resistance to their goals. Massive campaigns of expropriation, relocation, and banishment essentially decimated the Morisco population in Spain by the early seventeenth century, and similar "solutions" were proposed for dealing with the Irish. To what extent did the English recognize this similarity, even as they insisted on Spain's infinite cruelty and their own justice? How could they reconcile their denunciation of Spanish abuses in the New World and in the Dutch provinces with their mirroring of Spanish policies?

One imagines that the English might in fact have enlisted the grievances of the Moriscos against Spain in their own cause, as they did with the native peoples of the Americas or the Dutch, yet Spain was too attractive as a potential model of successful *imperium*, and the Moriscos too threatening, in the final analysis, to serve as poster children for Spanish cruelty. While the Indians, conveniently idealized as peaceful savages willing to embrace Christianity, could easily be cast as victims of Spain, the Moors, even when converted, remained the traditional enemies of Christendom, and thus more difficult to recruit for Elizabethan propaganda. Thus, while in anti-Spanish writings of the time the New World abuses are referred to again and again, the sixteenth-century persecution of the Moriscos rarely comes up. In fact, Spain itself is derided as a nation of Moors, and Roman Catholicism compared unfavorably with Islam.

Edward Daunce's "Brief Discourse of the Spanish State" (1590), for example, describes how the Spaniards "exercised all tyranny" in the West Indies, so that the natives, "hauing till then enioyed a long libertie, estemed the Spaniards more daungerous than wilde beasts."[21] Contemporary Moors are mainly discussed only in the context of the Inquisition, established "to looke into the corrupt life and maners of the Mores and Iewes of Spaine."[22] Yet Spain's Moorish past is described at great length, as Daunce stresses that Spaniards are genealogically "mingled with the Mores cruell and full of trecherie."[23] "The Anti-Spaniard" (1590), a pamphlet on the Spanish threat to France, suggests that the king of Spain tyrannizes his own subjects "with no lesse barbarous crueltie, then he spared not to intreate the Indians with all unchristian inumanitie," but does not pay any special attention to Moors or Jews.[24] The colorfully entitled "A Fig for the Spaniard" (1591) suggests, however, that the English were well aware of Spain's persecution of the Moriscos: "That [Philip II] is milde by nature, and seeketh no mans bloud, First aske his slaughtered sonne, and wife, ask the millions of Moores, and poor Portingales, aske thousands of Neapolitanes, and Dutchmen, aske Frenchmen, and Italians, yea and the English that have been tortured, and tormented to death by him."[25]

But "A Fig for the Spaniard," although an important piece of evidence of England's awareness, is the exception rather than the rule. During the war with Spain, it appears, English authors barely acknowledged Spain's persecution of the Moriscos, and certainly failed to note any similarity between it and English policies in Ireland. Only when the peace with Spain in 1604 somewhat attenuated the problems of identification—as well as the actual threat of a Spanish invasion via Ireland—could the similarities be more openly addressed in political discourse. In a 1609 report to the Privy Council, Arthur Chichester, in a kind of macabre wordplay, recalls the Spaniards' forced relocation and expulsion of the Moriscos, as well as the latter's rebellion in Andalusía:

> The O'Moores, together with some other Irish septs, their fosterers and followers in the Queen's County, are all removed from thence and dispersed into sundry remote places of Munster and Connaught; by which

it is to be hoped that others will be warned by their example to forbear such desperate and rebellious courses as they have often attempted. Only some young children of that name, without parents or other near kinsmen that have any care of them, are yet remaining among their fosterers in and about those borders. Wishes they were taken into England, to be put to occupations and other services, where they may forget their fierceness and pride, which they will otherwise retain, though they be but bastards of that name. This is a course not to be taxed, easy and incommodious to none, saving to such of this nation as are or shall be inclined to kindle the fire of rebellion, which has commonly been wont to be fetched or taken from those white Moores.[26]

Chichester's elision of the Celtic "O'" transforms the Irish *O'Moores* into ambiguous *white Moores* in order to justify the colonial repression he is advocating. Colonial quotation here equates not only the Irish to the Moors but also the *English* to the *Spanish*. Yet the rhetorical advantages of such a comparison seem to outweigh the disadvantages: English policies are implicitly authorized by Spanish precedent, and the othering of "Moores"—of whatever color—becomes more important than insisting on distinctions between England and Spain. At the same time, however, Chichester offers a hint that Irish difference may not be irreducible: if Irish children are indentured in England they may finally "forget that fierceness and pride" that is their birthright. The chiasmic exchange of servants for planters replaces the purported violence of the colonized with that of the colonizer, and Chichester's prescriptions for civility collapse under the weight of their own contradictions.

In 1610, shortly after Spain passes the first expulsion decrees against the Moriscos, John Davies, attorney general for Ireland, explicitly invokes the Spaniards as a model as he recommends to James the wholesale seizure of Irish lands and "transplantation" of the Irish in order to "make a civil plantation": "Lastly, this transplantation of the natives is made by his majesty rather like a father than like a lord or monarch. The Romans transplanted whole nations out of Germany into France; the Spaniards lately removed all the Moors out of Granada into Barbary, without providing them any new seats there."[27] The invocation of the Spanish model, coupled with the Roman precedent, authorizes Great Britain as simply one more empire, intent on achieving "civility."[28] It is interesting to note that Daunce's "Brief Discourse," explicitly condemns Spain's expropriation of natives in the New World as cruel and unprecedented.[29] Yet here the Black Legend seems temporarily forgotten, as Davies suggests that Spain might not be a bad model to follow. The image of James as a father—a metaphor of which the king himself was very fond—invokes a kindly, paternalistic regard for his subjects.[30] More importantly, however, it codes the king's power as arbitrary rather than legal, precisely when recommending an equivocal course of action.[31] Lastly, the image recalls the forcible fostering in England—via deportation and indentured service—recommended by Chichester in order to tame the children of the "white Moores" and, conveniently, to vacate Queen's County altogether for English occupation.

A VIEW OF THE PAST STATE OF SPAIN

As the above examples suggest, an explicit identification with Spain was possible for England after the signing of the peace. A generation earlier, I would argue, such models, though similarly fitting, could not be acknowledged in the same fashion. It was possible, however, to consider the perturbing parallels between England and Spain by means of a highly elliptical allusion. I turn now to Spenser's representation of the connections among England, Spain, and Ireland in two very different texts, *A View of the Present State of Ireland* (1598?, pub. 1633) and Book V of *The Faerie Queene* (1596) to suggest some of the ways in which the Spanish example made its insistent presence felt even as England explicitly denied any resemblance between its own actions and those of its greatest rival.

In *A View of the Present State of Ireland*, Spenser's two interlocutors spend a great deal of time discussing the provenance and ethnic origin of the Irish, which includes the Scythians and the Spaniards:

> IRENIUS: After this people [the Scythians] thus planted in the North . . . another nation coming out of Spaine arrived at the West part of Ireland, and finding it waste, or weakely inhabited, possessed it: who whether they were native Spaniards, or Gaules, or Africans, or Gothes, or some other of those Northerne Nations which did over-spread all Christendome, it is impossible to affirme, only some naked conjectures may be gathered, but that out of Spaine certainely they came, that do all the Irish Chronicles agree.[32]

The Irish genealogy that Irenius introduces is hardly innocent: the Scythian connection, often reiterated, will account for Irish savagery and nomadism; the Spanish connection, meanwhile, must be qualified and exposed as fraudulent in order to neutralize dangerous Irish pleas for Spanish help as England fights both of them simultaneously.

Initially, Irenius seems intent on criticizing the Spanish themselves as a "mongrel" people (49–50); when Eudoxius challenges him he qualifies his criticism, admitting that all Christian nations are now of mingled bloods.[33] Yet through his extensive description of the many peoples that make up Spain, as well as the multiple identification of Spain with "Gaules or Africans or Goths," Irenius foregrounds a diachronic view of Spain that serves to neutralize Irish recourse to Spanish allies while underscoring Irish otherness. Spenser's view of the present state of Ireland relies heavily on a *historical* view of both Irish and Spanish origins: for Spaniards, read "Moors"; for Spanish origins of Ireland, read Moorish or African origins. Irenius again emphasizes a historical ethnography in his description of Irish wailing, a custom that is "not proper Spanish, but altogether heathenish, brought in thither first either by the Scythians, or the Moores that were Africans, and long possessed that countrey" (61). Thus Spanish customs are collapsed into Moorish or African ones, transforming Irish claims to Spanish origins into markers of racial, as well as cultural, otherness. Instead of strengthening England's enemies, the Irish connection to Spain merely underscores their shared heathenism.

In his more extensive account of Irish customs derived from Spain, Irenius speaks repeatedly of the "*old* Spaniards," whose habits coincide with those of present-day "Mahometans":

> And this was the auncient manner of the Spaniards, as yet it is of all the Mahometans to cut off all their beards close . . . Also the woemen amongst the old Spaniards had the charge of all houshold affaires, both at home and abroad, (as Boemus writeth,) though now the Spaniards use it quite otherwise. And so have the Irish woemen the trust and care of all things, both at home, and in the field . . . Moreover the manner of their woemens riding on the wrong side of the horse, I meane with their faces toward the right side, as the Irish use, is (as they say) old Spanish, and some say African, for amongst them the woemen (they say) used so to ride: Also the deepe smocke sleive, which the Irish woemen use, they say, was old Spanish, and is used yet in Barbary: and yet that should seem rather to be an old English fashion: for in Armory the fashion of the Manche . . . is fashioned much like to that sleive. (65)

In this discussion, Spain becomes a highly unstable referent: if the Irish are like the Spaniards, it is only because the Spanish were once Moors; if the Irish are Moors—and sixteenth-century Christian Spaniards, as we have seen, actively persecute Moors—then the Irish clearly cannot appeal to Spanish allies. To obvious English advantage, both Spaniards and Irish are marked as savage others, and the striking resemblance between Spain's contemporary persecution of Moriscos in Granada and England's actions in Ireland is neatly elided. Yet the passage betrays a certain unease with this rhetorical tour-de-force: it signals its own hesitancy through the repeated qualification of truth as hearsay—*they say*—and ends with the admission of possible English origins for a custom that has been insistently othered through its location in, first, Ireland, then "old Spain," and, finally, Barbary, or North Africa. The ambivalence of these moments suggests how the resemblances identified obscure what cannot be expressed: the English are to the Irish as the Spanish are to the Moriscos.

Book V of Spenser's *Faerie Queene* reflects this problematic identification darkly, in an allegory that is even more unstable than the genealogies discussed above. This highly political section of Spenser's poem, full of violence yet announced as the "Legend of Justice," rehearses different and often contradictory subject positions for a personified imperial England. Book V considers the dynamics of *imperium*—what Elizabeth Fowler calls "dominion"—and colonization, as the Faerie Queene dispatches Artegall to save the helpless Irena from the ravages of Grantorto—the "great wrong."[34] Although the Irish mission is established at the beginning of Canto i, Irena largely disappears from the book, with the combat against Grantorto repeatedly postponed, and finally relegated to Canto xii, as Artegall takes on a number of other enemies and joins forces with Arthur. While these enemies have been read as straightforward political allegories of Elizabeth's foes, critics have generally been less willing to consider the implications of the multiple, and contradictory, contemporary identifications in this political book. I focus on the adventures that preface Artegall's encounter with the "strong tyrant" to argue that both knights must assume highly problematic roles before the poem finally reaches Ireland. These include identifying with Spain as the enemy of Islam, *as well as* opposing Spain as the tyrannical enemy of England, oppressor of the Dutch provinces, and of Ireland itself.

After administering a kind of Solomonic justice to the Squire and Sanglier in Canto i, Artegall must next vanquish the "cursed cruell Sarazin"[35] Pollente, who has captured a bridge and charges a steep toll to all who would cross. This liminal episode is part of Artegall's education in subduing tyrants and bullies, and recalls nicely the knight's need for constant movement past all obstacles toward his pressing chivalric obligations, even as he apparently forgets the larger purpose of liberating Irena. Pollente is modeled closely after Rodomonte, king of Algiers and foremost champion of the Saracens in Ariosto's *Orlando Furioso*. Rodomonte is, in fact, a Moor invading Europe, who retreats to his bridge after being spurned in love.[36] The rewriting of the *Furioso* in this liminal episode anticipates the multiple identifications of the Faerie knights with both English and Spanish champions. In his poem, Ariosto deliberately equates Spaniards and Saracens, in a none too subtle commentary on the burden of Spanish imperialism in Italy—there are no Christian knights from Spain to help Charlemagne fight the Moors, he implies, because the Spaniards *are* Moors. At the same time, however, Ariosto lavishes praise on Charles V for his conquests and advocates unified European action against Islam.

In fighting the Rodomontesque Pollente for the right to proceed, Artegall occupies a highly unstable position. On the one hand, he is fighting an Islam closely identified with Spain, prefiguring his many encounters with actual allegorical figures for Spain. On the other hand, Spain's own powerful myth of the reconquest of its territory from Islam—a myth contiguous with the story of Orlando that Ariosto tells—renders Artegall akin to a Spanish knight, removing Moorish obstacles to safe passage. The referents become even more complicated when Pollente's Saracen corpse falls into an Irish river, the Lee, "whose waters with his filthy bloud it stayned" (V.ii.19).[37] Thus the episode suggests the equation of England and Spain in a highly convoluted form: there is no overt identification of Moors with Irishmen, but instead an oblique suggestion that England can learn territorial control from Spain's war against the Moors.

Canto viii presents similar problems of polysemous context and unstable referents. In this episode, Artegall and Arthur meet as they rescue Samient, Queen Mercilla's messenger, from an embassy gone awry. Mercilla had sent her to negotiate with the tyrant Souldan, who "seekes to subuert her Crowne and dignity" (viii.18). After saving Samient from dishonor, the Faerie knights decide to "worke auengement strong/Vppon the Souldan selfe" (24), and opt for a strategy of "counterfet disguise" (25). The plot works: Artegall, "clad in th'armour of a Pagan knight," passes easily and enters Souldan's court. The actual combat with Souldan is marked as significant in a number of ways. First, the Briton Prince himself must fight the tyrant. Second, unable to reach Souldan "mounted in his seat so high" (33), Arthur must vanquish him with his magic shield, saved for "monsters huge he would dismay" (I.vii.34).[38] Third, the battle is described in mythological and even cosmic terms, with Souldan's horses fleeing from the glare of "the infants sunlike shield" in a fury that recalls "the firiemouthed steeds, which drew/The Sunnes bright wayne to *Phaetons* decay" (40–41). The simile suggests the universal import of this battle: the very order of the cosmos depends upon its outcome.

Critics have responded to the exaltation of the episode by associating it with England's "brightest moment." The defeat of Souldan has been related to Philip II and the Armada since 1758, when John Upton first noted the similarities between the tyrant's high war-chariot and the tall galleons attempting the invasion of England.[39] Further readings have expanded upon this doubtless accurate identification by noting not only the description of Souldan's weapons but the comparison to mythical characters who overreach their limits. More recently, critics have focused on the apocalyptic discourse—characteristic of the period after the Armada—used to describe the combat, and on the parodic substitution of Phaeton's horses running wild for Philip's Apollonian impresa, which featured the Sun god driving his celestial chariot across the sky.[40]

But this lengthy history of reading Souldan as Philip II has largely precluded any discussion of what is surely an alternative, though less historically specific, referent. So strong is the jingoistic Armada reading, in fact, that some editions never even point out the fairly obvious linguistic allusion: the term *souldan*—our modern "sultan"— can refer only to the ruler of an Islamic nation.[41] With alternate spellings, the term had been used in England since at least 1297 (OED, 2nd. edn., s. v. "sultan"). Spenser's recourse to a highly specific political term instead of the more generic "Paynim" or "Saracen" suggests that a historical and political reading of the allegory in terms of Islam is in order here.[42] In general critics have not known what to make of an Islamic souldan; although a few note that a sultan is a Muslim ruler, they fail to pursue the implications of the character's arresting title, and move on quickly to the identification with Spain. Mark Heberle's suggestive reading is the exception, in that it both takes seriously the strong allusions to Philip, and considers the Souldan as a representative of Islam. Heberle suggests that Spenser's "ideological mythmaking" here "identifies the greatest Catholic prince of Europe with his greatest Muslim enemy," demonizing Roman Catholicism by associating it with Islam.[43]

I want to argue that while this complex othering is certainly part of the point, the representation of Souldan as a figure for both Islam and Spain signals the episode's uneasy identification of *England* with Spain. The first equation, of Spain and Islam, operates via an implicit appeal to the same history foregrounded in the *View*'s Irish genealogies: what is Spanish now was Moorish not long ago. As I have shown in my reading of the *View*, that diachronic account of Spain offers specific political advantages for England. Critics who quickly read a "souldan" as Spanish thus unwittingly replicate the dynamics of early modern English propaganda, which relentlessly othered Spain as African and no better than the Infidel.

The vexed ideological context of imitation and contradistinction is reflected in turn in a second, and much more problematic identification: that of England with Spain. For if the Souldan remains the figure for a historical and threatening Islam, there are good reasons to identify his vanquisher with Spain—the nation that predicated its own self-construction largely on the Reconquista, and which, as Heberle reminds us, had recently and spectacularly defeated the Turkish sultan at the battle of Lepanto.[44] The poem itself acknowledges this identification by referring to Prince Arthur as the "Infant" as he confounds Souldan (41.2). While the OED gives one meaning of "infant" as "a youth of noble or gentle birth," the early examples are both from *The Faerie Queene* itself.[45] Surely the more relevant meaning here is "a prince or princess of Spain or Portugal."[46] The title makes the triumphant Arthur at once a British prince defeating Spain and a Spanish prince defeating Moors—a complex, and empowering, identification for an imperial England.

Yet if the identification aggrandizes Arthur's power, it also brings him dangerously close to what the poem anathematizes: the terrifying, monstrous power of Spain. Note that for all the emphasis on Souldan's fearful weapons, it is Arthur who has the unfair advantage. This is, moreover, an episode in which the Faerie knights resort to highly unchivalrous trickery, gaining entrance to Souldan's castle by having Artegall pass successfully as the Infidel other.[47] In Arthur's combat against Souldan, the erasure of difference confounds the frightful horseman, "like to the Thracian Tyrant, who they say / Vnto his horses gaue his guests for meat, / Till he himself was made their greedie pray" (31). When they turn "backe again upon themselves" (38) blinded by the shield's reflection, Souldan's horses cannot recognize the harm they are doing to their own master, who, "like as the cursed sonne of Theseus . . . of his owne steedes was all to peeces torne" (43). The *rapprochement* of Artegall's disguise, and the repeated emphasis on retributive and reciprocal fates—what Nohrnberg calls "reflexive mechanisms that destroy those who use them for evil ends"[48]—marks the mirroring of the other in the self as one of the canto's key preoccupations. If, on the surface, the erasure of difference seems to work to the Briton's advantage, it raises certain pressing questions as the episode ends and Artegall resumes his sally to Irena. How can England both identify with Spain and not have its own accusations of cruelty flung back in its face? Is it possible to pass as the other when convenient and yet retain both national and ethical integrity? What lessons are learned here that may apply in Ireland?

Like the less significant encounter with Pollente, the Souldan episode foregrounds the identification of Spain with a previous Islam, and elides that nation's violent contemporary persecution of Moorish subjects. At the same time, it subtly identifies England with Spain in a way that undermines the ostensibly transparent political allegories of the Legend of Justice. While Artegall is presented first carrying out and later witnessing violence against Moors as a kind of apprenticeship for his role in "saving" Ireland from Spain, the poem dissimulates any suggestion that this is "Spanish" behavior through the insistent allegorical figuration of Spain as the enemy. Although the culmination of the Book of Justice should feature the liberation of Ireland through the removal of the Spanish presence, Artegall's earlier adventures indicate that in fact a little of Spain arrives with him. Elizabethan England cannot acknowledge its Spanish model, but the instability of referents in Spenser's political allegory goes some length toward marking the *indistinctness*—both enabling and problematic—between the two rivals. It is by no means clear that the much-announced difference between England and Spain as colonial actors can keep apart what is joined darkly, in complex rhetorical avowals and disavowals of identification.

NOTES

A different version of this essay appeared as "Spanish Lessons: Spenser and the Irish Moriscos," *SEL: Studies in English Literature 1500–1900* 42. 1 (Winter 2002): 43–62.

1. For the dissemination of the Black Legend, see William S. Maltby, *The Black Legend in England: The Development of Anti-Spanish Sentiment, 1558–1660* (Durham: Duke University Press, 1971). In his *Colonial Writing and the New World 1583–1671: Allegories of Desire* (Cambridge: Cambridge University Press, 1999), Thomas Scanlan argues that England deploys the Black Legend in an effort to construct an alternative narrative of distinctively English national identity based on a difference in English colonizing practices.

2. Some of the more interesting recent studies include Andrew Hadfield, *Edmund Spenser's Irish Experience: Wilde Fruit and Salvage Soil* (Oxford: Oxford University Press, 1997); Christopher Highley, *Shakespeare, Spenser, and the Crisis in Ireland* (Cambridge: Cambridge University Press, 1997); and David Baker, *Between Nations: Shakespeare, Spenser, Marvell, and the Question of Britain* (Stanford: Stanford University Press, 1997). Three important exceptions to the disregard for the transatlantic context are Scanlan's recent

study, Nicholas Canny, whom I cite below, and Shannon Miller, *Invested with Meaning: The Raleigh Circle in the New World* (Philadelphia: University of Pennsylvania Press, 1998).

3. See my "Conquering Islands: Contextualizing *The Tempest*," *Shakespeare Quarterly* 48.1 (Spring 1997): 45–62.

4. For the problems involved in attempting to distinguish Englishmen from Spaniards in the colonial enterprise, see Louis Montrose's "The Work of Gender in the Discourse of Discovery," in *New World Encounters*, ed. Stephen Greenblatt (Berkeley: University of California Press, 1993), 177–217; Richard Helgerson, *Forms of Nationhood: The Elizabethan Writing of England* (Chicago: University of Chicago Press, 1992), 181–87, and Scanlan, *Colonial Writing*.

5. See, for example, Richard Eden's preface to his translation of Peter Martyr's *Decades of the Newe Worlde* (London: William Seres, 1555), where he expresses great admiration for Spanish achievements.

6. On the ways in which the *Laudabiliter* was gradually replaced by other justifications after the Reformation, see Hadfield, *Spenser's Irish Experience*, 93–95. In his *Lords of All the World: Ideologies of Empire in Spain, Britain and France, c.1500–c.1800* (New Haven: Yale University Press, 1995), Anthony Pagden points out that Spanish scholars themselves were uneasy about basing Spanish dominium in the New World on the pope's donation.

7. See one such episode in Edmund Spenser, *A View of the State of Ireland*, ed. Andrew Hadfield and Willy Maley (Oxford: Blackwell, 1997), 105. Subsequent references in the text are to this edition.

8. Highley, *Shakespeare, Spenser, and the Crisis in Ireland*, 50.

9. "The Coppie of a Letter sent from M. Rider, Deane of Saint Patricks, concerning the Newes out of Ireland, and of the Spaniards landing and present estate there" (London: Thomas Man, 1601).

10. Payne, *A Briefe Description of Ireland* [1589], 51. Cited in Nicholas Canny, *Kingdom and Colony: Ireland in the Atlantic World 1560–1800* (Baltimore MD: The Johns Hopkins University Press, 1988).

11. Payne's judgment is largely wishful thinking, as Irish exiles had long urged Philip II to launch an invasion of England from Ireland. See Niall Fallon, *The Armada in Ireland* (Middletown CT: Wesleyan University Press, 1978), 1–16.

12. Hakluyt was concerned with purveying colonial propaganda as much as with factual information. See, for example, his accounts of a "secret mappe" of Virginia's riches "made in Mexico . . . for the King of Spaine," and of "intercepted letters" that "acknowledge the Inland to be a better and richer countrey than Mexico" ("The Epistle Dedicatory in the Second Volume of the Second Edition, 1599," *Principal Navigations*, intr. by John Masefield [London: J. M. Dent, 1927], 39–40).

13. For a discussion of uses of the term in the period, see Pagden, *Lords of All the World*, 12–19.

14. The Spanish hysteria over *limpieza de sangre* ("clean blood") may be attributed in part to the difficulty of distinguishing recent Jewish and Moorish converts—the "New Christians"—from "Old Christians," who claimed to have been Christians even under Islam. See Deborah Root, "Speaking Christian: Orthodoxy and Difference in Sixteenth-Century Spain," *Representations* 23 (Summer 1988): 118–34.

15. As Hadfield points out, "The immediate advantage of the use of such a British origin-story is apparent: if the two islands are merged, as indicated, under the name of Britain, both can be regarded all the more easily as properties of the English monarch, who claimed to be a descendant of an ancient line of British kings" (*Spenser's Irish Experience*, 101).

16. Hadfield's detailed account of the Arthurian myths raises some intriguing questions. He describes the linguistic "proof" offered by John Dee, and by the character Irenius in Spenser's *View of the Present State of Ireland*, to claim a British presence everywhere from the New World to Ireland: etymological remains of the colonizers' language serve as markers of their previous dominion. Surely this proof-by-homonym is yet another, highly inventive, example of colonial quotation?

17. In the New World, the Spaniards attempted to justify the *Conquista* by analogy to the earlier *Reconquista* of territory from the Moors. The historian and colonial official Francisco López de Gómara claimed, in his 1552 *General History of the Indies*, that "The conquest of the Indians began after that of the Moors was completed, so that Spaniards would ever fight the infidels."

18. See K. Garrad, "The Original Memorial of Francisco Núñez Muley," *Atlante* 2.4 (1954): 199–226.

19. As reported by Ginés Pérez de Hita in his second part of the *Guerras civiles de Granada*, which describes how the Moriscos rebelled against such legislation, ed. Paula Blanchard-Demouge (Madrid: Bailly-Baillière, 1913), 2:3; the translation is mine.

20. "An Act for the English Order, Habit and Language" (28 Hen. VIII c.15), *Irish Statutes* (1786), 1:119–22. Reproduced in Constantia Maxwell, *Irish History from Contemporary Sources, 1509–1610* (London: Allen and Unwin, 1923), 112–14.

21. Edward Daunce, "A Brief Discourse of the Spanish State, with a Dialogue annexed intituled Philobasilis" (London: Richard Field, 1590), 14 and passim.

22. Ibid., 11.

23. Ibid., 36 and passim.

24. "The Coppie of the Anti-Spaniard . . . wherein is directly proued how the Spanish King is the onely cause of all the troubles in France" (London: John Wolfe, 1590), 31.

25. "A Fig for the Spaniard, or Spanish Spirits" (London: John Wolfe, 1591), B3.

26. *Calendar of the State Papers Relating to Ireland, James I, 1608–1610,* ed. C. W. Russell (London: Longman, 1874), 240.

27. Letter from Sir John Davies to the Earl of Salisbury, November 8, 1610, in Maxwell, *Irish History,* 281.

28. On the frequent allusions to Rome and its "civilizing mission" in the discourse on Ireland, see Canny, "The Ideology of English Colonization from Ireland to America," *William and Mary Quarterly* 30 (1973): 575–98.

29. "Setting the acts of Moses and Josua a part, I think there is no president that the godly haue rooted out the natural inhabitants of any country: but that the wicked have chastised sinners, many passages, both of divine and prophane writings haue testified" (Daunce, "A Brief Discourse," 20). Note that whereas Davies's models for his realpolitik are resolutely lay, Daunce appeals mainly to a religious rhetoric, with biblical precedents as the exception, and the Spaniards as the scourge of God.

30. See, for example, James's "Trew Law of Free Monarchies," in *James VI and I: Political Writings,* ed. Johann P. Sommerville (Cambridge: Cambridge University Press, 1994), 62–84. On the representation of royal authority during the Jacobean period, see Jonathan Goldberg, *James I and the Politics of Literature* (Baltimore, MD: The Johns Hopkins University Press, 1983).

31. Debora Shuger notes the connection between James's use of patriarchal imagery and his argument that the king is *properly* above the law: "a good king, although above the law, rules with 'fatherly love,' while a tyrant, equally above the law, rules in his own interest" (*Habits of Thought in the English Renaissance: Religion, Politics, and the Dominant Culture* [Berkeley: University of California Press, 1990], 156).

32. Spenser, *A View,* 45–46.

33. Cf. Daunce's extensive account of Spain as a mongrel nation in "A Brief Discourse."

34. I am indebted to Fowler for her wonderfully learned analysis of the relationship among character, dominion, and jurisprudence in "The Failure of Moral Philosophy in the Work of Edmund Spenser," *Representations* 51 (Summer 1995): 47–76.

35. Edmund Spenser, *The Faerie Queene,* ed. Thomas Roche (London: Penguin, 1978), V.ii.4. Subsequent citations are to this edition, by book, canto, and stanza numbers only.

36. The terms Saracen and Moor were often used interchangeably for Islamic peoples of North Africa in the period. The representation of a Moorish threat to Europe signals, I would suggest, enduring Christian fears of an expansionist Islam, as represented by the Ottoman empire and its Moorish allies. For Spenser's conflation of Paynim and Saracen, see William J. Kennedy's entry for "Paynims" in *The Spenser Encyclopedia*, ed. A. C. Hamilton (London: Routledge, 1990), 536.

37. In analyzing this episode, Hadfield focuses on how "the story that Spenser's narrator refused to tell at the wedding-feast [IV.xii]—that of the 'saluage countries'—is leaking out into the rest of the poem, colouring the Irish landscape with blood and so changing Faerieland into a bloody Irish landscape" (158–59). I would suggest that the violence spreading through the narrative has partly to do with the identification of the Irish with the Spanish Moriscos. Note that the reference to "filthy bloud," too, echoes directly the Spanish debates over *limpieza de sangre*, or "blood purity."

38. The shield is first used against Orgoglio and Duessa, in I.viii.

39. John Upton, *Spenser's Faerie Queene… With Glossary and Notes*, ii, 1758, 625–26; cited in *The Works of Edmund Spenser: A Variorum Edition; The Faerie Queene, Book V*, ed. Ray Heffner (Baltimore, MD: The Johns Hopkins University Press, 1936), 226–28.

40. For the triumph over Souldan as an apocalyptic battle, see Richard Mallette, "Post-Armada Apocalyptic Discourse," in his *Spenser and the Discourses of Reformation England* (Lincoln: University of Nebraska Press, 1997). For Philip's *Iam illustrabit omnia* and Spenser's parodic transformation of Apollo into Phaeton, see René Graziani, "Philip II's *Impresa* and Spenser's Souldan," *Journal of the Warburg and Courtauld Institutes* 27 (1964): 322–24; and Jane Aptekar, *Icons of Justice: Iconography & Thematic Imagery in Book V of* The Faerie Queene (New York: Columbia University Press, 1969), 82–83 and 218–19.

41. Roche's note in the Penguin edition reads: "[Adicia's] husband, the Souldan, probably signifies Philip II or the Pope, depicted as espousing injustice." More strikingly, Rosemary Freemar observes: "Not at all remote is the role of the Souldan. He probably represents Philip of Spain who made Ireland his political victim" (*The Faerie Queene: A Companion for Readers* [Berkeley: University of California Press, 1970], 284). Here the Armada reading has fully incorporated English propaganda and the Black Legend.

42. In his notes to the episode in the Longman edition of the poem [London and N. Y., 1977], A. C. Hamilton observes that Souldan is "the title of a Mohammedan or Egyptian ruler." He notes that "Since the term is used only in this episode, it may carry specific political reference," but fails to elaborate.

43. Heberle, "Pagans and Saracens in *The Faerie Queene*," in *Comparative Literature East and West: Traditions and Trends*, ed. Cornelia N. Moore and Raymond A. Moody (Honolulu: College of Languages, Linguistics and Literature, University of Hawaii, 1989), 81–87.

44. Ibid., 85.

45. The first reference is II.viii.56, where Arthur, having just defeated the Sarazin/Paynim Pyrocles and Cymocles, is referred to as the "infant." The second is to the very episode I discuss here.

46. In this case, the earliest uses of 'infant' recorded by the OED (Eden again, and Parsons) refer to Portugal, but the overwhelming preoccupation with Spain in Book V suggests that the more appropriate identification is with a Spanish prince. Hamilton, in his note, invokes the episode in Book II to suggest that "Arthur may claim the Spanish title, Infant or Prince, by defeating the Spanish power."

47. Aptekar, *Iconography*, 123.

48. James Nohrnberg, *The Analogy of* The Faerie Queene (Princeton: Princeton University Press, 1976), 362.

CHAPTER 3

"Those People far Surpass us": Gulliver, the Japanese, and the Dutch

Robert Markley

It is very usual for Civiliz'd and Polite Nations to look upon all others as barbarous.... Europe *now being the Seat of Learning, and Science, wherein learned Academies are set up for the Discovery of Hidden Secrets in Nature, we take all the Rest of Mankind for meer Barbarians: But Those who have Travel'd into* China *and* Japan, *must confess those People far surpass us in the endowments, both of body and mind.*

—*Jean Crasset*, The History of the
Church of Japan (1705)[1]

1

Books Two and Four of *Gulliver's Travels* have become key texts for postcolonial critics concerned with Swift's complicated attitudes toward European exploration, and exploitation, in the South Seas.[2] Book Three, in contrast, has received little attention—both because the hero's episodic adventures do not fit the pattern of European encounters with "barbaric" peoples (the Irish, Native Americans, and Pacific Islanders) and because Swift's satire is directed exclusively at European institutions (the Royal Society) and vices (luxury, political corruption, and absurd philosophies).[3] Gulliver's wanderings among

the imaginary islands of the western Pacific, however, are bracketed by
his only two encounters with natives of "real" realms: a Japanese pirate
captain and a Dutch pirate at the beginning of Book Three and the
emperor of Japan and the crew of a Dutch vessel at its end. In 1722,
after Swift had begun writing *Gulliver's Travels*, he noted that he was
reading "many diverting Books of History and Travels,"[4] and while
scholars have speculated about possible sources for his depiction of
Japan, only Anne Barbeau Gardiner has noted the significance of these
Japanese encounters in the context of Swift's vitriolic attacks on the
Dutch.[5] This essay examines Gulliver's voyage to Japan in the context of three important bodies of literature widely available in the early
eighteenth century: accounts of the short-lived English trading post
in Hirado (1613–23); histories of the expulsion of the Jesuits and
the extirpation of Catholicism in Japan; and narratives of the Dutch
willingness to perform the ritual of *yefumi*—literally trampling on
Christian icons—in order to maintain their trading privileges in Japan.
Gulliver's encounters with the Japanese suggest not only that Swift
knew this literature but that he was well aware of the deeply unsettling
implications that Japan posed for Eurocentric visions of trade, history,
and theology.[6] In their combination of fantasy and realism, Gulliver's
encounters with the Japanese register profound anxieties about the
limitations of English economic power, national identity, and morality
in a world that until 1800 was dominated economically by the empires
of South Asia and the Far East.[7]

Like many of his contemporaries, Swift recognized the limitations of
British economic and naval power in the Far East. Unlike Daniel Defoe,
however, who devotes (among other works) *The Farther Adventures of
Robinson Crusoe* (1719) and *A New Voyage Round the World* (1724) to
fantasizing about trading opportunities in China and the South Pacific,
Swift sets Book Three of *Gulliver's Travels* in the context of England's
failures to dent the Dutch monopoly of trade in either Japan or Southeast Asia. Like China, Japan presented fundamental challenges to the
rhetoric of European imperialism: it was a "heathen" empire that, after
the civil wars of the sixteenth century, had rejected Christianity, cut
off almost contact with Europeans, and yet continued to prosper. In
dedicating his translation of Engelbert Kaempfer's *History of Japan*
(1727) to George II, John Gaspar Scheuchzer, a Fellow of the Royal
Society, characterizes his subject as "a valiant and invincible Nation,
a polite, industrious and virtuous People, enrich'd by a mutual Commerce among themselves, and possess'd of a Country, on which Nature
hath lavish'd her most valuable Treasures."[8] Scheuchzer's language
reflects a consensus among European commentators that the Japanese

rivaled or surpassed the English, French, and Dutch in their standards of living, technological sophistication, and military prowess. Perhaps the most urbanized society in the early modern world, with a population that dwarfed that of any country in Europe, Japan boasted "cities that were infinitely cleaner and safer than anywhere else in the world"; water quality, sewage systems, and trash removal were more advanced and efficient than in London or Paris. Commoners "enjoyed a high degree of literacy," a "varied and nutritious" diet, "cheap entertainment," religious freedom (except for Christianity), and "relatively good and cheap medical care."[9] As Will Adams, the English mariner who became a samurai, put it in 1609, the Japanese "are good of nature, curteous above measure, and valiant in warre . . . They are governed in great Civilitie, I thinke, no Land better governed in the world by civill Policie."[10] For Adams as for Scheuchzer, the Japanese embody idealized, transcultural characteristics (good nature, courtesy) that the English both see as fundamental to their own sense of national identity and identify as universal standards of civility. Unlike the nations of Europe, wracked by warfare and the threat of war throughout the seventeenth and eighteenth centuries, however, Japan by 1720 had enjoyed peace and prosperity for a century.

Rather than being treated as a realm of Orientalist exoticism, then, Japan was considered an extraordinarily important economic power, the goal of European merchants since the sixteenth century. In one of most popular atlases of his day, Swift could have read that Japan

> abounds in all manner of Necessaries . . . with Mines of Silver and other Metals, and a great many fine Towns and Fortresses. The Emperor surpasses all the Monarchs of *Europe* in Splendor. The Kings, Princes, and Noblemen, who are his Vassals, have vast Riches in their Territories, which they spend in Luxury.[11]

Seventeenth-century voyages to Hudson's Bay searching for the Northwest Passage carried letters from James I to the emperor of Japan, and fifty years after the English had shut down their factory at Hirado, the East India Company mounted a costly voyage to Nagasaki to try to reopen this trade. The motivation for this venture was England's long-standing dream of finding a substantial Asian market for its broadcloth and thus stanching the flow of bullion from London to the East. The Company's instructions to its merchants declared that "our chiefest end of vndertaking the Iapon trade is the vent of Cloth, and other English Manufacture, and for the procuring of Gold, Silver & Copper for the supply of our other Factories in East India yt wee may not send Gold & Silver" from England.[12] For Swift's readers, Tokugawa Japan was both a promised land from which the English were banished and a reminder of the limits of England's commercial power.

Swift's decision to send Gulliver to Japan represents a crucial (if incomplete) inversion of Eurocentric discourses of colonialism, imperialism, and barbarism. Unlike contemporaries such as Leibniz or Voltaire who idealize Chinese civilization as a model for a corrupt Europe to emulate, Swift has little interest in trying to explain (or explain away) the paradoxical tag "heathen civilization" that was applied to both China and Japan.[13] Instead, Gulliver's audience with the emperor in Edo (Tokyo) marks a limit to visions of a European-dominated commerce and of Western morality. For Swift, the Tokugawa policy of *sakoku* (closed country) isolates Japan from the corruptions of modern Europe that are satirized throughout *Gulliver's Travels*. The emperor, however, is not the king of Brobdingnag or the Master Houyhnhnm, neither a satiric scourge nor an impossible ideal. Gulliver's audience with the emperor, in effect, offers a fantasy—conniving with the Japanese against the Dutch—which discloses *as fantasy* Eurocentric discourses of economic imperialism, moral probity, and technocultural superiority. Gulliver's Japanese encounters mortify English pride by revealing the *irrelevance* of the assumptions, values, and logic on which the self-congratulatory rhetoric of Eurocentrism depends.

2

In writing about Japan, European authors after 1640 confront a history of failed religious conversion and economic subservience. In the late sixteenth century, Jesuit missionaries had converted 220,000 Japanese (three percent of the population), and Portuguese merchants from Macao engaged in a lucrative trade that provided the silver bullion essential to their Asian commerce. Beginning in 1587, however, Hideyoshi and his successors, Ieyasu and Hidetaka, issued a series of edicts to clamp down on Christians who were suspected of political subversion.[14] Intensifying repression followed, and by 1615 missionaries had been deported, martyred, or chased underground; Japanese were forced to recant or die. In 1637 and 1638, confronted by famine and crushing taxes, peasants rebelled in the former Christian stronghold of Shimabara, resurrecting the rhetoric of apocalyptic Christianity as a rallying cry. Threatening to "slay all village magistrates and heathen bonzes [priests] without sparing even one; for judgment day is at hand," the rebels themselves were exterminated by the shogunate with the help of a Dutch warship.[15] The once-flourishing trade with the Portuguese ended, and Dutch merchants were confined to the tiny trading post on Deshima. The German naturalist, Engelbert Kaempfer (1651–1716), who was the physician on Deshima in 1691–92, described conditions on this tiny artificial island as "an almost perpetual imprisonment"; cut off from Nagasaki by armed sentries on the bridges to their outpost, the Dutch "patiently and submissively [had] to bear the abusive and injurious behaviour of these proud Infidels towards us" (325). The dominant European seapower in Asia was confined by the Japanese to a mercantile ghetto.

Japan, in short, provoked a crisis in seventeenth- and eighteenth-century historiography. Although in England, commentators such as Peter Heylyn could rely on anti-Catholic prejudices to mitigate the horror of Christian converts recanting their faith, Europeans had no ready-to-hand analytical vocabulary to explain either the suppression of Christianity or the abject behavior of the Dutch.[16] Besides Jesuit voices from a past that had been violently eradicated, the Dutch literature on Japan was both sparse and tightly censored by the Directors of the Dutch East India Company (VOC) who were intent on maintaining their monopoly on a still-profitable trade. The Dutch outpost was denied intercourse with all but a handful of Japanese, and communicated only through a hereditary guild of interpreters whose success was judged by the amount of money they could wring out of the red-haired barbarians. Before the publication of Kaempfer's *History of Japan* in 1727, the only eyewitness accounts published in England after the early seventeenth century were the short history by François Caron, a VOC merchant, and the compilation of Dutch reports collected and edited by Arnoldus Montanus and translated by John Ogilby as *Atlas Japanensis*.[17] Defoe characterizes Caron's history as "a tedious but very imperfect Account of the Country," and Montanus's work was never reprinted, although it frequently was cannibalized in geographies and atlases for a half century after its publication.[18] With the Japanese forced to swear an oath, in Kaempfer's words, "not to discourse with [the Dutch] nor to discover any thing . . . of the Condition of their Country," up-to-date information about Japan was a scarce and valuable commodity (ii).

Nonetheless, Swift and his contemporaries could read a fair amount of material on Japan, most of which reinforced views of the Empire as alien, alluring, and powerful. Purchas's *Pilgrimmes* included Adams's letters and the narratives of John Saris, the captain of the first trading venture to Japan in 1613, and Richard Cocks, the head of the English factory at Hirado 1616–23. In the atlases of the cartographer Herman Moll, English readers could find (in translation) short descriptions of Japan culled from Montanus and the Jesuits, such as a 1701 Latin entry by Johann Luyts, a professor at Utrecht: "The Japanese are reckon'd ingenious in Handicraft, just in Dealing, temperate, valiant and trusty, but at the same time addicted to Dissimulation and Cruelty, and are apt to lay violent Hands upon themselves; they are gross Idolaters, worshipping especially the Sun."[19] In this caricature, the Japanese embody contradictory qualities—"civilized" virtues (technological sophistication, honesty, temperance, and military prowess) and "barbarous" attributes usually displaced onto "heathens" (lying, cruelty, and idolatry). Luyts does not try to resolve these contradictory impressions, in part because the sources he cites offer no means to explain how the Japanese can dictate the terms of their contact with Europeans. Only "the Dutch," he continues, "by despising the Pictures and Images of the Virgin *Mary*, and other Fopperies of the Portuguese; and...delivering up their very Bibles to the Flames, [have] persuaded the Inhabitants, they were not Christians; and prevail'd upon them to permit Traffick there."[20] Luyts's strategy of labeling apostasy as Protestant iconoclasm failed to impress either English or Jesuit writers, who accused the Dutch of willingly sacrificing their beliefs to their lust for Japanese gold and silver.[21]

The most important of these Jesuit commentators was Jean Crasset, whose two-volume history of the Jesuit mission was translated into English in 1705 and ransacked by the anonymous author of the section on Japan in Moll's *A System of Geography* (1721). Writing a half century after the Jesuits had been expelled from Japan, Crasset devotes almost 1,400 pages to describing, with gruesome specificity, the tortures endured by Christian martyrs and trying to explain away the spectacular apostasy in 1633 of the Jesuit Procurator, Christovão Ferreira, who later served the Shogunate as an anti-Christian propagandist, translator, and interrogator.[22] Paradoxically, however, Crasset is more positive than Luyts in characterizing the Japanese. After praising this "most extreamly Courteous and Civil" people for their hatred of avarice, "their wonderful Courage in Adversity," the excellence of their education, and "their great Moderation," he declares that they "far surpass [Europeans] in the endowments, both of body and mind."[23] In effect, Crasset turns the Japanese into a heroic race who displace Western models of elegance and virtue, the equivalent of Swift's ancient worthies. In a telling comparison, he asserts that the Japanese "Language is grave, elegant, and copious, and surpassing without dispute both the Greek and Latine in the number of words, and variety of expressions" (1:6). Crasset displaces "the ancients"—the progenitors of Western civilization—as a source of cultural, linguistic, and secular authority. Japan wants only the spirit, and spiritual guidance is precisely what Catholic missionaries offer. Crasset ultimately conjures into being an imagined future, once "the Persecution blows over," of the resurrection of Christianity in Japan (2:547). This future spreading of the gospel represents the *only* contribution that Europeans can make to an otherwise superior people. The Jesuits see themselves reliving the early history of the Church when the faithful suffered martyrdom to bring true religion to the great empires of the ancient world. The heroism of Japanese converts in the face of bone-chilling tortures, in this regard, testifies to a national identity founded on courage, loyalty, and stoic endurance; the Japanese have become the spiritual heirs of an apostolic Christianity. Their martyrdom offers a powerful example to their European brethren who have fallen prey to heresy (Protestants), rivalry (Dominicans), and political and military conflict.

As armchair editors, Luyts and Crasset sift through evidence, shape their material, and make grand pronouncements about the country and its inhabitants. Like other seventeenth-century commentators, they lift passages from various sources, then transform the disparate experiences of priests, merchants, and officials into coherent and seemingly authoritative discourses. In contrast, Kaempfer's narrative in Japan emphasizes the psychological costs of being subject to the slights and abuses of "proud Infidels" (325). Although Kaempfer relies on his Japanese interpreter and judiciously placed bribes to gain access to dozens of Japanese sources to in order write his history, he also strives to give European readers a sense of what it is like to suffer the "shocking" indignities of subaltern status (325).[24]

Kaempfer's description of life on Deshima defines the relationship of the Dutch to the Japanese in terms of European *abjection*.[25] The Dutch do not simply comply with edicts from the Shogunate and regional authorities; they repeatedly demonstrate their "submissive readiness" to grovel before Japanese demands, including, in 1638, the order to aid in the "final destruction...of a people [the Christian rebels], with whom [the Dutch] otherwise agree in the most essential parts of their faith" (324–25). The reward for bombarding fellow Christians and then surrendering all of the ship's cannon to the Japanese are circumscribed trading privileges and confinement on an island the size of a baseball field. Although the Dutch claim that they have proved themselves "sincerely faithful to a foreign Monarch" by trampling on the crucifix, burning their bibles, and neglecting Christian worship, they never allay Japanese suspicions of their intentions (325). Their submission is neither a single act nor an annual tribute mission to Edo but an ongoing test of their willingness, at any and every moment, to sacrifice faith, honor, and weaponry to placate Japanese authorities. Kaempfer, an employee of the VOC, not a fellow national, is both complicit in Dutch rituals of abjection and critical of such compliance.

3

Although Kaempfer's history was published a year after *Gulliver's Travels*, the manuscript had been purchased by Sir Hans Sloane in 1723, and Scheuchzer had taken over its translation by 1725.[26] Subscriptions were being solicited by the end of that year, and it is tempting to speculate, as J. Leeds Barroll has done, that Swift added the Japanese episodes when he was in London in 1726 to a work otherwise substantially complete. Regardless of whether Swift knew of Kaempfer's work, he had read enough about Japanese in order to contrast their "heathen" virtues to the hypocrisy of the Dutch. By emphasizing Dutch malevolence and hypocrisy, he focuses the reader's attention on the moral failings of erstwhile Protestant allies rather than on the customs, language, or religion of the Japanese. Swift ignores much of what had been written about Japan: the warfare and political strife of the sixteenth century, the failure of the English factory, and the violent end to Japan's Christian century. The reader learns far more about Lilliput, Brobdingnag, the Island of the Houyhnhnms, Laputa, and Luggnagg than she does about Scheuchzer's "valiant and invincible Nation." Swift's depiction of Japan depends on the triangular dynamics of rivalry and exclusion: the Japanese are represented, in one respect, only in terms of their difference from the Dutch.[27] This dynamic is neither the byproduct of a "colonial imaginary" nor evidence of eighteenth-century Orientalism.[28] Japan resists representation precisely because it controls the cultural and economic terms of its encounters with red-haired barbarians. To participate in the discursive regime of the Japanese is to risk assimilation (Adams), martyrdom (the Jesuits), apostasy (Ferreira), or submission (the Dutch). Consequently, Gulliver cannot engage in extended conversations with the Japanese emperor as he does with the Brobdingnagian king or his Houyhnhnm master; he can only lie, connive, and evade the worst aspects of the subjection that have become an "essential" part of Dutch national character.

Gulliver's adventures in Book Three begin when he tries to enter the lucrative inter-Asian country trade; he leaves Tonquin in command of a sloop to engage in a trade with "neighbouring islands." Like his other endeavors, Gulliver's stint as a trader comes to an abrupt and unsuccessful end when his ship is captured by Japanese pirates who preyed on coastal shipping in the China Seas. The villain of this encounter, however, is not Japanese but Dutch:

> I observed among them a *Dutchman,* who seemed to be of some Authority, although he were not Commander of either ship. He knew us by our Countenances to be *Englishmen,* and jabbering to us in his own Language, swore we should be tyed Back to Back, and thrown into the Sea. I spoke *Dutch* tolerably well; I told him who we were, and begged him in Consideration of our being Christians and Protestants, of neighbouring Countries, in strict Alliance, that he would move the Captains to take some Pity on us. This inflamed his Rage, he repeated his Threatnings, and turning to his Companions, spoke with great Vehemence, in the *Japanese* Language, as I suppose, often using the Word *Christianos.*[29]

With the practice of Christianity a capital offense in Tokugawa Japan, the label "*Christianos*" is a death sentence. The Dutchman jabbers, threatens, and curses; his language lies beyond the pale of either civility or Protestant solidarity. During the years covered by Book Three (1707–09), England and Netherlands were allies in the war against France; but in his pamphlets of 1711 and 1712 Swift attacks the war, its staggering expense, and the self-serving behavior of the Dutch. The "Folly, the Temerity, the Corruption, [and] the Ambition" of the Whigs, he declared, was matched only by the "Insolence, Injustice, and Ingratitude" of the Dutch, who, he maintains, gained territory and trading concessions at England's expense.[30] The Dutchman, in short, embodies the pride, maliciousness, and avarice that Swift attributes to a nation that engages in "insolent Hostilities" against the English throughout "the *East-Indies.*"[31]

In contrast, the Japanese captain of one of the "Pyrate ships" is civilized and even merciful. He speaks "a little *Dutch,* but very imperfectly," and, having questioned Gulliver, refuses to allow the Dutchman to have him executed.

> I made the Captain a very low Bow, and then turning to the *Dutchman,* said, I was sorry to find more Mercy in a Heathen, than in a Brother Christian. But I had some reason to Repent those foolish Words; for that malicious Reprobate, having often endeavoured in vain to persuade both Captains that I might be thrown into the Sea (which they would not yield to after the Promise made me, that I should not die), however

> prevailed so far as to have a Punishment inflicted on me, worse in all human Appearance than Death it self.... I should be set a-drift in a small Canoe, with Paddles and a Sail, and four Days Provisions; which last the *Japanese* Captain was so kind to double out of his own Stores, and would permit no Man to search me. I got down into the Canoe, while the *Dutchman*, standing upon the Deck, loaded me with all the Curses and injurious Terms his Language could afford. (139)

The difference between the behavior of the Dutchmen and the Japanese captain hardly could be more marked. The Japanese captain is a man of his word, even "kind," doubling Gulliver's provisions "out of his own stores." He is the antithesis of the apostate Christian, a "Heathen" seemingly as virtuous as those figures called up from the dead later in Book Three as foils for a debased modern philosophy. The Dutchman is the evil genius of the pirate ships, cursing an innocent victim and demanding the severest punishment.

When Gulliver later lands in Luggnagg, he must lie to a "Customs-House Officer, by whom [he is] examined very strictly." Seeking to gain passage back to England, he admits that "I thought it necessary to disguise my Country, and call my self a *Hollander*, because my intentions were for *Japan*, and I knew the Dutch were the only *Europeans* permitted to enter into that Kingdom" (187). As Barroll suggests, aspects of the hero's stay in Luggnagg may be derived from Swift's sources on Japan: the custom-house interrogation was familiar to European merchants in Canton as well as Nagasaki, and Gulliver's description of his audience with the king of Luggnagg, "crawl[ing] upon [his] Belly, and lick[ing] the Floor as [he] advanced" and then "striking [his] forehead seven times upon the Ground" (189), satirically exaggerates the rituals of the Shogun's Court.[32] By posing as a Dutchman, Gulliver ultimately is able to avoid the protocols of abjection—*yefumi*, trampling on the cross—that define Dutch subservience to the Japanese. Ironically, he must assume the guise of his enemies in order to distinguish himself from them.

4

Gulliver's audience with the Japanese emperor resurrects nostalgic images of Englishmen at the Shogun's Court a century earlier, particularly the reception ultimately afforded Will Adams, the English pilot of a Dutch vessel who landed in Japan after a harrowing voyage through the Straits of Magellan and across the Pacific. Brought before Ieyasu, Adams found the Shogun "wonderfull favourable" and eventually convinced him that he was neither an Iberian spy nor a pirate, and that the English (or Dutch) would provide an effective counterbalance to the Jesuits (2:127). Adams spent the rest of his life in Japan as a translator and advisor to Ieyasu, rising to the rank of samurai, being given a substantial estate, and taking a Japanese wife.[33] Although, with Adams acting as a translator and intercessor, the English were allowed to establish a factory at Hirado, the audiences described by Saris and Cocks were paradoxically both nerve-wracking and anti-climactic affairs. No diplomatic breakthroughs were achieved and the Englishmen overestimated their importance to the Japanese.

In 1613, Saris traveled to Edo and had to be guided by Adams through his audience with the Shogun. Before Saris entered the audience chamber, he delivered "Presents sent from our kinge to the Emperour as alsoe those (which according to the custome of the countrie) I gave vnto the Emperour as from my self." These "Presents" (luxury items from England and South and Southeast Asia) signify differently for the English ambassador and the Japanese ruler: for Saris, they encode a reciprocal semiotics of civility that depends on idealized conceptions of exchange among equals; for the Japanese they are symbolic markers of the tributary status of another nation of European barbarians who nonetheless can be used to counterbalance the Catholic missionaries and their converts. After the Shogun takes his seat, Saris offers this brief description of his audience:

> Comminge to the Emperour, according to our English complements, I delivered our kinges letter vnto his Maiestie, who tooke it in his hande, and putt it vpp towardes his forehead, and commaunded his Interpretour whoe sate a good distaunce from him behinde, to will Mr Adams to tell me, that I was wellcome from a wearisome Iourney, that I should take my rest for a daie or two, and then his aunswer should be readie for our kinge. Soe takinge my leave of the Emperour, ... with my Attendaunts [I] returned to my lodgings.[34]

A bizarre figure with limited diplomatic skills, Saris apparently tried to hand-deliver James I's letter to Ieyasu, assuming that his "English complements" would satisfy Japanese protocol.[35] The Shogun's court, however, imposes a hierarchical regimen of discourses and protocols to elevate the Shogun well above a mere ship's captain. Even Adams must communicate through an official interpreter, and although he, like the Jesuits, constructs himself as an invaluable advisor and confidant to the Shogun, his status, like theirs, seems akin to that of a favorite pet.[36]

Englishmen in the Shogun's palace have roughly the same standing as Gulliver at the court of Brobdingnag.

Kaempfer's account of his audience in 1692 as a member of the annual tribute mission discloses the implications of seventeenth-century European embassies to Edo. Saris's sanitized fiction of diplomatic reciprocity for his superiors in the East India Company omits the experiential and psychological specificity that is a hallmark of Kaempfer's narrative. Kaempfer describes at length the passage of the Dutch through the palace before entering the audience chamber in which the Shogun, court officials, and women sit behind lattice work screens. The chief of the Dutch trade mission is granted the temporary rank of minor *daimyo* (feudal warlord) to elevate his status just enough to allow him to perform the ceremonies required of such vassals. The four Dutchmen (the ambassador, two merchants, and Kaempfer) "first [make their] obeyances after the Japanese manner, creeping and bowing our heads to the ground," and deliver their "most humble thanks . . . for having [been] graciously granted . . . liberty of commerce" (535). After this ritual is completed, however, "the succeeding part of this solemnity [becomes] a perfect farce." Although the ambassador is spared having "ridiculous and comical commands laid upon him," the other three Dutchmen are "ask'd a thousand ridiculous and impertinent questions" and then forced to perform for the amused nobility. The three Dutchmen are ordered to remove their

> Garment[s] of Ceremony, then to stand upright, that [the Shogun] might have a full view of us; again to walk, to stand still, to compliment each other, to dance, to jump, to play the drunkard, to speak broken Japanese, to read Dutch, to paint, to sing, to put our cloaks on and off. Mean while we obey'd the Emperor's commands in the best manner we could, I join'd to my dance, a love-song in High German. In this manner, and with innumerable such other apish tricks, we must suffer ourselves to contribute to the Emperor's and the Court's diversion. (535)

Kaempfer's description answers the question of whether the European subaltern can speak at the Japanese court—he can, but only according to a script that others write and direct for him. The commands to which the author and the two merchants are subjected render them farcical entertainers, and the accomplishments that might otherwise mark them as gentleman and representatives of a civilized nation—painting, dancing, and singing—are rendered ridiculous by being reduced to pantomime and farce. Kaempfer can articulate his resentment only after the fact.

If the situation were reversed—if a European monarch were ordering representatives from a small, far-off country to "speak broken" English or Dutch, and endure the indignity of performing "apish tricks"—postcolonial critics would have little trouble analyzing (and deploring) this spectacle. But Kaempfer's description of his audience points to the limits of narratives of Eurocentric "colonialism" or "imperialism" in the Far East. The postcolonial past, for most critics, remains centered on the Americas and Africa; the histories of those parts of Asia that can be made to fit traditional narratives of European colonization (the tiny islands of the Moluccas, the collapsing Moghul Empire, the late-eighteenth-century Ottoman Empire) reinforce old-school conceptions of European superiority over all of Asia, including Japan and China, in military power, technoscientific knowledge, economic sophistication, political organization, living standards, and social liberalization. The Japanese treatment of Kamepfer and his cohorts not only inverts the expectations generated by many postcolonial readings of European–Asian relations, it suggests the need for a complex rethinking of the semiotics, historiography, politics, and psychology of European abjection in the Far East. Gulliver's audience with the emperor of Japan, in this regard, becomes an important text precisely because it registers the cultural fantasies that Europeans develop to translate such "obeyances" into the languages of friendship and mutually beneficial exchange.

5

At the end of his adventures in Book Three, Gulliver takes a ship from imaginary Luggnagg to Xamoschi on "the South-East Part of Japan" (the region near Tokyo, marked on Moll's maps, that Swift takes for a "small Port-Town" [199]). The Japan that Swift imagines, however, is as much a fantasy as Luggnagg, though stripped of satiric description. Gulliver's letter of introduction from the king of Luggnagg to the emperor ensures that he is treated by the Japanese "as a publick Minister" and "provided . . . with Carriages and Servants" as well as expenses for his trip to Edo. There is no description of this journey; in a single sentence, Gulliver moves from his landing at Xamoschi to his audience with the emperor. Swift reduces the lengthy descriptions of the palace and the elaborate protocols of the Japanese court recorded by Saris and Kaempfer to a single phrase: Gulliver's letter is "opened with great Ceremony." Rather than licking the floor in ritual humiliation or experiencing endless delays, Gulliver is told simply "that [he] should signify [his] Request; and whatever it were, it should be granted for the sake of his Royal Brother of Luggnagg" (200). Swift's device of an alliance between a real empire and an imaginary island allows him to circumvent the problem of *sakoku*, which had closed Japan to all commerce except for the highly regulated Chinese and Dutch trade and forbidden all travel overseas by the Japanese. Rather than a xenophobic nation, ferociously resistant to international trade or friendship, Japan is engaged in "perpetual Commerce" with Luggnagg, a relationship cemented by royal friendship (200). Swift's radical departure from his sources has two effects: it brings Japan (or at least its emperor) within the idealized semiotics described by Crasset—Gulliver is again treated with civility and generosity, as he had been by the pirate captain; and it evokes the dream-like quality that characterizes Adams's version of his reception a century earlier.

Ironically, even though Gulliver is posing as a Dutchman, the sympathetic connection he forges with the emperor is founded on victimizing the Dutch. Having secured safe passage on a Dutch ship bound for Europe, he asks that the emperor,

> excuse my performing the Ceremony imposed on my Countrymen of *trampling upon the Crucifix*, because I had been thrown into his Kingdom by my Misfortunes, without any Intention of trading. When this latter Petition was interpreted to the Emperor, he seemed a little surprised; and said he believed I was the first of my Countrymen who ever made any Scruple in this Point; and that he began to doubt whether I was a real *Hollander* or no; but rather suspected I must be a CHRISTIAN. However, for the Reasons I had offered, but chiefly to gratify the King of Luggnagg, by an uncommon Mark of his Favour, he would comply with the singularity of my Humour; but the Affair must be managed with Dexterity, and his Officers should be commanded to let me pass as it were by Forgetfulness. For he assured me, that if the Secret should be discovered by my Countrymen, the Dutch, they would cut my Throat in the Voyage. (200–01)

With the connivance of the emperor, Gulliver avoids apostasy, the test of *yefumi* that all Japanese nationals and foreigners had to perform to demonstrate their rejection of Christianity and hence their loyalty to the Tokugawa Shogunate. Anti-Christian behavior and immorality are displaced onto the "*Hollander*[s]," continuing a tradition in the pamphlet literature of the 1670s anathematizing the Dutch for their "submissive readiness" to stomp on Catholic icons. Significantly, as the emperor's warning suggests, the Dutch are not temporizing when they perform this ritual: having internalized their abjection as a measure of self-identity, the Dutch elevate apostasy to a perverse article of faith.

Before the ship departs, Gulliver is "often asked by some of the Crew, whether I had performed the Ceremony," and escapes detection, without lying, only by "evad[ing] the Question by general Answers, that I had satisfied the Emperor and Court in all Particulars" (201). This Dutch obsession with *yefumi* suggests an inward corruption, a malevolence unmitigated by resentment directed at either the Japanese or at their own complicity in their humiliation. The Dutch no longer perceive themselves as Christians, but as submissive subjects. Although Gulliver's audience is mediated through the Emperor's relationship with the fictitious king of an imaginary country, the ultimate fantasy—one that Swift lets pass without overt satiric commentary— lies in imagining that the emperor is willing to circumvent the law in order to allow Gulliver to escape apostasy. This benevolence, even if its intended primary as a gesture to the king of Luggnagg, allows an (imaginary) Englishman to outwit the Dutch in one of the key outposts of their lucrative Eastern trade.

Gulliver's Japanese encounters, then, allow Swift to paper over internal political divisions within England by scapegoating a common adversary, the jabbering Dutchmen. Gulliver returns from Japan on a Dutch ship named *Amboyna*, and Swift's allusion, for his contemporaries, was unambiguous and chilling. For English writers in the seventeenth and eighteenth centuries, to write about the Far East is to confront the spectre of Dutch commercial and naval supremacy; this supremacy is symbolized by the trial and execution of twelve British merchants on the Southeast Asian island of Amboyna by the Dutch in 1623. This incident forced the underfinanced and underequipped British East India Company out of Spice Islands and, for a century, had marked the limits of British naval and mercantile power. For John Dryden, Defoe, and their contemporaries, the spectre of Amboyna haunted the coherence of a British national identity that depended, in part, on commercial success as a sign of providential favor.[37] The tendency to invoke Amboyna as both a rallying cry and a nightmare image of English abjection in the South Seas cut across political and religious divisions within England. By having Gulliver and the emperor outwit the Dutch, Swift offers his readers a satiric revenge fantasy for a century of indignities.

Framing the hero's episodic adventures in Book Three are the satires in Brobdingnag and Houyhnhnmland of European immorality, deceit, tyranny, violence, and hypocrisy. As the Brobdingnagian king tells

Gulliver after the hero has described the supposed virtues of England, "the Bulk of your Natives" must be "the most pernicious Race of little odious Vermin that Nature ever suffered to crawl upon the Surface of the Earth" (116). Gulliver's brief encounters with the Japanese raise questions about the extent to which such satiric judgments project into an imaginative or conceptual space what Europeans imagine must be going through the minds of the Japanese (and Chinese). To some extent, the attitudes toward red-haired barbarians ascribed to the Courts of Edo, Beijing, and Agra are refracted versions of European descriptions of the "savages" they encounter in the Americas, the Pacific, and Africa. A country "exceeding large, rich, and populous," Japan forces European writers to imagine an antipodal inversion of the rhetoric, values, and assumptions that define the colonization of the "New" World.[38] The fifteen or so primary sources cited in this essay represent a tiny fraction of the collections, histories, and memoirs on the Far East available to eighteenth-century readers. Donald Lach and Edwin van Kley count fifteen hundred works published in Europe between 1500 and 1800 dealing with Asia, and they admit to erring on the side of conservatism: widely reprinted and cannibalized reports (such as those compiled by Montanus) were recycled in atlases, travelogues, economic treatises, natural histories, and so on.[39] For Swift, Japan offers an ideal satiric foil for his anti-Dutch agitprop: a rich and populous land, both real and nearly inaccessible, that is inflexible in making the Dutch complicit in their own humiliation. Japan thus anchors and defamiliarizes Swift's satiric strategies by inverting the self-congratulatory rhetoric of European-driven trade: at the end of Book Three of *Gulliver's Travels* lies the possibility that, in Edo and Beijing, the "pernicious Race" of red-haired "vermin" have encountered an alterity more threatening to their self-conception than giants or talking horses.

NOTES

A different version of this essay, titled "Gulliver and the Japanese: The Limits of the Postcolonial Past," appears in *Modern Language Quarterly* 65.3 (2004): 457–79.

1. Jean Crasset, *The History of the Church of Japan*, trans. N. N. 2 vols (London, 1705), 5.
2. See Clement Hawes, "Three Times Round the Globe: Gulliver and Colonial Discourse," *Cultural Critique* 18 (1991), 187–214; Laura Brown, *Ends of Empire: Women and Ideology in Early Eighteenth-Century England* (Ithaca: Cornell University Press, 1993), 170–200; Claude Rawson, *God, Gulliver, and Genocide: Barbarism and the*

European Imagination, 1492–1945 (New York: Oxford University Press, 2001); Bruce McLeod, *The Geography of Empire in English Literature, 1580–1745* (Cambridge: Cambridge University Press, 1999), 181–86; and Anna Neill, *British Discovery Literature and the Rise of Global Commerce* (London: Palgrave, 2002), 110–19.

3. Douglas Lane Patey, "Swift's Satire on 'Science' and the Structure of *Gulliver's Travels*," *ELH* 58 (1991), 809–39; Robert Fitzgerald, "Science and Politics in Swift's Voyage to Laputa," *JEGP* 87 (1988), 213–29; and William Freedman, "Swift's Struldbruggs, Progress, and the Analogy of History," *SEL* 35 (1995), 457–72.

4. Jonathan Swift, *The Correspondence of Jonathan Swift*, ed. Harold Williams (Oxford: Clarendon Press, 1963), 2:430.

5. Anne Barbeau Gardiner, "Swift on the Dutch East India Merchants: The Context of the 1672–73 War Literature," *Huntington Library Quarterly* 54 (1991), 234–52. See Neil Rennie, *Far-Fetched Facts: The Literature of Travel and the Idea of the South Seas* (Oxford: Clarendon Press, 1995), 76–82; John A Dussinger, "Gulliver in Japan: Another Possible Source," *Notes and Queries* 39, n.s. (1992), 464–67; and Hermann Real and Heinz Vienken, "Swift's 'Trampling upon the Crucifix' Once More," *Notes and Queries* 30, n.s. (1983), 513–14.

6. Glyndwr Williams, *The Great South Sea: English Voyages and Encounters 1570–1750* (New Haven: Yale University Press, 1997), 208–12.

7. Andre Gunder Frank, *ReOrient: Global Economy in the Asian Age* (Berkeley: University of California Press, 1997); and Kenneth Pomeranz, *Europe, China, and the Making of the Modern World Economy* (Princeton: Princeton University Press, 2000).

8. Engelbertus Kaempfer, *The History of Japan*, trans. J. G. Scheuchzer (London, 1727), n.p. All quotations are from this edition.

9. Louis G. Perez, *Daily Life in Early Modern Japan* (London: Greenwood, 2002), 13, 15.

10. Samuel Purchas, *Purchas His Pilgrimmes*, 5 vols. (London, 1625), 2:128.

11. [Herman Moll], *Atlas Geographus*, 5 vols. (London, 1712–17), 3: 818. See also note 19 below.

12. David Massarella, *A World Elsewhere: Europe's Encounter with Japan in the Sixteenth and Seventeenth Centuries* (New Haven: Yale University Press, 1990), 356, see also 355–69; and John Keay, *The Honourable Company: A History of the English East India Company* (New York: Macmillan, 1991), 198–99.

13. Cf. Frank Boyle, *Swift as Nemesis: Modernity and Its Satirist* (Stanford: Stanford University Press, 2000), 61–77. On Voltaire and Leibniz, see David Porter, *Ideographia: The Chinese Cipher in Early Modern Europe* (Stanford: Stanford University Press, 2001).

14. See Mary Elizabeth Berry, *Hideyoshi* (Cambridge: Harvard University Press, 1982), 92–94; George Elison, *Deus Destroyed: The Image of Christianity in Early Modern Japan* (Cambridge: Harvard

University Press, 1973), 217–21; and C. R. Boxer, *The Christian Century in Japan: 1549–1650* (Berkeley: University of California Press, 1951).

15. From a circular of 1638, translated in Elison, *Deus Destroyed*, 220.

16. I discuss the significance of Heylyn's *Cosmographie* (London, 1652; eight editions before 1700) in "Riches, Power, Trade and Religion: The Far East and the English Imagination, 1600–1720," *Renaissance Studies* 17 (2003), 433–55.

17. Francis Caron and Joost Schorten, *A Description of the Mighty Kingdoms of Japan and Siam*, trans. Roger Manley (London, 1671); Arnoldus Montanus, *Atlas Japanensis: Being Remarkable Addresses by Way of Embassy from the East-India Company of the United Provinces to the Emperor of Japan*, trans. John Ogilby (London, 1670).

18. [Daniel Defoe], *Atlas Maritimus and Commercialis; or a General View of the World* (London, 1728), 200.

19. Herman Moll, *A System of Geography: or a New and Accurate Description of the Earth*, fourth ed. (London, 1723), 2:51. This work originally was published in 1721.

20. Moll, *System of Geography*, 2:51.

21. Gardiner, "Swift on the Dutch East India Merchants," 243–47.

22. On Ferreira, see Hubert Cieslik, "The Case of Christovão Ferreira," *Monumenta Nipponica* 29 (1974), 1–54; Elison, *Deus Destroyed*, 185–88; and Jacques Proust, *Europe through the Prism of Japan: Sixteenth to Eighteenth Centuries*, trans. Elizabeth Bell (Notre Dame: University of Notre Dame Press, 2002), 44–56. Montanus, *Atlas Japanensis*, 343–47, 357–58 includes a long description of Ferreira, hectoring captured Jesuits in 1643.

23. Crasset, *History of the Church of Japan*, 1:5; 1:13. All quotations are from this edition.

24. See Paul van der Velde, "The Interpreter Interpreted: Kaempfer's Japanese Collaborator Imamura Genemon Eisei," in *The Furthest Goal*, ed. Bodart-Bailey and Massarella, 44–70, and, in the same volume, Beatrice M. Bodart-Bailey, "Writing *The History of Japan*," 17–43, on Kaempfer's use of VOC sources.

25. On the complexities of this term, see Julia Kristeva, *Powers of Horror: An Essay on Abjection*, trans. Leon S. Roudiez (New York: Columbia University Press, 1982).

26. See Derek Massarella, "The History of *The History*: The Purchase and Publication of Engelbert Kaempfer's *The History of Japan*," in *The Furthest Goal: Engelbert Kaempfer's Encounter with Tokugawa Japan*, ed. Beatrice Bodart-Bailey and Massarella (Folkestone, Kent: Japan Library, 1995), 96–131. See also J. Leeds Barroll, "Gulliver in Luggnagg: A Possible Source," *Philological Quarterly* 36 (1957), 504–08; and,

on Swift's friendship with Carteret, Irvin Ehrenpreis, *Swift: The Man, His Works, and the Age*, 3 vols. (London: Methuen, 1962–83), 3:437.

27. See Michel Serres, *The Parasite*, trans. Lawrence Schrer (Baltimore: Johns Hopkins University Press, 1982).

28. Shankar Raman, *Framing "India": The Colonial Imaginary in Early Modern Culture* (Stanford: Stanford University Press, 2001).

29. Jonathan Swift, *Gulliver's Travels*, in *Prose Works of Jonathan Swift*, ed. Herbert Davis, 14 vols. (Oxford: Shakespeare's Head Press, 1941), 11:138. All quotations are from this edition.

30. Swift, *Conduct of the Allies* (1711), in *Political Tracts 1711–1713*, volume 6 of *Prose Works of Jonathan Swift*, ed. Herbert Davis (Oxford: Shakespeare Head Press, 1951), 15.

31. *Some Remarks on the Barrier Treaty* (1712), in *Prose Works of Swift*, 6: 97. On Swift's anti-Dutch attitudes, see Ian Higgins, *Swift's Politics: A Study in Disaffection* (Cambridge: Cambridge University Press, 1994), 183–90.

32. Barroll, "Gulliver in Luggnagg," 504–08.

33. See Massarella, *A World Elsewhere: Europe's Encounter with Japan*, 71–130, and Giles Milton, *Samurai William: The Adventurer Who Unlocked Japan* (London: Hodder and Stoughton, 2002), 106–14; 291–97.

34. John Saris, *The First Voyage of the English to Japan*, ed. Takanobu Otsuka (Tokyo: Toyo Bunko [The Oriental Library], 1941), 184.

35. See Milton, *Samurai William*, 194–97.

36. On pethood, see Srinivas Aravamudan, *Tropicopolitans: Colonialism and Agency, 1688–1804* (Durham: Duke University Press, 1999), 33–49.

37. On Amboyna, see Markley, "Violence and Profits on the Restoration Stage: Trade, Nationalism, and Insecurity in Dryden's *Amboyna*," *Eighteenth-Century Life* 22 (1998), 2–17; and Bridget Orr, *Empire on the English Stage 1660–1714* (Cambridge: Cambridge University Press, 2001), 157–59.

38. Josiah Child, *A treatise Wherein is Demonstrated . . . that the East-India Trade is the Most National of all Trades* (London, 1681), 9.

39. Donald Lach and Edwin J. Van Kley, *Asia in the Making of Europe*, 3 vols. (Chicago: University of Chicago Press, 1965–93).

Part II

Early Modern Europeans on India

CIVILIZATION AND THE PROBLEM OF RACE: PORTUGUESE AND ITALIAN TRAVEL NARRATIVES TO INDIA

Dorothy Figueira

INTRODUCTION

A study of the initial encounter of the West with India effectively demonstrates that all heterologies, all investigations of the Other, seek to distinguish between what is deemed "civilized" as opposed to "barbarian." This chapter compares early Italian and Portuguese accounts of voyages to and from India[1] to consider first of all how these narratives reflected or differed from the classical sources. Questions of race and racial construction featured centrally in these discussions. An insistence on distinguishing the civilized from the barbaric also characterized the Church's contributions to these debates. The influence of this alternative hegemonic structure in the representation of the "Other" adds a significant component to the study of the rhetoric and politics of empire building in India.

CLASSICAL AND BIBLICAL REPRESENTATION

In classical accounts, the actual location of India mattered less than its symbolic function. When Alexander the Great invaded India in

326 B.C., he thought that he had reached the Nile at the Indus. Even though Megasthenes had arrived at the court of Chandragupta in 303 B.C., India was often not distinguished from Ethiopia. All that was clear was that India existed beyond the borders of civilization, stamped as a land of marvels. Ktesias (fourth century B.C.) repeated stories reminiscent of Homer, adding new elements to the repertory: India was a land inhabited by pygmies, sciopods, cynocephali, headless beings, giants, and fabulous races. His account, as well as that of Megasthenes, survives in Pliny (A.D. 28–79) and Arrian (A.D. 92?–175). In the *Anabasis of Alexander* (A.D. 130?–180), Arrian described Indians in terms of how they differed from black races: they are taller and blacker than the rest of mankind, with the exception of the Ethiopians.[2] In the practical science of Strabo (63 B.C.–A.D. 19) and the mathematics of Ptolemy's *Geography* (second century A.D.), racial descriptions only occasionally enter into the "rational" conception of the world. In Strabo's *Geography*, for example, the color of the Indians' skin is attributed to the effects of the sun. Their hair is straighter than the "wooly" hair of the African, because India is more humid than Africa. In these descriptions of India, however, there is no racial antipathy. Although the Ancients noted racial difference, they were primarily concerned with one's membership within the *polis*. In this respect, they differed considerably from the Hebrews who were interested in the genesis of families and their relationship to human origin.

According to the Old Testament, humanity was divided with Japhet's descendants populating Europe, Shem's sons peopling the region of the Indian Ocean, Chaldea and Armenia, and Ham's descendants inhabiting Egypt, Libya, and Africa. Ham's exile to the far reaches of the earth was in punishment for having been the only one of Noah's sons to have gazed upon his drunken father's nakedness. By relegating Ham to Africa, the Old Testament associated sin with racial difference. Noah's curse of perpetual servitude on the offspring of Canaan, the son of Ham (Genesis 9:25), condemned the Africans who were supposedly his descendants. Because of its interchangeability with Ethiopia, India thus took its place in the Old Testament genealogy, where sin became embodied racially. Because sin was spatially configured, the biblical rendition of human descent coexisted nicely with the Greek belief that "civilization" was tied to the body's relationship to the community.[3] Physical alterity could now be associated with moral difference.

In the course of time, the ecclesiastical Christian order absorbed the Greek conception of what it meant to be civilized, thus characterizing citizens not by virtue of their membership in the *polis* but as willing partners in the Christian community. In Pauline letters, the ethnic Other was no longer a non-Greek barbarian, but the heathen who did not share in the body of the faithful in Christ. When Augustine (354–430) wrote *De civitate Dei*, a new political context emerged. The Goths had sacked Rome a few years earlier and barbarians, who had been on the edges of civilization, now occupied the epicenter of politics. Still Augustine resisted a racialist argument.[4] If monstrous races existed and were human, then they must have been descended from Adam. If they descended from Adam, we have no right to pass judgment on them (8.16). Henceforth, Pliny's and Aulus Gellius's descriptions of Indian monsters were no longer regarded as wholly reliable. Accounts of the monstrous had to be treated with circumspection, since all men born of Adam were rational and moral, whatever physical form they took. It did not matter if one was speech-gifted or mute, barbarian, black, or white (16.8). It only mattered if one was a willing partner in the sacrament that brought membership in the mystical body of the faithful in Christ.

The classical conception of India as a land of fabulous races continued into the fifteenth and sixteenth centuries—well after actual physical encounters had cast their existence into doubt. Even with their new-found knowledge, Europeans were unwilling to give up their dreams of monsters. Early explorers went to distant countries with a preconceived idea of what would be found. Since they knew their classical authors, Christian encyclopedias, natural science treatises, romances, and maps, it is not surprising that the lands they discovered and described conformed to the world that had previously been configured in the classical and cartographical literature. This world was still divided into antitheses of the civilized and the barbarian, with monsters occasionally making an appearance. Civilization was determined by one's ties to a community, now defined as much by reference to the *ecclesia* as to the *polis*. Attempts to establish anatomical, physiological, and geographical relationships among various human and animal populations did not produce a fully developed idea of race, since there was no proper anthropology, natural history, or biology to support it.[5] When the idea of race appeared in travel narratives, it was only an occasional element.

The early voyages of discovery did, however, offer a variety of new reasons to account for startling differences Europeans encountered in the lands they "discovered." Since civilization entailed membership in a social community, travel narratives investigated public governance and contrasted it to the brutishness of private existence in realms bereft of a legitimate public dimension. They also examined civilization (or lack thereof) in both the personal and public space. On the private level, brutishness often expressed itself in extravagant sexual practices.

In the public realm, civilization could sometimes be revealed by what constituted the nobility in such lands. Most importantly, the accounts of travel to India in the late fifteenth and early sixteenth century marked the presence of civilization by the presence of Christians. All these discussions, however, were framed by the traditional discourse that described India in terms of monsters and marvels.

Indian Christians and Monsters in Early Travel Literature

Niccolo de'Conti set out for the East in 1416 with a strong desire to go to India, where it was said that the inhabitants worshipped Christ. The account of his journey appeared in *India recognita* (1492). In this small volume, general information concerning Indian geography, customs, and natural resources merely forms the backdrop to de'Conti's larger thematic regarding Indian Christians and his personal need to engage them. During his travels, de'Conti had renounced or was forced to renounce his faith. Legend has it that Pope Eugenius exacted from de'Conti the narration of his memoirs as penance for his apostasy. De'Conti's comments on Indian Christians must be read within the context of this personal spiritual crisis.

In de'Conti, the myth of Indian Christians effects the movement from self-estrangement to self-realization. The Christian Indians appear as narcissistic objects resolving the lack experienced in the Self. They are consistently described as just like us, only better. They lead exemplary lives, are of sober demeanor, and excel in humanity and refinement. They are our equals in lifestyle and civilization. By constituting paradigms for model behavior, Indian Christians present the means by which the lost, apostatized de'Conti reconstitutes his religious Self. The reader, in turn, is meant to be edified by his tale of divine providence.

Poggio Bracciolini, the papal secretary and leading humanist, first edited *India recognita* in 1448. Poggio had been involved in both the Council of Constance and the Council of Ferrara-Florence-Rome and had obviously shared their aims of reconciling Eastern and Western Christians. During Eugenius's pontificate (1431–47), Poggio gathered material for a dialogue in Latin entitled *On the Vicissitudes of Fortune,* in which de'Conti figured prominently. De'Conti's life story provided Poggio with the central illustration of the beneficent aspects of fortune and he was the principal informant for Book 4 replying to Poggio's questions regarding Indian peoples, customs, and religion. Although *On the Vicissitudes of Fortune* differs considerably from

India recognita in tone, it too has de'Conti's apostasy as its subject.[6] Because de'Conti renounced his religion, he tends to identify Christianity with all that is good. The odd customs and perversions of the Indians, that he lovingly and humorously describes, are not, he assures us, practiced by Indian Christians. Notably, de'Conti chose to extol Christian virtue in a context that exploits the erotic and intentionally aims to titillate the audience. Neither de'Conti nor his editor Poggio, who as a papal secretary had written a collection of licentious anecdotes, feared the risk of diffusing their message by embedding it within pornographic minutiae.

Travel literature provides the necessary geographical and cultural distance from which criticism could be directed against Europe. As Poggio demonstrates, de'Conti had, indeed, discovered paradise in India.[7] Like Gaul, India is divided into three parts. The third India, the area beyond the Ganges and the Indus rivers, includes the south, the site of Saint Thomas's tomb. Here dwell the virtuous Christians that de'Conti encounters, identifies as Nestorians,[8] and represents as a civilization far more splendid and accomplished than Europe.[9] Like the Jews who are scattered throughout Europe, Christians are found throughout India, although they are more numerous in the south.[10] They were gentle and wise. Their material wealth was equal to that of Renaissance Italy. Poggio leaves little doubt as to the broadly satirical thrust of his polemic. He effectively juxtaposes de'Conti's account with the commentary of a fictive Indian who has come to the West. Poggio relates how this Indian came to the pope to "get information about the Christians" who "were rumored to live in the West." He is thus able to compare the Western Church and prelate unfavorably to an ideal Christian India.

De'Conti's image of ideal Indians Christians, whose virtue he himself sought to emulate, was embedded within tales of monstrosities: pig-headed elephants, fish-men, phoenixes, and androgynes. In Vijayanagar, the site of the most sophisticated Hindu kingdom of its time, de'Conti focused on those inhabitants who took pleasure in mortifications of the flesh, self-sacrifice, and sexual aberrations. On the Andaman islands, he described the behavior of cannibals.[11] In Cochin, he encountered monstrous fish-men. He emphasized that Indians could be monstrous both on a moral plane as well as on a biological level. In a particularly descriptive and self-deprecating passage, de'Conti described customs of male genital mutilation performed in order to satisfy the monstrous lusts of the Indian female population. Throughout the narrative, de'Conti returns to the theme of moral difference amidst talk of phoenixes and androgynes, exempla of physical difference.[12] In other words, de'Conti made sure to round out his detailed descriptions regarding the geographical, social, and economic conditions with erotic anecdotes in order to entertain as well as educate his readers. We are led to understand that the Indians, although they possess virtues, are sorely in need of management. The Indian Other is defined through the double optic of the Christian and the monster, the civilized and the barbarian. This binary opposition informed not only travel narratives, such as that of de'Conti, but also animated the popular literature of the time.

Giovanni Battista Dati, a pious priest who would become the bishop of San Leone in Calabria, popularized the myth of a utopian India populated by Christians in a two-piece song cycle (1493–95). The first song was entitled a "Treatise on the Supreme Prester John, Pope and Emperor of India and of Ethiopia," the second was simply "The Second Song of India." These poems were inspired by the translations of Columbus's supposed discovery of India, as described in the famous letter to Sanchez (February 14, 1493).[13]

Dati was a mediocre versifier, writing with the tone and style of the *cantastoria* or ballad-singer. Wholly popular in nature, his songs were destined to be recited publicly in the markets and squares. Although inspired by Columbus's letter, Dati did not rely on the information furnished by the admiral, nor did he present any images of the lands Columbus had discovered. Rather, he recycled the classical literary and cartographic image of India.

The first poem opens with the enumeration of the ten Christian nations in which India figures prominently (stanza 3). Although Indian Christians may err in their beliefs, the poet claims that they are more sincere in their faith than their more orthodox European brethren and they exist in great numbers (stanza 42). They have been in contact with the West through embassies to Pope Eugenius (stanza 43). Prester John is presented as the incarnation of power and splendor (stanzas 10–18), expressing in a popular form the same vision of a Christian utopia as found in de'Conti and serving the same purpose: Amidst battles for supremacy of the papacy, individual dynasties, and republics, India represents the ideal locus of peace as well as material and moral well-being. It figures a just, tolerant, and pious sovereign who happens to be the most potent and richest emperor on earth, serving God with humility and governing his people wisely. All the political, social, and domestic virtues that did not predominate the real world are projected onto Dati's fictive India.

In the "Second Song of India," Dati presented the flip side of the Indian equation. Here, we have the barbarian India in the form of a traditional teratology or tale of monsters (stanza 10). Dati's second poem follows the classical tradition of the monster, a tradition articulated primarily in biological and moral terms. Like Polyphemous, Indians live in physical isolation from civilization defined by a bountiful nature (stanza 7). They fit Aristotle's biological definition of a monster as 'ανόμοιον (different): without mouths (stanza 12), with one eye located in the middle of their chest (stanza 14), acephali (stanza 15), pigmies (stanza 18), sciopedi (stanza 21), monuculi (stanza 24), hermaphrodite (stanza 25), cynocephali (stanza 29), cannibals (stanza 31), mermaids (stanza 39), and human serpents (stanza 43). But, even here, India appears as a political and social utopia, eliciting devout sentiments and pious considerations. India is blessed with natural resources and Dati implores God to preserve its Christian faith.

De'Conti's and Dati's works resemble each other in an important respect. In both authors, the two myths, one identifying Indian Christians, the other presenting a theology of the monstrous, function as cultural allegorizations of India. One myth presented India as predominantly populated by Christians, descendants of those heathen who had been converted to the faith by Saint Thomas, thus creating a portrait of civilization in order to elicit sentiments of affinity and posit an ideal alternative to existing society. It provided both refuge and solace to Europeans beset by internecine wars and threatened by Moslem encirclement.

The myth of the Indian Christian, by allowing the Other to return to the same, explained the unknown through the known. The India inhabited by monsters justifiably could be marginalized as Other. Through a symbolic positioning of the body of the monster, certain areas in India could be differentiated as pagan and barbarian. Prior to Columbus, a double discourse of alterity operated: The civilized and the barbarian were represented by the Christian and the monster. Literature followed the classical taxonomy, where civilization was tied to community membership. The early travel narratives identified a community either in terms of the *polis* or the *ecclesia*. Usually, the civilized were members in both communities. After Columbus, however, talk of the physically monstrous had to cease, since the travelers could not produce specimens. The imaginary monsters were replaced by humans deemed monstrous on a moral, ethical, or spiritual plane.

In Ludovico de Varthema's *Itinerario* (1510) describing his journey to Egypt, Arabia, Ethiopia, Persia, and India,[14] we find many familiar elements. Here too, India appears as a series of edenic sites.[15] Gujarat is a cornucopia, rich in fruit, spices, and precious stones. The dry

Deccan is described in terms of its opulence, a veritable storehouse of diamonds. Centacola abounds in peacocks, flowers, and fruits. The air is fragrant and the inhabitants are long lived. Vijayanagar is literally a second paradise.[16]

In India, Varthema encounters many Christians. He also comes in contact with many virtuous heathens. Varthema informs his readers that, unlike other pagans (and certainly unlike the Moors), Hindus should be baptized, since they are a truly good and virtuous people. There is a direct analogy drawn between the virtue and nobility associated with Christian prelates and the character of brahmin yogis. Varthema claims that Hindu holy men are saint-like and lead the life of penitents. He contrasts them to the many barbarian Muslims he encounters.[17]

In Bengal, there are Christians who are just like us, with the same beliefs and rituals. In Calicut, Varthema finds Saint Thomas Christians for whom the sacraments are performed every three years by priests who come from Mesopotamia for that very purpose. They hold to the regular rites and holy days. The king of Portugal has made life difficult for these Christians because of his constant warring with the Moors. In retaliation, the Moors have taken to kill the Christians. They attack them secretly to avoid the wrath of the king of Narsinga (Vijayanagar), who is a friend to the Christians and protects them because of the miracles that Saint Thomas still performs in his realm.[18]

According to Greek notions of what is meant to be civilized—living in a community, cultivating the land, and establishing social structures—Varthema's Indians clearly pass muster. They live in walled cities after our fashion, farm, bank, and trade commodities. Their economy and mode of warfare are sophisticated.[19] Varthema makes little overt mention of race. However, each people is described in terms of color. We learn that the Deccani and Gujarati are of a tawny complexion. Moreover, Varthema minutely enumerates the castes and delineates their distinctions. He describes the precautions that upper castes take to prevent defilement from outcastes. His description of the untouchable Poliars as beast-like creatures immediately precedes a description of the various animals one finds in India. They are described as beasts. The cover their children in dirt, so that they resemble little buffaloes and appear as misshapen creatures fed by the devil.[20]

For Varthema, the Indian barbarian appears within the context of the larger discussion on caste, and most specifically, racial contamination. Some low castes were simply degenerate, both morally and physically. Through contact with such castes, civilized Indians underwent racial decay. Varthema also claimed that Indians from different castes degenerated from exposure to foreigners. For example, the demarcations of culture, as tied to the production of bread, vegetarianism, and settled communities living in proper dwellings, disappeared from those areas where Indians came into contact with the Portuguese.[21] Those sites allegedly lapsed into a barbarous condition. Civilization was also absent in the primarily Moslem zones.[22] Believing that the Portuguese had conflated them, Varthema clearly distinguished the Hindus and Christian Indians from the Moors.

In the *Suma Oriental* of 1515, Tomé Pires brings the racialist argument to the forefront of this narrative. Pires enumerates those areas populated by whites and contrasts them to the black inhabitants of Malabar.[23] Because of their color, the Nayars, a warrior caste whom Pires described as knight-like, must be aborigines. He enumerates the various low castes and provides an in-depth discussion of the rules regarding caste pollution. Pires contrasted them with the "purer" blooded brahmins whom he described as pacifist vegetarians. Their profession, bellicosity, and skin color distinguish them from the Aryan fold. Their racial impurity is, however, most noticeable in the behavior of their women. Nayar women, Pires informs his readers, are not virtuous. They are also not domestically inclined. They cannot sew or work. They collect multiple sexual partners and they take the upper position during sexual intercourse. They spend their time eating and amusing themselves.[24]

As in other travel accounts, India also appears in Pires as a paradisiacal site, rich in abundance. Its inhabitants exist in a prelapsarian state. There are good, virtuous, clever, prudent, and honest heathens as well as an abundance of Christians. In Malabar, Pires counts some 15,000 of the faithful. However, Christians are only found among the higher castes, the noblemen, merchants, and craftsman. They live in fortified communities as cultivators. In Pires's narrative, civilization is marked racially, by one's position within a well-defined social hierarchy, and by adherence to Christianity.[25]

From this brief *aperçu* of late-fifteenth-century and early-sixteenth-century accounts of voyages to India, one might draw several tentative conclusions. In both the Italian and Portuguese descriptions of India, the classical binary civilized/barbarian is still largely operative. Civilization was marked by membership in the *polis* and its Christian reconfiguration the *ecclesia*. Christians must exist in India either as Christians *avant la lettre* or as actual Christians. The Italian Varthema identifies as civilized those Indians left to their own devices who live in communities as Christians. These Indians degenerate into barbarians upon prolonged contact with the Portuguese. The low castes are presented as racially and morally inferior. The Portuguese Pires, likewise, established an idyllic prelapsarian India where civilization is tied to social structures and long-standing membership in the Church. Here too, barbarism is tied to racial indicators, such as skin color, sexual impurity, and caste.

Indeed, other Portuguese travelers of the period stressed the issue of caste. Duarte Barbosa's long enumeration of the myriad castes of the Indian subcontinent especially comes to mind. The case could be made that Portuguese travel narratives consistently focused on delineating the various castes they encountered throughout India. Here too, we might want to compare Pires's examination of caste with the manner in which caste was discussed in the narratives of Varthema and other Italians. Varthema and his compatriots describe the various castes with a view to the manner in which they interact with each other. Pires is far less descriptive. He focuses primarily on the moral dimension of caste and on the problems raised by Portuguese interaction with the various castes. In particular, he emphasized the moral dangers involved in racial miscegenation in the form of breeding outside one's own caste. Portuguese concern with racial miscegenation was not limited to the prejudices of a given author or mere theoretical speculation, it had very practical ramifications. The fantasy of Indian Christians, embedded as it was in speculation regarding racial identity, could not help but inform policy regarding the establishment of the Church in India. This myth would also sabotage any hope of dialogue between Eastern and Western Christians, as an embassy from Prester John amply demonstrates.

DAMIÃO DE GÓIS AND THE ENCOUNTER WITH "INDIAN" CHRISTIANS

In 1514, Damião de Góis (1502–74), a 12-year-old page at the court of Manuel I of Portugal, witnessed the arrival of an embassy that was said to have come from Prester John, identified as the emperor of India. For twenty years, there was no written testimony on this embassy until the then grown-up Damião de Góis wrote his account entitled the *Legatio magni Indorum imperatoris Presbyteri Ioannis ad Emanuelem*. This work presents the text of a letter sent by the court of Ethiopia, then thought to be part of India. It also relates the story of the embassy's sojourn in Lisbon and offers details, in the form of questions posed to Matthew, the ambassador, as well as his responses. These questions dealt with issues regarding the religion, patriarch, kingdom, court, and emperor of the Indians. Matthew claimed that, although his people differed in rites, laws, customs, and ceremonies, they were in accord with Christian nations and Catholic doctrine in all other matters pertaining to the faith. The Portuguese believed that Dawit II, the king who had sent the embassy, was the elusive Prester John of the Indies, believed to be the heir of Saint Thomas who had gone to India to spread the Gospel. Since the eleventh-century *Epistola Presbyteri Iannis*, Europe had fantasized about this mysterious Oriental potentate. It was believed that he could be an Eastern ally for Christianity in a definitive confrontation with Islam.[26] This fantasy was, of course, politically expedient.

Sometime between 1514 and 1527, Dawit II's envoys returned to Ethiopia accompanied by the first Portuguese embassy. A second embassy was subsequently dispatched and when it returned home to Portugal, its chaplain, Francisco Alvares, was accompanied by an Ethiopian priest named Sagâ za-Ab (Zagazabo), whom Dawit had sent with letters to João III and Pope Clement. In 1533, Góis had the opportunity to meet Zagazabo in Lisbon, where he had been detained by the king. The Portuguese had not allowed the Ethiopian emissary either to convey his letters to Rome or even return home. Zagazabo was angry, since he had already been in Lisbon for seven years and had not been allowed to take communion or fulfill his emperor's commission to describe his country to the West. He welcomed the opportunity to speak to Góis. For his part, Góis, who knew full well the limitations and errors of his *Legatio*, welcomed this opportunity to correct the record. Zagazabo provided Góis with the information necessary to emend Matthew's initial articles. Góis then published Zagazabo's statements in 1540 under the title of *Fides, religio, moresque Aethiopum*.[27]

In the introduction to the *Fides*, Góis addressed a statement to Pope Paul III, who had succeeded Clement VIII in 1534, deploring the state of Europe and rejoicing in the hope of new additions to Roman Catholicism. Góis stressed the geographic polarity between India and Ethiopia. He also held open the possibility of union between Ethiopian and Indian Christians and European Catholics.[28] The first section of the *Fides* recounts the history of the Portuguese search for Prester John up to the 1527 legation. It includes the exchange of letters among Manuel, Dawit, João, and the Pope. It then provides a direct translation of Zagazabo's rectification of Matthew's original articles. Zagazabo's treatise on Ethiopia's religious beliefs, rites, and customs supplements Matthew's information on the country, its patriarch, and emperor.

At various points in the narrative, Zagazabo complains that he was not sent Westward to dispute small points of doctrine with prelates, but rather to begin a friendship between Catholic peoples. He affirms that the Ethiopians recognize the pope and hope for one religion, one flock, and one shepherd. He views the trivial discussions that have detained him and sabotaged his mission as unimportant. What was necessary, he felt, was the need to sustain the Eastern Christians. Matthew thought that it was useless for him to justify his rituals, since all Christian brothers, as sons of one baptism, were bound together in one faith. This argument might have been difficult for his interlocutors to appreciate, since this religion that Matthew claimed was the same as theirs included married clergy and female circumcision and lacked indulgences. Zagazabo's responses suggest that the Ethiopians also realized the political advantages of embracing the Prester John legend for diplomatic purposes. Zagazabo responded performatively; he tailored his comments to suit what he believed to be both the theological substance of Christianity and its political context.

The *Fides* champions the cause of Ethiopia and Portugal's role in the long-dreamt reconciliation between Eastern and Western Christianity. Although Portuguese imperialism is defended as a divinely inspired crusade to spread the Gospel, the text challenges Rome's refusal to accept other Christian churches. The subject, however, was not the Portuguese humanist, but the Ethiopian Christian, whose message had not been allowed to be heard for seven years. In both the *Legatio* and more so in the *Fides*, Góis gave voice primarily to the Ethiopian informants, unaccompanied by any commentary and uncensored by Góis himself.[29] Clearly the time for such messengers and such a message had not yet come. Exposing and championing an alternative form of Christianity did nothing to promote a union between the Eastern and Western Churches. In fact, it contributed to their ultimate schism. Once the facts concerning Ethiopia were more or less known, Catholic opinion was that the Monophysite Church was heretical and its king and resources were not as great as one had once imagined. The fabulous Prester John was clearly not the same as the "real" one and the fantasy Christians did not resemble those found in Ethiopia.

In fact, the Ethiopians were clearly *barbari*.[30] Even though they were Christian, Góis runs down a virtual checklist of attributes from medieval and early modern ethnographers to judge them as civilized or barbarian. The very questions put to Matthew in the *Legatio* sought to determine whether the "Indians"/Ethiopians ranked among the civilized or the barbarian according to Aristotle's criteria. To prove whether they live a proper civil life (in cities with institutions), the articles focus on the existence of written laws, courts, and magistrates (#14,

16, 18–19), marriage and family life, inheritance (#23), commerce (#4, 25), possession of written history (#15), taxes (#20), proper clothing, and social distinctions (#2–3). Their eating habits are investigated to show whether they might be bestial in what was eaten and the manner in which it was cooked. Matthew was questioned about the emperor's wives to elicit information on possible bestial sexual practices such as matriarchy, polygamy, and promiscuity (#3, 7). As tolerant and ecumenical as Góis was, the humanist held to classical taxonomy. He did not relinquish the Aristotelian typology.[31]

Either one was civilized or barbarous: Ultimately, the determining factor in judging people rested on their military might. This is the point at which reality confronted fantasy. When the Ethiopians were discovered to possess insufficient defensive strength against their own enemies, to the degree that they sought aid from the West to contain their Moslem neighbors, they were relegated to the class of barbarians. When they were found to possess insufficient wealth and engage in unorthodox practices, they were deemed insignificant Christians at best, heretics at worst. Civilization, defined as force of arms and the standard faith, formed the package of Christianity in this literary geography. Once one or more of the components failed, the entire construct crumbled. At that point, race and especially, caste became important factors in determining access to the Church and its hierarchy.

Race and the Consolidation of Religious Power

Official documents and private correspondence bear witness to the Portuguese obsession with "limpeza" or "pureza de sangue." In the heart of the empire, war and sea travel had considerably thinned out the ranks of white males.[32] Even as early as the voyage of Pires, it was impossible to furnish a full complement for the fleet without raising it from a class lower than that of the peasants. Convicts were enlisted to work out their terms in Indian forces. As sources of free labor diminished, slaves became a necessity as did intermarriage.[33]

Very few white women went to India. A ship of 800 men would perhaps have a dozen women.[34] Those women who survived the journey tended not to be fertile or to live long. In other words, miscegenation became more the rule in India than it would be in Brazil or Africa. In a letter to Ignatius Loyola, the Jesuit Nicholas Lancilotto (December 5, 1550) decried the cross-breeding that was common from the beginning of the Portuguese presence in India.[35]

Alfonso de Albuquerque inaugurated the policy governing mixed marriages in 1510, that is, at about the time that Pires concluded his voyage. Albuquerque encouraged the Portuguese to marry the white and, preferably, beautiful widows and daughters of the Moslems they had killed in the battle for Goa. In other words, Albuquerque tried to limit marriage to women of Aryan origin who had been forcibly converted to Christianity. It was not desirable for the Portuguese to breed with the black women of Malabar, who were dark-skinned Dravidians. However, in Goa, most did in fact "marry negresses."[36]

Miscegenation among the populace was one thing, diluting the blood of the clergy quite another. Alexandre Valignano, the celebrated reorganizer of the Jesuit missions in Asia, categorized the mixed breeds according to their percentage of European blood.[37] The pure breeds born in India, Eurasians, half-breeds, and Indians were all deemed unsuitable candidates for admission in the Society of Jesus. The pure breeds born in India were thought to be illiterates, the rest were weak, vice-ridden, and stupid.[38]

The Portuguese ideology of white superiority was thus borne out by the behavior of the Portuguese religious orders and their refusal to admit persons of color and half-caste recruits. Jesuits who originally had no color bar, adopted one under Portuguese pressure. Where efforts were made to relax color prejudice, they were usually the work of Italian, and not Portuguese members of the Society of Jesus. Among the Indian secular clergy, brahmins exclusively filled the ranks. They had retained their racial pride; they were not born from intermarriage with lower castes or debased Portuguese. Moreover, lower caste converts to Christianity tended to retain their fear and respect for brahmins, whether they be Hindu or Catholic priests.

The official line was that religion, not color, should be the criterion for Portuguese citizenship and that all Asian converts to Christianity should be treated as equal to their Portuguese coreligionists. Laws were promulgated to this effect in 1562 and 1572. Race, however, continued to be a concern and inhibited the immediate implementation of these racial laws. Two hundred years later, Pombal's decrees of 1761 and 1774 once again declared that all baptized Asian subjects of the Portuguese crown had the same legal and societal status as white persons who were born in Portugal. Even so, Pombal's decrees were ignored for thirteen more years. History reveals how deeply the Portuguese in India held to their race consciousness.

As historians have noted, the much vaunted Portuguese not to be color-prejudiced was a myth. This chapter has shown how the Portuguese concern with racial degeneration entered into discussion as a remainder on the edges of discourse, as a leftover from the selection of materials that the traveler chose to investigate. In the case of Pires, the textual production, his discussion on caste, substitutes for the presupposition absent from the textual product, namely Portuguese fear of miscegenation. The important thing to note is that Portuguese attitudes regarding their "Indian" coreligionists could never be isolated from a concern over racial contamination or moral and racial decay. This fatal combination derailed any attempt to forge a reunion between the Eastern and Western believers.

CONCLUSION

What happened to the monsters that inhabited India in the classical texts and tarried there well into the age of discovery? This chapter has demonstrated how the literal monsters faded away as discussion turned to descriptions of figurative monsters, the sexually aberrant, racially degenerate, and spiritually perverse. However, the monster, barbarian, and outcaste share a common aim in the heterological process. As implicit devices in the representations of the New World produced by the texts themselves, these tropes were transported along with their authors across the ocean, and circulated in Portuguese and Italian culture. Indian Otherness was thus transformed into the continuous text of European knowledge—a presentation of a natural world as a transitional site between savagery and civilization. These figures represent exempla of those very points that Michel de Certeau has found most evocative—where the effects of the transformative operation seem most precarious, where the textual seam is torn. They appear in the text as traces of what falls outside language's operative capacity to bring what lies outside back into "sameness." They function as waste products of the interpreter's constructural thought, what is repressed, yet ultimately becomes the Other.[39]

In general, the Indian and Ethiopian Other serves to confirm and reinforce a European sense of identity that culminates, for the Portuguese, in an obsession with purity of blood and fears of sexual chaos. The established identity of the Portuguese conqueror as a civilized, Christian upholder of bloodlines became codified in the myth of Portuguese racial tolerance. However, it produced a residue that returns insistently as a fantastic Other (monster, barbarian, black outcaste whore) putting in jeopardy the stable figures of both the Other and the Self, blurring their distinction, like the Freudian repressed, and upsetting an aesthetic construction. The traveler is, therefore, no longer secure in a detached position of contemplation, but inhabits an ambivalent realm of seduction and fascination. Our assurances regarding contracts between the subject and the Other are thus shaken as are the divisions drawn between unauthorized knowledge and its textual absence, fantasies of strength, and fears of weakness.

Protestantism was in the air, offering a real experience of how dangerous difference could be and what enormous havoc it could wreak. The Ethiopians were different and proof arrived in the form of returning travelers and their companion Zagazabo. The sympathetic efforts of Góis and the ecumenicism of the Ethiopian Christian notwithstanding, the dream of unity was hopelessly shattered by prosaic reality. And so, tolerance toward this area never thrived. Portuguese military, naval, and commercial activity in the West Indian Ocean isolated Ethiopia from Cairo, just as the Saint Thomas Christians would become cut off from Mesopotamia, the source of their bishops. In both areas, the Portuguese would insist on conformity with practices of the Roman Catholic Church. Their demands could not be met. In the decades following 1540, a significant number of Christians dwelling in Ethiopia and India would be lost to the dream of Catholic unity.[40] Classical literature, and early travelers had all confused these two realms. However, once they became truly known, it was of little consequence. They were, after all, just the same place of difference. The ideology of alterity prevailed. Rather than provoking a reconsideration of the fantasies of difference, the light of new truth provided instead an excuse for rejection. This squandered opportunity represented a failure of European consciousness on multiple levels: a failure of political intelligence, religious values, and imagination.

Notes

1. By the term "India," I signify what was then loosely considered as the expanse encompassing Ethiopia as well as the area that today comprises the modern nations of India and Pakistan.
2. Arrian described the Indians as tall and slender, lighter in weight than other men. Also see R. G. Majumdar, *The Classical Accounts of India* (Calcutta: Mukhopadhyay, 1960).
3. Ivan Hanneford, *Race: The History of an Idea in the West* (Baltimore: Johns Hopkins University Press, 1996), 88.
4. Augustine, *De civitate Dei*, "The deserts of souls are not to be estimated by the qualities of bodies," *The City of God*, trans. Marcus Pods (New York: Random House, Inc., 1950), 11.23.
5. Hanneford, *Race*, 183.

6. Lincoln Davis Hammond, ed., *Travelers in Disguise: Narratives of Eastern Travel* (Cambridge, Mass.: Harvard University Press, 1963), 6.

7. Richard Henry Major, ed., *India in the Fifteenth Century* (London: Hakluyt, 1857), 13.

8. Hammond, *Travelers in Disguise*, 10.

9. Ibid., 25.

10. Ibid., 10.

11. Ibid., 11, 32.

12. Ibid., 14.

13. In June 1493, Dati printed in Rome a rhymed version of Columbus's letter, with the title *Lettera delle isole nouvamente ritrovate*. In a relatively authentic form, Dati's poem provides information concerning events that from the end of March 1493 had been spreading through the commercial *aziende*.

14. Varthema undertook his voyage between 1503 and 1510.

15. Hammond, *Travelers in Disguise*, 150–54.

16. Ibid., 120, 115, 122–23, 125, 127.

17. Ibid., 116, 119, 199, 122. For a discussion of the many Muslims he encounters, see also ibid., 13, 145, 164, 176.

18. Ibid., 116, 119, 122.

19. Ibid., 115, 121, 144, 154, 155–56.

20. Ibid., 118, 125; 116, 123; 138–39, 157.

21. See, in particular, his description of Cannanore (ibid., 125).

22. See in this regard his descriptions of Tornapatani (ibid., 132), Calicut and Quilon (ibid., 163).

23. Tomé Pires, *The Suma Oriental. An Account of the East from the Red Sea to Japan*, ed. Armendo Cortesão (Nendeln, Lichtenstein: Kraus, 1967), 48, 51, 57.

24. Ibid., 57, 67, 68, 69, 70, 71, 72.

25. Ibid., 55, 58, 59, 73.

26. Pope Eugenius had written to Prester John as early as 1439 seeking an alliance (Francis X. Rogers, *The Quest for Eastern Christians* [Minneapolis, Minnesota: University of Minnesota Press, 1962], 137).

27. Damião de Góis, *Fides, Religio, Moresque Aethiopium sub Imperio Preciosi Iounnis* (Louvain: Rutgerus Rescius, 1540). This work barely scooped Alvares's own account of the encounter published under the title, the "Verdadera informacam das terras do Preste Joam."

28. As he had done in the *Legatione magni Indorum Imperatoris Presbyteri Ionnis ad Emanuelem Lusitaniae Regem Anno Domini 1513* (Antwerp: Iaon. Grapheus, 1532), here too Damião de Góis made an appeal for the Lapps and the need to bring them, like the Ethiopians, into the Roman Catholic fold.

29. Jeremy Lawrance, "The Middle Indies: Damião de Góis on Prester John and the Ethiopians," *Renaissance Studies* 6.3–4 (1992): 320.

His authorial stance, by the way, would cost him dearly when he later came under the surveillance of the Inquisition.

30. Ibid., 319.
31. Ibid., 322, 323.
32. C. R. Boxer, *Four Centuries of Portuguese Expansion 1415–1825: A Succinct Survey* (Berkeley: University of California Press, 1969) and C. R. Boxer, *The Portuguese Seaborn Empire: 1415–1825* (London: Hutchinson, 1969).
33. K. G. Jayne, *Vasco da Gama and His Successors: 1460–1580* (London: Methuen, 1910), 286–87.
34. C. R. Boxer, *Race Relations in the Portuguese Colonial Empire* (Oxford: Clarendon, 1963), 58.
35. Antonio da Silva Rego, ed., *Documentacão para a história das missões do Padroado português do Oriente. India*, 12 vols. (Lisbon: Agência Geral do Ultramar, 1947–58), cited in ibid., 61.
36. Ibid., 65.
37. The Reinol was the Portuguese born in India of pure European heritage of which there were few in number. The casticos were born of a European father and a Eurasian mother. The Mesticos were the half-breeds.
38. Boxer, *Race*, 62–63.
39. Michel de Certeau, *The Writing of History*, trans. and intro. Tom Conley (New York: Oxford University Press, 1988), 227.
40. Rogers, *Quest*, 169.

CHAPTER 5

ENGLAND IN MOGHUL INDIA: HISTORICIZING CULTURAL DIFFERENCE AND ITS DISCONTENTS

Paul Stevens

No recent work better exemplifies the postcolonial proposition that Western historicity empowers colonial habits of thought than Bernard Lewis's bestseller *What Went Wrong? The Clash Between Islam and Modernity in the Middle East.*[1] As his title suggests, Lewis imagines the Islamic world of the Arabs as a culture or polity that is by definition premodern—a world whose emergence from the Middle Ages was stillborn or at best monstrously stunted or deformed. Lewis's message is clear. What the Arabs are, we could have been had it not been for the miracle of modernity. Indeed, modernity defines the West. The problem for the Islamic world is not technological or even political, but historical and ideological. At the heart of Lewis's neoliberal understanding of modernity is a familiar, Enlightenment conception of freedom. Freedom is not simply a matter of political independence, but a historically specific way of being:

> To a Western observer, schooled in the theory and practice of Western freedom, it is precisely the lack of freedom—freedom of the mind from constraint and indoctrination, to question and inquire and speak; freedom of the economy from corrupt and pervasive mismanagement; freedom of women from male oppression; freedom of citizens from tyranny—that underlies so many of the troubles of the Muslim world.[2]

At its most positive, then, freedom means the ability of an individual or society to question, inquire, and speak, that is, to practice the "industry of free reasoning" so idealized by Milton and others in the seventeenth century.[3] Freedom is reason and reason is but choosing, the kind of choosing whose antitheses are "Custom" from without and "blind affections" from within (*CPW* 3:190). Clearly, so Lewis feels, the Arabs were made more than sufficient to choose reason and so improve themselves, though free to fail. Like Milton's God, he looks down on the Islamic world and offers its denizens this choice—accept modernity, that is, "the theory and practice of Western freedom," or continue to stagnate in poverty, violence, and failure. He ends his eloquent monologue with these ominous words: "For the time being the choice is their own."[4] Published in paperback just before the Anglo-American invasion of Iraq, Lewis's book, as Francis Robinson was quick to point out, reads like "a historian's manifesto for regime change."[5]

One of the many ironies of *What Went Wrong?* is that it dramatically confirms the charges laid against Lewis by the late Edward Said over twenty-five years ago.[6] Again, Lewis's reluctant critic Robinson makes the point—the book "will, I fear, become a *locus classicus* for the Orientalism thesis of Edward Said."[7] For Said, the Orientalism of Lewis and others means emphasizing difference and recreating the East in the image of all the negatives that define Western identity. What continues to make this improbably totalizing thesis so compelling is the pervasive force of Western historicity, for Orientalism means historicizing cultural difference—that is, it reveals the distinctively Western, epistemological habit of comprehending cultural difference in terms of historical development. Distance in space is routinely represented as difference in time.[8] What they are, we were. As the record of Western colonialism suggests, historical knowledge even at its most restrained or objective, to the extent that it imagines the patterns of development it perceives as "our" knowledge, that is, to the extent that it is driven by the identity thinking at the heart of ideology, always encourages solipsism and serves as a function of power. Nowhere is this more apparent than in the kind of historicism the Enlightenment theorization of historicity produced. There, according to Said, the one human history or progress uniting all humanity imagined by Enlightenment historicism always culminated in or was observed from the vantage point of Europe, and what was neither observed nor documented by Europe was either lost or felt to be of no consequence.[9] Non-European societies were routinely dismissed in Marx's infamous words as "passive," "unresisting and unchanging"[10] and, according to Michael Hardt and Antonio Negri, this "negative construction of non-European others" had and still has a certain kind of inevitability, for it "is finally what founds and sustains European identity."[11] The irony is that the more insistently Lewis makes his case the more effectively he confirms this argument, happily fuelling the postcolonial suspicion that the relation between Western historicity and domination is not simply possible but necessary or absolute. In this view, "modernity" is not so much the answer as the mode of thinking and acting that is in large measure responsible for the problem.

By examining early modern English responses to the East, specifically to Moghul India, what I want to do in this essay is critique both the neoliberal and postcolonial positions. First, I want to do justice to the postcolonial proposition that historicity empowers colonial thinking by explaining something of the force of the habit of historicizing cultural difference as it emerged in early modern times—suggesting how, especially in the case of a thinker like Milton, this way of knowing encouraged citizens of what Hardt and Negri would call the new national empire states of Europe to imagine Moslem India as a specific example of the old medieval empire states from which their polities were evolving. Second and more importantly, I want to suggest the limitations of the postcolonial proposition by indicating how in over-emphasizing this and other "Orientalist" patterns of representation recent scholarship has underestimated their instability and the degree to which they are put at risk by various equally historically determined, countervailing patterns of representation. Historicity itself in the form of a close analysis of English travelers' experience in Moghul India makes the relation between historicity and domination seem less than inevitable and certainly not necessary, and it does so, I want to argue, by revealing moments of surprising contingency. Let me begin with the emerging habit of historicizing cultural difference.

STEALING HISTORY

One of the defining characteristics of the Renaissance or early modern period in Europe is the emergence of a new sense of historical consciousness or what we've been calling historicity. This does not mean that history had no past, but rather that the cultural or ideological assumptions that determined how the past was to be recorded or history was to be written began to change. According to R. G. Collingwood, for instance, medieval historiography is distinguished by a radical split between the human and the divine. History is the book of God's acts—all real agency and significant change is purely a matter of divine providence, that is, of a universal design outside time. The chief intellectual aim of medieval historiography is, says Collingwood, "the task of discovering and expounding this objective or divine plan."[12] All human action independent of the plan is by definition meaningless and time itself is only of value to the extent that it yields those moments when we come to see the oneness of things in God's design. The most dramatic representation of such a moment in medieval writing is, of course, Dante's *Divine Comedy*. In Scripture, these moments are called typological or messianic; in the neo-religious writing of the 1940s, when Collingwood's book, *The Idea of History*, first came out, they appear as T. S. Eliot's "timeless moments," "moments in and out of time," or Evelyn Waugh's epiphanic understanding that the elegiac human story of Charles Ryder and his world is only of significance to the extent that it bears witness to the enduring presence of Brideshead's sanctuary lamp. The antithesis of messianic time is calendrical time—what Walter Benjamin calls "homogenous, empty time."[13] For a thorough-going historicist like Collingwood, however, calendrical time is anything but empty—it is the "temporal process" through which human energy and achievement can be measured. For Collingwood, the problem with the messianic time of medieval historiography is that it denies this process and turns human history into "something passive, shaped by a timeless force working on it from without."[14] In other words, what Hegel and Marx credit to non-European history, medieval historiography assigns to all human history. It is this denial or lack of interest in the larger significance of human history independent of God's providential design that explains medieval anachronism—why in Giotto, for instance, first-century biblical figures routinely appear in contemporary dress, or why in Chaucer, ancient Troy is represented without the slightest trace of self-consciousness in terms of the chivalric court of Richard II. Over the course of the Renaissance, all this was to change.

One of the most effective ways of capturing the force of this newly emerging sense of historicity was to describe the temporal process it foregrounded in terms of travel. The past, in a way it never had been for Giotto or Chaucer, became a foreign country. In acknowledging this development, Collingwood quotes Descartes on the dangers of cultural relativism implicit in historicity or time traveling:

> To live with men of an earlier age is like traveling in foreign lands. It is useful to know something of the manners of other peoples in order to judge more impartially of our own, and not to despise or ridicule whatever differs from them, like men who have never been outside their

native country. But those who travel too long end by being strangers
in their own homes, and those who study too curiously the actions of
antiquity are ignorant of what is done among ourselves today.[15]

In order to comprehend cultural difference and at the same time protect themselves against the relativism imagined by Descartes, early
modern travelers tended to invert the time–distance metaphor. While
traveling to non-European countries in fiction might be utopian, traveling in practice almost always turned out to be a matter of traveling
back in time. Nowhere is this more graphically illustrated than in
Theodore de Bry's now familiar engravings for the 1590 edition of
Thomas Harriot's *Briefe and True Report* on Virginia, where images
of Algonquin Indians are juxtaposed with those of Ancient Britons
in order to show how, says Harriot, "the Inhabitants of the great
Bretannie have been in times past as sauvage as those of Virginia."[16]
The savages the Algonquin now are, we were. The cultural centrality
of this historicizing trope is, as I've argued elsewhere, most dramatically seen in an early modern rewriting of Scripture like *Paradise Lost*.[17]
The central act of the poem is the fall of humankind. As Adam and Eve
exclude themselves from the community of grace, they become people
of the woods, *silvatici* or savages, specifically contemporary American and south Asian Indians. What the contemporary inhabitants of
"*Malabar* or *Decan*" are now in 1667, says Milton, Adam and Eve
were at the beginning of human history.[18] It is difficult to overestim-
ate the importance of Milton's trope—it functions as a palimpsest in
which the timeless Christian design of medieval historiography is now
written over by the calendrical markings of the new historicity. The
timeless fall of humankind, timeless because the original act of sin is
repeated every day in the quotidian failings of all postlapsarian souls,
is now historicized in such a way as to insist on the cultural and moral
inferiority of contemporary Indians.

India, it needs to be emphasized, however, is not America, and
Milton makes an important distinction between American and south
Asian Indians. The latter, though every bit as subject to "sensual
Appetite" (9.1129) and as "unclean" (9.1098) as the former, are associated with the ingenuity of Adam and Eve in sewing together their new
covering of fig leaves. Depending on which time scheme one wishes to
emphasize, our first parents either anticipate or imitate the ingenuity
of the "*Indian* Herdsman" (9.1108): just as Adam and Eve would
cover their shame and protect themselves from heavenly creatures, the
most important of whom will be the Son of God, "Insufferably bright"
(9.1084) with their newly sewn fig leaves, so the Indian tends his herds

and protects himself from the physical sun by sheltering in the pillared shade of the fig tree and cutting loopholes through its leaves. In the context not only of fallen humankind's shame but of India itself, however, ingenuity is not quite the positive it might at first seem; it is in fact one of the ways early modern European travelers routinely transformed their initial admiration of Indian culture into derogation. Sir Thomas Roe's chaplain, Edward Terry, for instance, recounting his experience in India between 1616 and 1619, praises Hindu craftsmen for the "most excellent Ingenuity expressed by their curious Manufactures."[19] He tells the story of how, after Roe had given Emperor Jahangir the present of "a curious neat small oval Picture," Jahangir had his artists reproduce it so precisely that the English ambassador was unable to distinguish the copy from the original. But this was "no Marvel," says Terry, because the "truth is, that the Natives of that Monarchy are the best Apes for imitation in the world, so full of ingenuity that they will make any new thing by pattern, how hard soever it seem to be done."[20] The implication is that there is something profoundly illusory or inauthentic about the marvels of Indian civilization—indeed, as postcolonial critics have stressed, for early modern Europeans, inauthenticity belies all India's achievements and is evident in everything from Hindu idolatry to Moghul absolutism. Jyotsna Singh and others have drawn attention to the European emphasis on the counterfeit quality of Hinduism: she quotes Henry Lord's 1630 judgment that Hindus violate true religion with extraordinary ingenuity, "with notable forgery Coyning Religion according to the minte of their own Tradition."[21] At the same time, Richmond Barbour and others have drawn attention to the English emphasis on the theatricality of the Moghul court and the abject hypocrisy it produces: he quotes Roe's contempt for the Persian ambassador who first appears at court rather as "a jester or jugler than a person of any gravity, running up and downe, and acting all his words like a mimick player. Now indeed the *atashckannoe* [audience place] was become a right stage."[22] For Roe, a former member of James I's obstinate "addled" Parliament of 1614, the splendor of the court masks a kind of slavery worse than feudal since, so he believes, subjects hold nothing in fee: "for as all his Subjects are slaves, so is he [the emperor] in a kind of reciprocall bondage," having to obey the endless theatrical customs of public appearance and deliberation.[23] Most importantly, over the course of the seventeenth century, despite considerable confusion over property rights, India's perceived inauthenticity, her superstition and despotism, increasingly comes to be associated not just with the past in general or the abominations of the Old Testament, but much more specifically with the recent past, that is, the "medieval" world European historicity had just begun to create and from which Renaissance Europe felt itself to be emerging. To claim as Roe does, to a readership as sensitive to the role of the law in governance as the English in 1616, that "[t]hey have no written Law," that "[t]he King by his owne word ruleth" (*Roe*, 110) is to medievalize India.

Milton develops the point in his 1654 *Second Defence of the English People* by identifying the recurrent failures of English common people to throw off the dead weight of medieval custom with contemporary Indian idolatry.[24] For a Renaissance historicist like Milton, the English Civil War was meant to continue the work of the Reformation in separating the present from its medieval past. The war was a revolution against custom and feudal enslavement, against the tyranny of kings and the superstition of priests. In the past, in an England "made small" by medieval historiography, by the "unskilfull handling of monks and mechanicks" (*Reason of Church-Government*, CPW 1:812), the common people had "sunk to a barbarism fouler than that which stains the Indians, themselves the most stupid of mortals" (*CPW* 4:551). While Hindus "worship as gods the malevolent demons whom they cannot exorcize," the common people of England had, in "blind superstition," established "as gods . . . the most impotent of mortals" and made "a sacred institution" of tyranny (*CPW* 4:551). In their idolatry, what the Hindus are, the English of feudal and some even of recent times were. It soon becomes apparent that almost all Milton's allusions to India in *Paradise Lost*, to the world "Beyond the *Indian* Mount" (*PL* 1.781), imply the threat of illusion, specifically the kind of illusion occasioned by blind affections, by imagination operating independently of reason or Christian revelation—that is, the kind of illusion that Milton's mentor, Sir Francis Bacon, sees as the distinguishing feature of medieval or scholastic learning. For Bacon, scholastic learning is by definition a matter of error and it is no accident that the allegorical figure of Sin in *Paradise Lost* reproduces not only the allegorical figure of Error from Spenser's *Faerie Queene* but also the same figure from *The Advancement of Learning*.[25] Nor is it an accident that when both Eve and Satan are surprised by Sin and her medieval originals, they are associated with India. When Eve, deluded and deflowered after she has eaten the forbidden fruit, bows in "low Reverence" before the Tree of Knowledge "as to the power/That dwelt within" (*PL* 9.835–37), she reenacts the fantastic superstition of the Hindu women in the Italian traveler Pietro Della Valle's account who "fall to their adoration" before the great fig tree of the goddess Parvati at

Surat.[26] Similarly, when Satan displays his proud imaginations "High on a Throne of Royal State, which far/Outshone the wealth of *Ormus* and of *Ind*,/Or where the gorgeous East with richest hand/Show'rs on her Kings *Barbaric* Pearl and Gold" (*PL* 2.1–4), he reenacts the fantastic theatricality of Jahangir who on new year's day from a chair of estate "most rich to behold" is presented with "the rarest jewels and toyes" his nobles can find[27] and on his birthday is balanced on a golden scales against his own weight in precious metals and stones (*Roe*, 411–12). In Milton's representation of India, not only are we given a digest of travelers' tales, but a particular argument: in Milton's India, the inauthenticity, illusions of fancy, or failures of reason, which governed medieval Europe, are given a local habitation and a name. In the India of Milton's contemporary, Francois Bernier, the name stands as a warning for what Europe could become should it backslide into its medieval ways, specifically should the modern European nation state fail to respect the rights of its private citizens to their own property. "Take away the right of private property in land," Bernier admonishes Louis XIV's finance minister, Colbert, "and [as the example of Moghul India makes clear] you introduce, as a sure and necessary consequence, tyranny, slavery, injustice, beggary and barbarism...the road will be opened to the ruin of Kings and the destruction of Nations."[28]

When one reads mid- and late-seventeenth-century writers like Milton and Bernier, there seems little question of historicity's formidable power to reinforce Christian and other modes of othering a "heathen" culture like that of Moghul India. In a recent essay on Camoens's *Lusiads*, Shankar Raman emphasizes the point by suggestively outlining how with the emergence of Europe's new historical consciousness, God's providential plan is incipiently assimilated into the Western nation state's own imperial master narrative.[29] So powerful is this new nationalist ideology, argues Raman, that it offers the indigenous no means of resistance. Hegel is both anticipated and made possible by Camoens. The problem is, however, that in Raman's desire to demonstrate the continuity between early modern and nineteenth-century colonialism, neither he nor for that matter any other postcolonial scholar writing on Moghul India shows much interest in contingency. The beginning is shaped by their knowledge of the end, and so the recurrent fascination of early modern travelers with the Moghul empire's policy and practice of religious toleration, for instance, gets scant attention. While there is little question of English travelers' inclination to derogate and subject by historicizing cultural difference, there are also powerful countervailing tendencies, and it is central to my argument that these and the possibility of real agency only become available through historical analysis, that is, through the practice of historicity itself. This is implicit in Ranajit Guha's understanding of "counter-history." According to Guha, the doyen of Indian subaltern studies, "the appropriation of a past by conquest carries with it the risk of rebounding on the conquerors."[30] This sense of risk is a roundabout way of conceding the power of historicity's contingencies, all the unpredictable data that allow the perception or construction of disruptive counternarratives. The point is historicity is not historicism, whether Enlightenment or neoliberal, and the power of its contingencies are not to be underestimated. And it is on one of these contingencies that we now focus.

CONTINGENCY AND COUNTER-HISTORY

In November 1558, two years after Akbar became Moghul emperor, Elizabeth became queen of England. Five years later in 1563, in the same year that the Moslem emperor revoked the tax on Hindu pilgrims, Elizabeth completed the first phase of her religious settlement with a new Act of Uniformity. These two polities, Moghul India and Protestant England, are classic examples of what Hardt and Negri, deeply engaged with the arguments of Benedict Anderson, mean by patrimonial and national empire states. In European history, so these neo-Marxist critics feel, the latter evolves out of the former and the two kinds of empire are most easily distinguished from each other by the displacement of sovereignty from the person of the monarch to the concept of "the people."[31] For a liberal scholar like Liah Greenfeld, this displacement of sovereignty is at the heart of her argument that Protestant England is the prototype of the modern nation state, the embryo out of which modern Western democracies with their emphatic distinction between religious and secular spheres of action developed, the states Bernard Lewis wishes the Arabs would emulate.[32] However persuasive these various interrelated master narratives might be, popular sovereignty and religious toleration were not obvious characteristics of Elizabethan England, and the irony we need to consider is Lord Tennyson's in his poem "Akbar's Dream"—that Akbar's "tolerance of religions and abhorrence of religious persecution put our Tudors to shame."[33] That is, at precisely the same time the "new" nation state reembarked on a policy of rigorous and increasingly brutal religious uniformity,[34] the "old" patrimonial empire initiated a policy of toleration.

Unlike his grandfather, Babur, the central Asian monarch who founded the Moghul empire, Akbar was a native of India. Although he spent much of his childhood in Afghanistan, he felt at home in India, and in his late teens he married into a distinguished Rajput family without insisting that his bride, Man Moti, convert to Islam.[35] Man Moti became the mother of Akbar's son and successor, Jahangir. For the old Timurid emperor, Babur, India was always a foreign country: "It is a strange country," he complained, "[c]ompared to ours, it is another world."[36] Akbar thought differently, but his sympathy for his Hindu subjects was not simply a matter of individual genius—it grew out of a sensitivity to a long-standing process of cultural integration and assimilation. In sixteenth-century India, as John Richards points out, after generations of contact, in both Hinduism and Islam "many mystics, scholars, intellectuals, and more ordinary folk were actively seeking some form of synthesis." Especially, "[i]n folk culture," he continues, "there was substantial sharing of customs, ceremonies, and beliefs between ordinary Muslims and Hindus. Such practices as the worship of the smallpox goddess Sitla were often practiced as ardently by Muslims as Hindus in the countryside."[37] For many members of the imperial elite, though certainly not all, Hindus as Hindus had become members of the imagined community—a community not defined in national but in increasingly world or universalist terms. Akbar's minister and biographer, Abu 'l Faizl, explains the universalism that drove the emperor's reforms. The poll-tax or *jizya* on non-Moslems was abolished in 1564 "as the foundation of the arrangement of mankind" in "the administration of the world" (*Akbarnama* 2:316). The tax on Hindu pilgrims was revoked the year before because "although the folly of a sect might be clear, yet as they had no conviction they were on the wrong path, to demand money from them, and to put a stumbling block in the way of what they had made a means of approach to the sublime threshold of Unity and considered as the worship of the Creator" was contrary to both "the discriminating intellect" and "the will of God" (*Akbarnama* 2:295). These reforms were only the beginning, and what they suggest is not so much the shadowy type of Victorian Christianity imagined by Tennyson as a polity confident enough in its wealth and efficiency to tolerate and respond imaginatively to the cultural diversity it had inherited. The toleration rooted in the experience of diversity, precipitated by a genuinely religious desire for synthesis, and idealized in various forms of political universalism was more than evident when English travelers began to arrive in Moghul India in the late sixteenth and early seventeenth centuries. The travelers I want to concentrate on are the members of the group that found itself at the court of Jahangir between 1615 and 1619, most importantly James I's ambassador and the East India Company's agent, Sir Thomas Roe, and his chaplain, Edward Terry.

Unlike their reaction to so much they encountered in Moghul India, the response of these travelers to the experience of religious toleration was profoundly conflicted. On the one hand, it was dismissed as confusion, while on the other, it was welcomed and grudgingly admired. After explaining in some detail the "medievalism" implicit in the religion of both Moslems and Hindus, that they "ground their opinions on tradition, not reason," Terry, for instance, concluded with a sense of security bordering on satisfaction that "[a]ll religions [in Jahangir's empire] are tolerated, and their priests [held] in good esteeme. My selfe often received from the Mogol himselfe the appellation of Father, with other many gracious words, [and] with place amongst his best nobles."[38] Terry is especially interesting because in traveling to India he travels back to a melange of medieval and biblical times—a melange that suggests how, as in Milton, the othering of the old historiography is being written over by the markings of the new historicity. Over and again in Terry, images of what strike him as a medieval culture also realize Old Testament scenes: for instance, *sati* or the superstitious practice of widow-burning, he explains, is not unlike "the custome of the Ammonites, who, when they made their children passe through the fire to Moloch, caused certain tabret or drums to sound, that their cry might not be heard."[39] At the same time, however, despite this intense drive to derogate by historicizing difference, Terry continues to enjoy the empire's religious freedom. After describing a daring public affront to Islam made by his friend, the traveler Thomas Coryat, an affront that in any other Moslem country would have cost Coryat his life, Terry confidently reflects: "But here every man hath libertie to professe his owne religion freely and, for any restriction I ever observed, to dispute against theirs with impunitie."[40]

This confidence in toleration is important not simply because it offers security or opportunities to proselytize but because it reveals how toleration appeals to these humanist-educated travelers' sense of civility. Civility, it needs to be emphasized, is a cultural imperative every bit as powerful as historicity in early modern Europe, and the irony here is that in the intermittently recognized civility of the Moghul state's policy of religious toleration the patrimonial empire complicates Western historicity's tendency to represent the East as an image of its own medieval or monkish past. The irony is that in the civility of its toleration, a counter-historian might argue, the empire of Akbar and Jahangir functions not as a shadowy type of what the modern West will provide but as a real model of what so many early modern Europeans actually desire, especially those spirits like the Montaigne of the essay on cannibals or the John Donne of *Satyre 3* who hunger and thirst after release from wars of religion or Elizabethan persecution.

The force of this irony seems unavailable to so much recent scholarship on England in Moghul India. Even a critic as acute as Kate Teltscher sees the early modern mode of understanding and representing India as a closed system. Travel writers, she argues, know their readers, and those readers "only believe what they want to be told; they want to hear of the strangeness, difference and barbarity of abroad to flatter their own sense of civilization at home."[41] That is, they want cultural difference to be historicized. A writer like Sir Thomas Roe, she feels, however potentially open to experiences that might decenter his own culture, is always conscious of just how unreceptive his public might be and so is careful to censor his own text. But if this is the case, then it is not clear why Roe and others talk in the way they do about religious toleration to the close-minded "public" she imagines for them. A more immediate problem with this argument, however, is that the text of Roe's that Teltscher uses is from *Purchas His Pilgrimes*. There Roe is certainly censored—but not by himself so much as by Samuel Purchas. What most obviously gets lost in Purchas's edition is any clear sense of Roe's text as a journal—a text in which entries are written day by day, as they occur, not for the pleasure of the public but primarily for the practical use of the East India Company. Because of this, events and observations in Sir William Foster's more diplomatic edition of Roe often read quite differently. Most importantly, the one example of cultural instability in Roe that Teltscher concedes turns out in Foster's edition to be a story as much about civility as Christian humility.

The passage Teltscher focuses on is Roe's moving account of Jahangir's encounter with a "professed Poore holy" beggar on December 18, 1616.[42] There, she argues, because Jahangir's act of humility in conversing and eating with the beggar and then raising up his filthy body in his arms realizes the biblical ideal of Yahweh raising up the poor in Hannah's song against the arrogance of the mighty (1 Samuel 2:8), the heathen prince's extraordinary virtue seems to unsettle Roe's confidence in "Christian certainties."[43] In Foster's more faithful edition, however, this incident appears not so much as a "submerged challenge"[44] but as the occasion of an explicit and angry denunciation of Christian failure: "I mention [this incident]," Roe says, "with envye and sorrow, that wee having the true vyne should bring forth Crabbes, and a bastard stock of grapes: that either our Christian Princes had this devotion or that this Zeale were guided by the true light of the Gospell" (*Roe*, 367). The denunciation opens a radically disturbing fissure that Purchas moves to contain. He deletes Roe's angry sentence and adds a marginal gloss: "Humilitie and Charity superstitious, and therefore blind" (4:386). He may not be able to close the fissure entirely but he does mask Roe's anger. That anger is important, because in the context of the sequence of daily events edited out by Purchas it indicates why the Company's business is failing. Roe comes across Jahangir and the beggar because he is on his way to see the emperor about a breakdown in relations between Moghul officials and East India Company factors at Surat reported to him on December 9—a breakdown occasioned by the incivility of the English. Roe lays it down as a rule that "wee can never live without quarrell . . . untill our Commanders take order that noe man come to Suratt but on Just occasion and of Civil Carriage . . . . For what Civil Town will endure a stranger to force open in the streetes the close Chayres wherin their weomen are Carried (which they take for a dishonor equall to a ravishment)?" (365). No matter how strange their customs are, Roe insists, *civility* demands they be respected. In this context, the civility of Jahangir, the respect and "kindnes" he shows the beggar (366) together with the many "just and gratious" words he offers Roe himself and others (416), stands as a model to be emulated by the English. It is true that Roe's confidence in Jahangir will wane as the possibility of securing a comprehensive trade treaty fades, but at this point, he feels sure that both his hope and security rest in the civility of the emperor—"I stand on very fickle termes [here]," he writes to his friend George Abbot, the Archbishop of Canterbury, on October 30, 1616, "though in extraordinarie Grace with the King, who is gentle, soft, and good of disposition" (*Roe*, 310). Roe despises the emperor's weakness for drink, but at this point even in drink Jahangir's idealism is remembered warmly as he makes it clear that one of the chief marks of imperial sovereignty is the civility of religious toleration: "The good king fell to dispute of the lawes of Moses, Jesus and Mahomet," Roe says, "and in drinck was so kinde that he turned to mee, and said: Am I a king? You shall be wellcome: Christians, Moores, Jewes, hee meddled not with their faith: they Came all in love and hee would protect them from wrong: they lived under his safety and none should oppresse them" (382). My point is that civility and the security it affords is the cultural imperative that enables conventional Christians like Terry and Roe to value the Moghul policy of toleration even while they despise most of the actual religions it tolerates. Civility is the countervailing tendency that disrupts, if it does not completely prevent, their inclination to derogate cultural differences by historicizing them. The experience of reading these travelers is not one of encountering a closed system, but one of listening to people who seem unmoored, unable to make up their minds. This is evident even in a Christian as vehement and outspoken as Coryat.

When Terry looks back in 1655 over his experience of England in Moghul India, he travels back in time to the Old Testament experience of Israel in Egypt. But what comes to mind is not the epic story of Israel's exodus from the house of bondage; it is rather the romance story of Joseph and his clan reunited in an empire of extraordinary promise. It is true that Jahangir may have been difficult to deal with in business matters, Terry concedes, "[y]et we Englishmen did not at all suffer by that inconstancy of his, but there found a free trade, a peaceable residence, and a very good esteem with that King and people; and much better (as I conceive) by reason of the prudence of my Lord Ambassador, who was there (in some sense) like Joseph in the Court of Pharaoh, for whose sake all his nation there seemed to fare the better" (quoted in Foster's edition of Roe, 45). This image epitomizes the unmooring I have been trying to suggest. Over the course of the Hebrew scriptures, especially as they are reproduced in the Christian Old Testament, Pharaonic Egypt functions as one of the principal representations of the demonic other against which Israel defines itself, but in the story of Joseph and his brothers, the story Terry finds most appropriate to explain his experience, the teleological momentum of Israel's divine history is disrupted by the contingency of Egypt's plenitude and Pharaoh's civility. At that moment, the moment when Pharaoh welcomes Joseph's family and Jacob blesses Pharaoh (Genesis 47:1–12), Egypt is no longer Israel's defining other. Similarly, in the innumerable moments of conflictedness, moments felt in response to the unexpected experience of toleration and civility, the old patrimonial empire of the Moghuls ceases to function as the new English nation state's defining other. Historicity itself reveals that in the testimony of these English travelers the drive to *derogate* by historicizing cultural difference is anything but seamless and indeed is left in some disarray among the fragmentary glimpses of a peaceable kingdom.

To an extent that has received surprisingly little attention, there is some evidence to suggest that those glimpses of real knowledge of another culture did affect England's future. Coryat's letters circulated among the group of intellectuals that had begun meeting at Sir Robert Cotton's library from 1612 onward—a group that included members of his Mermaid Tavern fraternity like Ben Jonson and the most eloquent spokesman for religious toleration in the early seventeenth century, John Selden. At the same time, Roe became increasingly interested in toleration, expressing outrage at the Laudian persecution of Prynne, Bastwick, and Burton in 1637, and committing himself wholeheartedly in the early 1630s to John Dury's plans to develop a tolerant reunion of Protestant factions across Europe.[45] For Akbar and Jahangir, toleration was an intensely religious response to the experience of diversity. For Akbar's minister, Abu 'l Faizl, it was also pragmatic. He explains how economically unnecessary the poll tax on non-Moslems was: "Moreover the prime cause of levying the tax in old times was the neediness of the rulers and their assistants. At this day when there are thousands of treasures in the store-chambers of the world-wide administration, . . . why should a just and discriminating mind apply itself to collecting this tax?" (*Akbarnama* 2:317). In 1641, echoing the pragmatism of Abu 'l Faizl, Roe made a speech to Parliament arguing the economic cost of intolerance—that "the decline of the clothing trade in England could not be halted until 'the pressure on tender consciences' . . . had been relaxed."[46]

CONCLUSION

Let me conclude by returning to the principal theme of this essay—historicizing cultural difference and its discontents. The discontents I wish to identify are twofold. First, the habit of understanding other cultures by turning them into images of the West's past has been and still is the solipsistic cause of enormous suffering and injustice in the world. Even as we speak, we are told over and again by so many of those in power, by conservative admirers of Lewis like Richard Perle or Paul Wolfowitz, for instance, that any culture or polity that opposes or even differs from the values of the West is "on the wrong side of history," and, in Perle's chilling words, must be "put at a distance" until they learn to change. The second and more immediate discontent is the refusal by those of us who most want to resist this crude but still astonishingly powerful kind of historicism to see that it is not a necessary or defining function of Western identity. The example of England in Moghul India demonstrates just how unstable or risky are the enslaving fictions of historicism—not least when they are subjected to a sense of historicity always willing to identify and exploit the power of contingency.

NOTES

Versions of this essay were delivered at the Northwest Pacific Renaissance Society conference in Nanaimo BC, May 2003, and the Canadian Society for Renaissance Studies conference in Halifax NS, May 2003. I am grateful for the many helpful responses I received on those occasions. I am especially grateful to Rahul Sapra.

1. Bernard Lewis, *What Went Wrong? The Clash Between Islam and Modernity in the Middle East* (New York: Perennial, 2003). For the relationship between historicity and colonial habits of thought, see, for instance, Edward W. Said, *Orientalism* (New York: Vintage, 1978), 31–36; "Orientalism Reconsidered," *Race & Class* 27.2 (1985): 1–15; Homi K. Bhabha, "Signs Taken for Wonders," in *The Location of Culture* (London, Routledge, 1994), 102–22; and Robert Young, *White Mythologies: Writing History and the West* (London: Routledge, 1990), passim.
2. Lewis, *What Went Wrong?*, 159.
3. John Milton, *Complete Prose Works of John Milton*, gen. ed. Don M. Wolfe, 8 vols. (New Haven: Yale University Press, 1953–82), 2:224. Hereafter cited as *CPW*.
4. Lewis, *What Went Wrong?*, 160.
5. Francis Robinson, "Thoroughly Modern Muslims," *Times Literary Supplement* (April 11, 2003): 26.
6. Said, *Orientalism*, esp. 315–21.
7. Robinson, "Thoroughly Modern Muslims," 26.
8. Cf. Anthony Pagden, "*Ius et Factum*: Text and Experience in the Writings of Bartholome de Las Casas," in *New World Encounters*, ed. Stephen Greenblatt (Berkeley: University of California Press, 1993), esp. 95.
9. Said, "Orientalism Reconsidered," 10.
10. Marx on India is the *locus classicus* for this view of Enlightenment historicism's acts of oblivion: "Indian society has no history at all, at least no known history. What we call its history is but the history of successive intruders who founded their empires on the passive basis of that unresisting and unchanging society" ("The Future Results of British Rule in India" [1853], in K. Marx and F. Engels, *The First Indian War of Independence, 1857–59* [Moscow: Foreign Languages Pub. House, 1959], 32). For a telling critique of Said's use of Marx on India, see Aijaz Ahmad, *In Theory: Classes, Nations, Literatures* (New Delhi: Verso, 1992), 221–42.
11. Michael Hardt and Antonio Negri, *Empire* (Cambridge, Mass.: Harvard University Press, 2000), 124.
12. R. G. Collingwood, *The Idea of History* (Oxford: Oxford University Press, 1956), 53.

13. Walter Benjamin, "Theses on the Philosophy of History," in *Illuminations: Essays and Reflections*, trans. Harry Zohn, ed. Hannah Arendt (New York: Harcourt, Brace & World, 1968), 261.

14. Collingwood, *The Idea of History*, 54.

15. Quoted in ibid., 59.

16. Thomas Harriot, *A Briefe and True Report of the Newfoundland of Virginia* (London, 1590), sig. G.

17. See Paul Stevens, "*Paradise Lost* and the Colonial Imperative," *Milton Studies* 34, ed. Albert C. Labriola (1996): 3–21 and "Milton and the New World: Custom, Relativism, and the Discipline of Shame," in *Milton and the Imperial Vision*, ed. Balachandra Rajan and Elizabeth Sauer (Pittsburgh: Duquesne, University Press, 1999), 90–111.

18. Milton, *Paradise Lost*, in *Complete Poems and Major Prose*, ed. Merritt Y. Hughes (New York: Macmillan, 1957), 9:1067–142, 1103. All Milton's poetry is quoted from *Complete Poems*.

19. Quoted in *Travel Knowledge: European "Discoveries" in the Early Modern Period*, ed. Ivo Kamps and Jyotsna G. Singh (New York: Palgrave, 2001), 189.

20. Ibid., 190.

21. Quoted in Jyotsna G. Singh, *Colonial Narratives/Cultural Dialogues: "Discoveries" of India in the Language of Colonialism* (London: Routledge, 1996), 21. See also John Michael Archer, *Old Worlds: Egypt, Southwest Asia, India, and Russia in Early Modern English Writing* (Stanford: Stanford University Press, 2001), 139–92.

22. Quoted in Richmond Barbour, "Power and Distant Display: Early English Ambassadors in Moghul India," *Huntington Library Quarterly* 61.3 & 4 (1999): 365. See also Kate Teltscher, *India Inscribed: English and British Writing on India 1600–1800* (Delhi: Oxford University Press, 1995), 20–23.

23. Sir Thomas Roe, *The Embassy of Sir Thomas Roe to the Court of the Great Mogul, 1615–19*, ed. Sir William Foster, 2 vols. (London: Liechtenstein, 1899), 107–08. Hereafter cited as *Roe*.

24. Cf. Pompa Bannerjee, "Milton's India and *Paradise Lost*," in *Milton Studies* 37 (1999): 154.

25. See Paul Stevens, *Imagination and the Presence of Shakespeare in Paradise Lost* (Madison: University of Wisconsin Press, 1985), esp. 118, 120–21 and Catherine G. Martin, "The Sources of Milton's Sin Reconsidered," *Milton Quarterly* 35.1 (2001): 1–8.

26. *Travels of Pietro della Valle in India*, trans. G. Havers, ed. Edward Grey (London: Printed for the Hakluyt Society, 1892), 9:35–39.

27. William Hawkins, in *Travels in Early India, 1583–1619*, ed. Sir William Foster (London: Oxford University Press, 1921), 60–121, esp. 117–18.

28. Francois Bernier, *Travels in the Mogul Empire, 1656–68*, ed. Archibald Constable (Westminster: A. Constable, 1891), 238.

29. Shankar Raman, "Back to the Future: Forging History in Luis De Camoes's *Os Lusiados*," in Kamps and Singh, 134–47.

30. Ranajit Guha, *Dominance without Hegemony: History and Power in Colonial India* (Cambridge, Mass.: Harvard University Press, 1997), 3.

31. Hardt and Negri, *Empire*, 102–03.

32. See Liah Greenfeld, *Nationalism: Five Roads to Modernity* (Cambridge, Mass.: Harvard University Press, 1992), 14–17, 29–87.

33. Headnote to "Akbar's Dream." Tennyson is quoted from *The Poems of Tennyson*, ed. Christopher Ricks (London: Longmans, 1969).

34. See, for instance, John Guy, *Tudor England* (Oxford: Oxford University Press, 1988), 290–308 and Eamon Duffy, *The Stripping of the Altars: Traditional Religion in England 1400–1580* (New Haven: Yale University Press, 1992), 565–93.

35. Abu 'l Faizl, *Akbarnama*, 2 vols., trans. H. Beveridge (Calcutta: Asiatic Society, 1907–39), 2:240–43; hereafter cited as *Akbarnama*.

36. Babur, *The Baburnama: Memoirs of Babur, Prince and Emperor*, trans. and ed. Wheeler M. Thackstun (New York: Oxford University Press, 1996), 332.

37. John F. Richards, *The Mughal Empire* (Cambridge: Cambridge University Press, 1993), 34.

38. Edward Terry, in Foster, *Travels in Early India*, 325, 331.

39. Ibid., 323.

40. Ibid., 315.

41. Teltscher, *India Inscribed*, 28.

42. See Samuel Purchas, *Hakluytus Posthumus, or Purchas His Pilgimes*, 20 vols. (Glasgow: MacLehose, 1905), 4:386–87 and Roe (Foster's edition), 364–67.

43. Teltscher, *India Inscribed*, 27.

44. Ibid.

45. See W. K. Jordan, *The Development of Religious Toleration in England*, 4 vols. (Gloucester, Mass.: P. Smith, 1965), 2:364–65.

46. Quoted in ibid., 4:344.

CHAPTER 6

THE BRITISH AND THE DUTCH IN INDIA, 1751–99

Florence D'Souza

Trade was the major initiating drive that led various European powers to undertake overseas voyages to Asia and create monopolist trading companies. As time passed, changing political and economic circumstances caused them either to withdraw completely from the Asiatic zone with the dissolution of their trading companies, or to modify their approaches to meet the new challenges in Asia. This essay proposes to compare the evolution of two European overseas trading companies (the British East India Company and the Dutch Veereinigde Oostindische Compagnie or VOC) within the geographic region of India from 1751 to 1799. The British Company expanded to become the supreme European power in India over this period, while the Dutch VOC followed an opposite trajectory, suffering decline from the 1740s and completely dissolving by 1799. The aim here is to understand the reasons for the differences and the similarities in the ways these two European powers developed over the second half of the eighteenth century. This study is based on the published travel accounts of two Dutchmen and three Englishmen who were present in India during this period.

Britain and the Netherlands had already fought three wars against each other from 1652 to 1654, from 1665 to 1667, and from 1672 to 1674. This last war of 1672–74 was terminated by the Treaty of Westminster and an Anglo-Dutch commercial agreement. All three wars were explosions in a struggle for trade supremacy in which the Dutch held the upper hand over the British in the Caribbean, in Asia, and in Europe. However, by the 1750s, the English were already emerging as the dominant European power in India with the recall of the French governor, J. F. Dupleix, to France in 1754, and Robert Clive's victory against the Nawab of Bengal at Plassey in 1757. Although still the foremost European trading power in Asia,[1] the Dutch were beginning to suffer losses in their overseas trading returns.[2] At home, they were just returning to Orangist rule in 1747 with the restoration of the Dutch Stadholder William IV after a long period of republicanism from 1702 to 1747 without any Stadholder in power.

1751 marked the death of William IV and the beginning of the sixteen-year regency of the infant Stadholder William V. As the Netherlands suffered economic decline between 1751 and 1799, the VOC's overseas trade also began to decline. The Dutch principle of free seas, free ships, and free goods added to British frustrations during their Seven Years' War against the French (1756–63), when Dutch ships blatantly assisted French coastal trade in Europe and French overseas trade in the Caribbean and in Asia.[3] Nevertheless between 1751 and 1799, the debts of the VOC rose to unmanageable proportions so that it was completely dissolved in 1799, although a Dutch colonial presence (with free trade for private Dutch traders) was maintained in Indonesia. The British occupied the VOC's settlements in India and Ceylon from 1781 till 1784, and then again from 1810 to 1815 under the Napoleonic Wars, before taking them over completely in 1824 under the Anglo-Dutch Treaty of London. As a European power in Asia, the Dutch were left only with their settlements in Indonesia.

In Britain, the period from 1751 to 1799 saw the final years of the reign of George II (1727–60), followed by the long reign of George III (1760–1820), studded by the Seven Years' War with France (1756–63), the American War of Independence (1776–83), and the Fourth Anglo-Dutch War (1780–84). The period was also marked by appeals for the reform of the British East India Company in the British Parliament, leading to the 1773 Regulating Act under the prime ministership of Lord North and to Pitt's India Act of 1784.[4] In India, the British East India Company had moved from outsider trading to deliberate meddling with Indian politics and territorial acquisition.[5]

The first to land in India of the five late-eighteenth-century witnesses whose accounts are investigated here was Johan Splinter Stavorinus (b. Middelburg, June 4, 1739–d. Middelburg, November 9,

1788, aged forty-nine).[6] He started boarding Dutch ships in the Schelde in 1749, was appointed an ordinary captain by the admiralty of the Dutch province of Zeeland in 1766, and made his first voyage to the Dutch East Indies under Commandant Van Braam. He compiled a detailed account of two subsequent voyages to Asia (1768–71; and 1774–78), published posthumously in Dutch at Leiden in two volumes in 1793 and 1797. An English translation in three volumes appeared in London in 1798.[7] Stavorinus's voyage of 1768–71 covered the Cape of Good Hope, Batavia, Bantam, and Bengal, while his voyage of 1774–78 took him via the Cape of Good Hope to Batavia, Amboyna, and Surat and again from Surat to Batavia, then back to the Coast of Malabar, before his final return to Europe via the Cape of Good Hope in 1778. Stavorinus was later promoted to rear admiral in the Dutch Navy. He died at a relatively young age, before reaching fifty. His texts provide observations on the Dutch and the British in India and in Far East Asia during the 1760s and the 1770s.

William Hodges (b. London 1744–d. Brixham, Devonshire, 1797, aged fifty-three) established himself in London as a landscape painter. From 1772 to 1775, thanks to the influence of Lord Palmerston, Hodges had participated in Captain Cook's second expedition to the South Seas as the official draughtsman. He spent six years in India from 1778 to 1784, "under the patronage of Warren Hastings."[8] Hodges brought back to England several views of India as well as his travelogue, published in London in 1793.[9] After retiring from the painting profession in 1795, he settled at Dartmouth and then died of gout at Brixham. Hodges's observations on India during the 1770s and the 1780s are particularly revealing.

William Hickey (b. London, June 30, 1749–d. London, May 31, 1830?, aged eighty-one)[10] was the eighth child of Joseph Hickey, an Irishman established as a London attorney. After studying at London's Westminster school, and failing in 1769–1770 to become a cadet of the British East India Company in Madras, and later failing again to establish himself as an attorney in Jamaica, Hickey finally returned to India where he stayed for twenty-seven years between 1777 and 1808. He returned only once to England, in the period of 1779–1783, when he presented a petition about trial by jury from the Bengal Council to the London House of Commons. Hickey practised as a private attorney at the Calcutta Supreme Court. The 742 manuscript pages of his personal memoirs, published by Alfred Spencer between 1913 and 1925 in four volumes, reveal a whole fresco of European personages, social practices, and personal anecdotes.

Jacob Haafner (b. Halle, 1755–d. Amsterdam, 1809, aged fifty-four years) was the son of a doctor who was a native of Colmar in Alsace.[11] He sailed for several years on VOC ships in the Indian Ocean and the South China Seas. Though lacking a formal education, he learned several Asian languages, could express himself fluently in four European languages, and mastered the VOC's complex accounting methods. From 1773 to 1785, he occupied various VOC clerical posts in India and traveled through India and Ceylon. He eventually returned to Europe in 1785 at the age of thirty, after nineteen years of absence from Europe. He died in Amsterdam, some twenty-four years later. Before his death, he published in Dutch two volumes, in 1806 and 1808 respectively, recounting his travels from Madras to Ceylon via Tranquebar and along the coasts of Orissa and Coromandel. The books offer a wealth of information on India in the 1770s and 1780s. The French translation of Haafner's texts appeared in Paris in 1811.

Thomas Twining (b. London, 1776–d. Twickenham, 1861, aged eighty-five) was the son of Richard Twining, Senior (1749–1824)—the proprietor of the family tea firm "Mary Twining and Son" in London from 1771 to 1824 and one of the twenty-four Directors of the English East India Company in London in 1810. Thomas Twining spent thirteen years in India as a civil servant of the British East India Company (from 1792 to 1805) from the age of sixteen to twenty-nine. He could speak Hindustani and Persian. He visited Madras in 1792, served on the staff of Cornwallis, helped to reform the Calcutta Customs at the Budge Budge Fort near Calcutta, and functioned as the deputy of the English resident, while also fulfilling the role of Judge in the Santipore district that lay sixty miles north of Calcutta. His "Travels in India," published in 1893, contains valuable observations on India in the 1790s.[12]

Investigations of the five narratives produced by these travellers enable comparisons of the ways in which the British and the Dutch pursued their trade interests, interacted with the other European powers present in Asia, related to the local peoples, and formulated justifications for their actions and strategies in the region. One of the striking differences between the British East India Company and the Dutch VOC concerns the operations of their administrators within the institutions. While accompanying the British Governor General Hastings on a river tour to Patna, Ghazipur, and Benares in 1781, the British landscape artist William Hodges noted the contrast between Hastings's personable interactions with both the Indian and British peoples and the formalities they observed in receiving him (Ho, 44). William Hickey mentions the official examination he underwent in

London before his departure for India in 1769 with "three old Dons of the Committee of Directors" in the Company's Leadenhall Street headquarters (Hi, I: 119, 124). This detail reveals the importance of the East India Company's twenty-four London directors in a two-tiered administrative structure divided between London and Calcutta. Hickey also comments on the "absurd dress" worn by the English East India Company officers in India whose woolen double-breasted coats must have been very uncomfortable in India's hot summers (Hi, I: 120). He reports, moreover, on the procedures of the Bengal Supreme Court (in his capacity as an attorney) (Hi, II: 130, 134). Details on the fortifications at Fort St. George (Madras) in August 1792, and on the British East India Company's Customs Houses at Fyzabad (near Patna) and at the old Fort within the city of Calcutta, (renamed the Customs-House Wharf) are furnished by Thomas Twining (Tw, 65, 74, 202–06), who also vividly describes the trade volume of commodities leaving India on East India Company ships in the 1790s.

Reports on the different European powers in Bengal by the Dutchman, Stavorinus, include depictions of the English as bullying blackguards (St, I: 482; 490–92; 497), and observations on the decline of the Dutch transactions in Surat in the 1770s (St, III: 105–29; 148–61). He is critical about the excessive formality of VOC officials, which he contrasts with the relative ease prevalent in the British trading stations (St, I: 145–46):

[At Calcutta]... the conversation was carried on at table, in a free and unconstrained manner, without the company being under any fear or restraint, from the presence of the governor, or of other great men. The spirit of liberty, which animates a Briton in his own country, is repressed as little here, as there. This freedom and ease, is diametrically opposite to the stiff and obnoxious formality, which takes place at Batavia, in the company of the Governor-General and the counsellors of India.

Jacob Haafner, who resided in India from 1773 to 1785, does not touch upon the inner functioning of the VOC management in the Netherlands, but gives instead a field view of certain Dutch settlements in India and Ceylon that he actually visited. The settlements include Sadraspatnam, where he practised the double-column book-keeping used by the VOC (Ha, I: 10), and witnessed the unprovoked destruction of the Sadras fort by the British in June 1781 (Ha, I: 41, 55); Madras, where he encountered British officials, including the governor Macartney in November 1782 (Ha, I: 110–18); and Jaffanapatnam in 1783, where he correctly predicted that all of Ceylon would soon pass under British domination (Ha, I: 348–74). Though

Ceylon, temporarily under French occupation, was restored to the Dutch in 1784, it was taken again by the British in 1795 and definitively ceded by the Dutch to the British in 1802. Indeed, by the 1790s, the British had completely taken over the Dutch trade in textiles and piece goods in India and the cinnamon trade in Ceylon, leaving the employees of the VOC no recourse but to turn to private trade on British ships. This accelerated the complete closure of the VOC by 1799.[13]

Accounts of the interactions between the British and the Dutch on the subject of their Asian trade include Hickey's report that he changed from the British ship *Nassau* to the Dutch ship *Held Woltemade* for the remainder of the return journey from the Cape to Europe. Hickey landed at Amsterdam in the Spring of 1780, met the Wilkinson partner of the British agency house of Pye, Rich, and Wilkinson, and visited the VOC headquarters in Rotterdam, known as the Dutch East India House. He made the following observations about the Dutch and other vessels in Rotterdam harbor (Hi, II: 239–40):

> [The VOC East India House is] . . . a superb building, delightfully situated upon the edge of a noble river that runs through the city, upon which were laying at anchor innumerable vessels of all sizes and of every nation in Europe, altogether constituting one of the grandest scenes I ever beheld. Though in every respect very superior, it brought to my recollection our mild and gentle Thames at Chelsea.

Another difference emerging in comparisons of the five travelers' narratives is the greater flexibility of the British in contrast to the rigidity of the Dutch in their respective approaches to private trade, to new trade commodities, and to navigating instructions. The more lenient attitude of the British East India Company toward its employees engaging in private trade enabled the official British Company to stay afloat when its own trade returns ran into difficulties and when huge expenditures for wars of conquest in India were needed from the 1770s on. By contrast, because the VOC forbade private trade among its employees, the VOC's official trade incurred huge losses and debts by the 1790s, thus reducing the Dutch Company's factories to "empty shells" (LB, 207). Four of the five travelers, namely Hickey, Twining, Haafner, and Stavorinus, allude to triangular private trade. In March 1770, while escorting the departing Dutch director of Chinsura to his Europe-bound ship in Fulta, Stavorinus seized the opportunity to transact "some affairs of my own" at Calcutta, and returned to Chinsura with the new Dutch director, Mr. F____, after "having done what I wanted for myself, at Calcutta" (St, I: 156–57). We are left to guess whether these affairs concerned Stavorinus's own private investments in country cargoes on private British ships plying in Asia, since his affairs could only be transacted in Calcutta and not in any Dutch settlement. Again during a halt at Surat in the early days of January 1776 prior to his departure for Batavia, Stavorinus declares (St, III: 187):

> The remainder of the time which I staid at SURAT, was devoted to the settling of my own concerns, to the receiving a return-cargo for BATAVIA, on board of my ship, and to parting entertainments, which several of the members of this direction were pleased to give on my account, so that I had no further opportunity of going to see anything more of importance.

This extreme circumspection about any link between Stavorinus's "own concerns" and the "return-cargo for Batavia" may be attributed to the VOC's instructions prohibiting its employees from private trading. Strikingly, the Englishmen, Twining and Hickey, speak much more freely about private trade. Hickey refers bluntly to the private European country traders who rented warehouses from Chinese owners on the wharves of the Canton-Whampoa port in 1770, and to the British "Compredor" there, who acted as intermediary between the Chinese authorities and merchants and the passing British crews interested in buying or selling private cargoes (Hi, I: 195, 219). He also mentions several personal acquaintances in Calcutta who returned to Britain with considerable personal fortunes after a few years of lucrative private trade in Bengal—in silk, in piece goods, or in indigo for example (Hi, II: 360; III: 162; III: 269; III: 301–02; III: 349). Thomas Twining likewise observes on his first arrival at Calcutta a great many "country ships" in the Calcutta Harbor (Tw, 74):

> all manned with native sailors, but commanded principally by English captains and chiefly belonging either to these captains or to British Houses of trade established in Calcutta. These vessels, called "country ships," were employed in the Indian seas exclusively, principally between Bengal, China, and Bombay, never going nor being allowed to go, beyond the Cape of Good Hope, unless by a specific license from the East India Company, who possessed, by their Charter, a monopoly of the trade to Europe.

VOC trade politics and practices were decidedly different from those of the East India Company. Stavorinus, for example, refers

explicitly to certain anomalies created through the private trade prohibitions of the VOC on its own employees. He mentions that at
Bantam although a Dutch fiscal official was especially appointed "for
the purpose of preventing the illicit or smuggling trade," the VOC
commandant himself there was suspected of private trade dealings with
the English from Bantam, reputed for its pepper supplies (St, I: 69).
In October 1769, Stavorinus observes that a Dutch officer was posted
fulltime at Fulta at the mouth of the Hugli river to check "the illicit
or smuggling trade" (St, I: 124). In 1776–77, Stavorinus comments
on the institutionalized practice in the Banda islands of exacting percentage trade premiums on all the sales of imported goods as well as
on all the trade commodities exported on VOC ships, as regular commissions to every level of VOC employee from the governor down
to the VOC ships' crews (St, I: 332–33; 363–64). Abuses of these
trade premiums had led to the VOC's ships often being "crammed
with the private property of the crews" for resale in Europe or in
Asia. This seems to contradict VOC principles forbidding any illicit
trade. At another place, Stavorinus denounces the corrupt practice
among the VOC employees of prohibiting transfers of precious metals
through the Cape of Good Hope. He thereby voices the free trade
ideology that was beginning to dominate financial circles in Europe
(St, III: 461–62):

Although the colony [at the Cape] is thus a yearly heavy charge upon the
[VOC] Company, it amply compensates for the expenditure of 300.000
gilders per annum, by its excellent position for a place of refreshment,
for the outward and homeward bound India ships. It is likewise much
frequented for that purpose by ships of other nations, which do not contribute in a slight degree, to the advantage of the colony, both by their
daily expenditure at the Cape, and by their affording a vent for its pro-
ductions; and which, in my opinion ought rather to be encouraged than
discountenanced, as they, in general, pay ready money, and we, by that
means, draw the specie of other nations into our hands. Indeed, the pro-
hibitory regulations, in this respect, serve, at present, no other purpose
than that of filling the pockets of those who are appointed to prevent a
clandestine trade.

Political considerations have, probably, prevented the Company from
granting the freedom of trade and navigation to the colonists of the
Cape; for I imagine that they cannot have failed to perceive that nothing would more contribute to lessen the charges of the settlement, or
to increase the revenues against them, and to add to its power and
importance, than such a measure.

While Hodges, Hickey, and Twining make only passing reference to the Dutch, showing that the Dutch did not occupy a place of importance for them at all, both Stavorinus and Haafner repeatedly criticize the role played by the British in India, which they viewed from the perspective of Dutch trading interests. For example, Haafner regrets that the future of the Dutch in India is doomed "because the trade in textiles of the VOC on the coasts of India, which was formerly so considerable, and brought in such great profits, is now greatly hampered by the English, in whose hands it is, so to speak, entirely" (Ha, I: 364–65). As a result, Haafner perceives the British as "the enemies and the oppressors of our [Dutch] commerce, at least in the East Indies" (Ha, I: 373).

Stavorinus also refers to the detrimental effect on the VOC's trade of British commercial rivalry (a) in Malacca for the sale of opium; (b) all over India for purchasing piece goods; (c) in Ceylon for the procurement of cinnamon; (d) in Macasser for the sale of Indian piece goods; (e) in Surat for sugar imports; (f) on the Malabar coast for pepper purchases; and (g) at Batavia, the very headquarters in Asia of the VOC, for private English trade in "all sorts of commodities both Indian and European" (unofficially encouraged by Dutch officials) (St, (a) I: 295–97; (b) I: 364; (c) II: 366; (d) II: 276–82; (e) III: 105–29; (f) II: 272; III: 188–202; (g) I: 368). Stavorinus's overall attitude toward the English is expressed in the following passage (St, III: 129):

> The instances that I have thus slightly touched upon, are enough to shew the arrogant and arbitrary disposition and conduct of a nation whose inveterate hatred of the Dutch is too notorious to admit of dispute; and likewise the unpleasant and cruel situation in which our [VOC] Company are placed both here [in Surat] and in Bengal.
>
> It would be a most desirable circumstance, if the English were shut out from trading to other places, where we are possessed of the territorial power; or, at least, that their trade were not preferably encouraged both by the [VOC] Company and by individuals.

The greater flexibility of the English East India Company is also visible in its approach to the two new trade commodities for European trade in Asia in the late eighteenth century: opium from India and tea from China. The VOC responded to the entry of various European private traders (mainly British) into the growing opium trade between Bengal and Bihar on the one hand and China on the other hand by creating under the governor generalship (1743–50) of Gustaaf Willem baron Van Imhoff (1705–50), the

Batavia Opium-Trade Society. The shareholders thereof undertook to sell in Batavia all the opium that the VOC would transport annually from Bengal to Batavia for a fixed rate payment to the VOC. The VOC hoped thereby to halt the undercutting by private European traders of the opium market in Batavia. However, in the 1770s, Stavorinus informs us that a flourishing contraband opium trade in Far East Asia by English and other European (including private Dutch) traders was already depleting the Dutch Batavia Opium-Trade Society's profits and capital. Ultimately by 1795, the Dutch Opium-Trade Society was completely dissolved (St, I: 295–97).[14] Stavorinus also mentions the VOC's attempts to enter the Tea trade with China from the 1770s, when they established a Dutch factory at Canton (St, I: 362) to purchase tea supplies. Until the implementation of Pitt's India Act of 1784, which drastically reduced the British import duties on Tea, the VOC and private Dutch traders were able to conduct illicit and highly profitable sales of tea in Britain. Dutch exports by way of the Hague and Rotterdam of their tea cargoes from Canton, to other markets of Europe, were also adversely affected by Pitt's India Act. By the 1790s, therefore, the British were in full command of the tea imports into Europe from the Far East, and the Dutch were deprived of a lucrative source of trade profits (Tw, Introd., 13).[15] Hickey mentions the private tea cargo in chests on board the English East India ship, the *Plassey*, in 1770 and adds that his acquaintance Humphry Howorth returned to Britain in 1780 with a fortune made from opium contracts (Hi, I: 250; III: 315). Twining also refers to the British East India Company's procurement of opium from Patna in the 1790s "for sale to the Chinese" (Tw, 195; 202–06) as an obviously profitable venture. Thus Stavorinus, Hickey, and Twining illustrate the point suggested by the historian Leonard Blussé about British private trade being the cuckoo of the East India Company in Asia, which paradoxically enabled the Company to screen its deficits through the triangular trade with China and through a complex system of remittances of funds from India to London via Canton. According to Blussé, it was this so-called "cuckoo" of private trade that offset the British East India Company's bankruptcy and rescued it from insolvency (LB, 211).

While they certainly differed, the British East India Company and the Dutch VOC nevertheless shared certain perspectives. They seem to have been quite alike in their adoption of an ostentatious life style in their Asian settlements. For example, Haafner notes the merrymaking among his friends at the Coromandel VOC settlement of Palicolé (eighteen miles north of Masulipatnam) (Ha, I: 88–89), and admires the whitewashed stone mansions of the British officials in Madras (Ha, II: 387). Hodges is attracted in the early 1780s to the type of coaches used in Calcutta, while he finds the houses of the Dutch VOC officials at Chinsura and Hugli of a "handsome appearance" (Ho, 16, 42). Stavorinus remarks with interest on the pleasure afforded by the colonial-style Botanical Gardens at Cape Town and at Surat (St, Cape Town I: 547–56; III: 432–44; Surat II: 465–78; III: 165). William Hickey provides details about the sprawling living quarters and leisure activities in various European settlements. For example, he describes the grandeur of Mr. Hall Plumer's town mansion and country residence near Madras, his friend Robert Pott's mansion five miles from Calcutta, and his own lavishly furnished home on Calcutta's Esplanade (Hi, II: 194; III: 140, 358). Hickey also mentions concerts, theater plays, racecourse outings, subscription assembly Balls, annual dinners, and fireworks displays (Hi, II: 196; III: 154, 180, 244, 279). Twining partook of boar hunting in Cossimbazar Island, and while accompanying the British commander-in-chief Sir Robert Abercromby on an inspection tour up the Ganges valley in June 1794, witnessed a fancy dinner with splendid entertainment, rounded off with fine Mocha-imported coffee provided by a specialized Parsi trader particularly for that occasion (Tw, 97, 106–07). Ultimately, there was no difference between the British and the Dutch in their indulgence of pleasures that India could offer.

Lavish living in British and Dutch settlements contrasted distressingly with the famines that both confronted. Stavorinus witnessed two famines during his first voyage to Asia (1768–71): at Chinsura in October 1769, and then again in February 1770. He observed people being devoured alive by jackals, and attributes the 1770 food shortage to crop failure, to monopolistic rice hoarding by the British, and to small pox (St, I: 115–16; I: 151–55). Hodges, having been in India from 1780 to 1783, reports secondhand on the 1770 famine suffered throughout Hindustan, his information having been gleaned from District Records and hearsay. He mentions the "huge loss of human lives," and underlines the benevolent role played by leading Indian gentlemen in Murshidabad and Bhagalpur in efforts to preserve the lives of poor victims during the famine (Ho, 94–95). Haafner was in Madras during the 1782 famine. He claims to have witnessed the arrival in Madras of ships from Bengal laden with relief provisions to the joy of all the famished victims in the British settlement, but at the same time he alludes to British monopolists who delayed the unloading of the relief vessels and obstructed the distribution of the foodgrains to the population with the aim of increasing grain prices (Ha, I: 79;

II: 360; II: 381–82). Hickey refers to two different famines. First, he recalled that during the 1783 famine, the road outside Madras was "strewed on both sides with the skulls and bones of the innumerable poor creatures who perished from want of food." Yet the table of the British governor in Madras, Lord Macartney, lacked nothing even if it displayed an "indifferent fare," Hickey observes (Hi, III: 97, 108). Again in 1789, Hickey witnessed the effects of crop failure on the laboring poor in Bengal and Bihar and noted that the British inhabitants of Calcutta offered relief through "a voluntary subscription" and special "stations" for delivering food (Hi, III: 344). As if to reassure the reader, Hickey declares: "Everything in the power of liberal individuals was done for their relief." Twining, not having witnessed any famine personally between 1792 and 1805, feels obliged to mention the 1767 famine, experienced in the Santipore district north of Calcutta and Murshidabad. He emphasizes the one million victims in 1767 "in those districts alone of which Murshidabad may be considered the centre," and attributes the food shortages to "destructive incursions of the Mahrattas." He thereby justifies the "political subjection" of the Bengal, Bihar, and Orissa region to the British on the basis that the British had successfully prevented future incursions. That several famines devastated the region after the British takeover in 1765, does not seem to disturb Twining (Tw, 110).

All the European powers in the eighteenth century felt the need to introduce the Enlightenment ideal of justice for all in their overseas settlements by establishing the European form of law courts, complete with judges, advocates, and attorneys. Stavorinus briefly refers to the VOC Council of Justice, which assisted the VOC's civil council in Chinsura by meting out sentences after conducting trials of offending Dutch members in Bengal. Any "capital executions" were thereafter to be carried out only at the VOC Asia headquarters in Batavia (St, I: 502–11). Haafner is more critical as he sees the host of judicial punishments carried out by European courts in India as "juridical murders" (Ha, I: 141–43). He criticizes the British for their ruthless enforcement of religious and civil laws in the areas under their control, and observes that in the Indian-administered territories, the traditional judicial officials, the Kotwals, tended to be lax and overlooked the crimes committed by Europeans (Ha, I: 144–62). Hickey describes the chambers of the Calcutta Courts, near the Central Bazaar, where British judges and British attorneys dealt with complaints registered by natives. The place was nicknamed "Ragamuffin hall" since it was frequented mainly by Indian waifs and vagabonds (Hi, III: 225–27). In 1790, Hickey participated in a case of cheating and fraud filed by "an eminent Mogul merchant," Hadjee Mahatee by name, against his European agent. As an attorney, Hickey, worked with the barrister William Burroughs and they won the case for Hadjee Mahatee under the acting chief justice, Sir Robert Chambers. This judicial victory did wonders for William Burroughs's reputation as a barrister, according to Hickey (Hi, III: 335–36).

This brings us to the justifying discourses on foreign domination. In an interesting reflection on the decline of empires, Stavorinus acknowledges the "seeds of destruction" within an Empire visible through "the conquest of countries and the increase of territory," which cost " a great expenditure of blood and incalculable treasures" and brought only "an imaginary advantage" to the conquering power. He elaborates (St, III: 417, 423):

> Were the prosperity of the [Dutch] East India Company only in a state of decline, from the circumstances we have mentioned, hopes might be entertained of relief and restoration. A fortunate chance of war, or a favourable peace in Europe might afford sufficient opportunities of engaging men enough to supply, in a very ample manner, the deficiency of people now laboured under. But many other circumstances concur, if not to render the restoration of the Company's affairs, a matter of impossibility, at least, to afford the most unfavourable prospects respecting them. . . .
>
> The evil which has its origin, in the constitution of the body politic itself, is irresistibly augmented, when accidental extraneous circumstances concur to drag to perdition, the state or institution which thus totters on its base.
>
> Both the interior leven (*sic*) of corruption and external adventitious evils, have taken place, and still exist, with regard to the [VOC] Company.

Thus already in 1777, twenty-two years before its final dissolution, Stavorinus anticipated the ruin of the VOC. Haafner likewise exposes the injustices of exerting political control over foreign territories—either through outright massacre or war, or the forging of manipulative alliances, or through false accusations indigenous allies (Ha, I: 356). While casting suspicion on any show of generosity by European powers toward indigenous peoples, Haafner judges the Dutch and the British tactics as equally abhorrent (Ha, II: 370–74). He condemns all European officials in Asia for "depredations of all kinds" against the indigenous people under their control, and for circumventing all the checks on their own actions by their home authorities in Europe (Ha, II: 413). Hodges is the most optimistic of our three British observers about the possible justifications for European intervention in Asian affairs. He views the situation philosophically, from an Enlightenment perspective, and considers all the manifestations of human genius in art and architecture, whatever their geography or cultural origins, as equally valuable in forming parts of the same unified whole of universal creativity. So any exchanges among different cultures could only be enriching (Ho, 65, 75). Hickey makes two ambivalent comments on the justifiability of foreign intervention in the internal functioning of a distant land. In 1776, he appears completely convinced of the validity of the activities of White European plantation owners in Jamaica, after the few months he spent there from October 1775 to April 1776. Despite his awareness of the existence of brutal overseers, he believes that "moderation and gentleness" usually triumphed over tyranny in Jamaican plantations (Hi, II: 49–55). Then, ten years later in Bengal in January 1786, when the new governor general, Charles Cornwallis, launched equity suits to recover sums of which individual contractors working for the British East India Company had cheated the Company (in the form of commissions on every contract granted), Hickey makes it clear that even this form of legal redress was a source of profit to him personally as an attorney (Hi, III: 306–08). Twining in the 1790s is the most conscious among our observers of the paradox of foreign settlements in Bengal, a matter that touches on the complex question of land appropriation that had already occupied European jurists in justifying settlement in North America. Twining declares about Bengal: "... It comprehends also the foreign settlements of Chinsurah, Chandernagore, Serampore and Bandel, bearing the flags of Holland, France, Denmark and Portugal—as if this peopled and fertile region had been an unappropriated waste on which every nation might plant its standard and take a share" (Tw, 124).[16] Twining also evokes the dilemma of the need for East India Company government investment for infrastructural construction. For example, the widening of river beds or the building of new canals needed to be blended with local knowledge and practical experience in order to ensure against the sterility of "those utopian systems of theoretic legislation," which, in Twining's opinion, would subvert the very foundations of the British Empire in the East, "to the chief misfortune perhaps of India itself" (Tw, 343–44).

To conclude, each European trading company devised its specific ways of taking advantage of the field conditions it encountered, based on its unique history and the circumstances of its involvement in Asian affairs. Yet the different companies had in common their aims of earning profits in Asian trade and their need to justify their actions in the field to their respective home authorities. These similarities and differences were further complicated by institutional rivalries and individual collaborations between the British and the Dutch in India. The net result by 1799 was that the European financial center had shifted from Amsterdam to London, but far from any monolithic imposition of any Machiavellian, preconceived, worldwide system by any single power (LB, 212), the different competing world powers at the time were each trying to adapt to a world scene that was changing fast in commercial, technical, and political terms.

NOTES

1. Albert Hyma, *The Dutch in the Far East* (Ann Arbor: George Wahr, 1942), 54; henceforth cited as AH.
2. D. K. Fieldhouse, *The Colonial Empires: A Comparative Survey from the Eighteenth Century* (London: Weidenfeld and Nicholson, 1966), 145.
3. Alice Clare Carter, *Neutrality or Commitment: The Evolution of Dutch Foreign Policy 1667–1795* (London: Edwin Arnold, 1975), 79.
4. Philip Lawson, *The East India Company—A History* (London: Longman, 1987), 86–144.
5. Vidya Dhar Mahajan, *India since 1526* (New Delhi: S. Chand & Co., 1978), esp. 605–06.
6. *Biografisch Archief Van de Benelux* (München: K. G. Saur, n.d.), Series No. I-644, 414–17. Note by Frederik Nagtglas, *Levensberichten van Zeeuven* (Middelburg: D2, 1891), 9.
7. John Splinter Stavorinus, *Voyages to the East Indies, translated from the original Dutch by Samuel Hull Wilcocke, with notes and additions by the translator, the whole comprising a full and accurate account of all the present and late possessions of the Dutch in India, and at the Cape of Good Hope, illustrated with maps, in three volumes* (London: G. G. & J. Robinson, 1798); henceforth cited parenthetically as St.
8. Leslie Stephen and Sidney Lee, eds., *Dictionary of National Biography* (London: Smith, Elder & Co., 1891), 27: 61–62; note by Lionel Cust, FSA.
9. William Hodges, *Travels in India During the Years 1780, 1781, 1782 & 1783* (London: J. Edwards, 1793); henceforth cited as Ho.
10. Peter Quennell, ed., *Memoirs of William Hickey* (London: Hutchinson & Co., 1960), 9–18; C. S. Nicholls, ed., *Dictionary of National Biography—Missing Persons* (Oxford: Oxford University Press, 1993), 309–10, note by P. J. Marshall. See also Alfred Spencer, ed., *Memoirs of William Hickey, in 4 Volumes* (London: Hurst & Blackett, 1913–25); henceforth cited as Hi.

11. Jacob Haafner, *Voyages dans la Péninsule Occidentale de l'Inde et dans l'Ile de Ceilan* (Vol. I), suivis de *Voyage fait par terre le long des Côtes d'Orixa et de Coromandel* (Vol. II), translated from the Dutch by M. Jansen (Paris: chez Arthus-Bertrand, Libraire, 1811). See: "Notice sur la vie de M. Jacques Haafner par M. Jansen," I: ix–xii; henceforth cited as Ha.

12. Thomas Twining, *Travels in India a Hundred years Ago, with a visit to the United States, being notes and reminiscences by Thomas Twining, a civil servant of the Honourable East India Company, preserved by his son, Thomas Twining of Twickenham, and edited by the Rev. William H. G. Twining, Vicar of St. Stephen's, Westminster* (London: James R. Osgood, Mc Ilvaine & Co., 1893), 525–29; henceforth cited as Tw.

13. See Leonard Blusse, "The Run to the Coast: Comparative Notes on Early Dutch and English Expansion and State Formation in India," *ITINERARIO*, Vol. 12, special issue, *The Ancien Regime in India & Indonesia* (Leiden: Grafaria, 1988), 195–214; henceforth cited as LB.

14. See Om Prakash, *European Commercial Enterprise in Pre-Colonial India, The New Cambridge History of India*, Vol. II, 5 (Cambridge: Cambridge University Press, 1998), 282–86.

15. See Earl H. Pritchard, *The Crucial Years of early Anglo-Chinese Relations, 1750–1800*, Research Studies of the State College of Washington, Vol. 4: 3–4 (Pullman, Wash.: State College of Washington, 1936), 180–83, on the system of remitting money from Bengal via Canton to London at this time.

16. See David Armitage, *The Ideological Origins of the British Empire* (Cambridge: Cambridge University Press, 2000), 92–99.

PART III

EARLY IMPERIALISMS: EAST AND WEST

CHAPTER 7

EMPIRE AS COMPOSITE: THE OTTOMAN POLITY AND THE TYPOLOGY OF DOMINION

Daniel Goffman and Christopher Stroop

> *It is far from clear whether separate religious identity, however powerful, is, taken by itself, similar to nationalism. The modern tendency is to assimilate the two, since we are no longer familiar with the model of the multi-corporate state, in which various religious communities coexist under a supreme authority as in some senses autonomous and self-administering entities; [sic] as under the Ottoman Empire.*
>
> —*Eric J. Hobsbawm*, Nations and Nationalism (1990)[1]

Neither "empire" nor "nation-state" is an easily defined concept.[2] The first often is loosely conceived as any political formation that answers to no earthly authority and is neither a city-state nor a nation state; the second is rather sloppily imagined as a state and society that boasts a citizenry that is homogeneous in language and identity.[3] The terms come together because many believe that the nation-state is a successor to, and consequently implicitly superior to, the empire as a way of organizing society. The place where this transformation is said to have occurred is Western Europe; the time was the fifteenth through the eighteenth centuries.

Not only has Western Europe been at the center of investigations of this change in political formations, but the normative models for such undertakings also have been culled from Western civilization. We typically take the Roman Empire to represent the archetypal model of empire and the British Empire to represent the normative modern case.[4] We study the modern French, English, Italian, and German polities, meanwhile, as exemplars of the construction of nation-states. In this schema, we tend to measure modern states outside of Europe against a European standard, and we are inclined to consider them to be malformed to the degree that they veer from the European ideal. In much the same way, scholars tend to measure African, Asian, and American empires against either the Roman or the British ones, and conceive divergences as defects.

Tendencies to study even borderlands, middle grounds, marches, and frontiers in terms of the encounters between European empires and others further color our understanding of the term.[5] Borderlands in colonial and early national America typically are conceived in terms of conflict and negotiation between European empires—the English versus the Spanish, or the French versus the English, or, later, the United States versus one or another European power. Sophisticated and powerful understandings and models have emerged out of these studies.[6] Nevertheless, such conceptualizations are problematic in part because they sometimes assume that the specific case is generally valid.

Theories of empire are problematic also because other state formations that we call empires—such as the Aztecs or the Chinese—developed in complete isolation from the Roman tradition. How can we simultaneously call the Roman example definitive and continue to name such entities in Africa, the Americas, and Asia, which evolved autonomously, empires? We either need to develop more sophisticated and inclusive understandings of terms such as "empire" and "borderlands" or come up with a better vocabulary to replace them.

Even our examinations of European empires have suffered from our tendencies to view all empires from a Western European perspective. One historian of the Habsburg Empire, for example, has written that "owing perhaps to its extreme complexity and diversity, the development of the Habsburg Empire is seldom given its due importance in general accounts of modern European history." We believe that the author is mistaking unfamiliarity for complexity in his suggestion that the Habsburg kingdom is more complex than other polities. Rather, just as Western scholars, politicians, and journalists often label what they do not understand as exotic, he also is representing difference from an implicit norm as being of inordinate complexity. On the one hand, he is correct in the sense that the Habsburg Empire certainly appears to be complex to a scholarly world that has framed Western

European states as the standard against which to measure other states. On the other, he is mistaken to suggest that it is definitionally more complex than other political entities. In addition, there is irony in the fact that, while he demands that the academy pay more attention to the role of the Habsburg Empire in European history, he writes from the same paradigm as historians of other European polities, namely, a paradigm in which the Habsburg Empire must be seen as abnormal.

The same author further explains that the Habsburg Empire's "development in the seventeenth and eighteenth centuries is usually brought in only as background material for the study of other European states or general trends. As a unit, to be studied *per se*, the Habsburg Empire is usually brought in only in the nineteenth century, when it was already in decay."[7] One implication of this statement is that the Habsburg Empire becomes significant to most historians only when Western Europe directly influenced it, and only in the age of modern nationalism, when this polity can easily be viewed as backward. A second, and we think more interesting, implication is that scholars have tended to apply the characteristics of the nineteenth-century empire to its earlier career, thereby imposing upon it a deceptive appearance of static timelessness, and robbing it of much of its potential for development, change, or variation.

Another historian discusses such ahistorical appropriation of the Habsburg past from a different perspective in his examination of the early modern *Altes Reich*. He asserts that post-unification nationalist scholars have ignored concepts of nationhood and empire as they existed in the Holy Roman Empire in favor of Prussia's "mission" to create a centralized nation.[8] In other words, researchers have tended to examine predecessors to the modern German and Austrian states for precedents and antecedents, rather than in terms of those polities' own times and realities. In short, the twin prongs of Western-centered learning and national ideology have sometimes subverted study of the early modern Habsburg Empire.

If assumptions of abnormality have sabotaged our understanding of the Habsburgs, at least most scholars who study that empire know and have undertaken research in its languages, and have immersed themselves into the residue of its civilization in Austria, Hungary, or Germany. Such is typically not the case with the Ottoman Empire, where Western scholars almost routinely assess its composition, its policies, and its personality through the prism of earlier Western sources, commentators, and literary figures, who themselves usually wrote about the Ottomans from afar. Consequently, not only has much scholarship relegated the Ottomans to a supporting role both in terms of its historical place in Europe and also in terms of its possible contributions to theories of empire, but it also has done so without engaging Ottoman society directly. American, English, and French literary critics and historians tend to examine Western representations of Ottoman life—by diplomats, travelers, divines, playwrights, and political philosophers—and use such alien perspectives either to situate the "Turk" (the identifier used for both Ottoman and Muslim in most of their sources) in Western European worldviews, or to reconstruct a (plainly invented) early modern Ottoman world.[9]

The most recent scholarship on the idea of empire maintains such biases. The important edited volume *Theories of Empire*, for example, limits itself to the development of European thought and politics in the early modern period.[10] In his introduction, its editor outlines some basic theories of empire in early modern Europe, including the European understanding of the Latin *imperium* and its etymological evolution. And in another work, he writes: "Few polities could legitimately claim direct descent from the Roman Empire; only the [Holy Roman] emperor and the pope could plausibly claim even a restricted form of universal rulership."[11]

It certainly is appropriate to begin a discussion of Western theories of empire with Rome, since many later Western rulers and political philosophers looked to Rome for legitimization. Nevertheless, this particular discussion remains problematic because some early modern empires usually deemed non-Western, including both the Russians and the Ottomans, also drew upon a Roman legacy in defending their own legitimacies. Both these putative empires claimed Roman succession on the basis of Mehmed II's conquest of Constantinople in 1453. In the Ottoman case, it was as direct geographical heir to the Byzantine Empire. By 1453, the Islamic entity had virtually superimposed itself upon the Orthodox one, as both the sultan who conquered the city and the pope who failed to rally forces to raise the Ottoman siege realized. Mehmed's very title reflects his awareness of the political and ideological significance of the conquest. His predecessors had referred to themselves as *begs*, that is, as nobles of distinction; Mehmed began calling himself a sultan, a great lord, and a great prince, and after 1453 simply dropped the title of *beg*. Pius II, meanwhile, referred to the Ottoman conqueror as "legitimate emperor of the Greeks and the Orient," a clear acknowledgment of the validity of Mehmed's claims as successor to Byzantium, despite their Islamic basis.[12]

The rulers of the Russian empire, supported by Russian theologians, also saw the Ottoman conquest of Constantinople as a critical event in the development and legitimization of the Russian state (if for very different reasons than their Ottoman nemesis). For them, the conquest was divine punishment for Byzantium's willingness to reunite with the Catholic heretics. For many Russians, in 1453, the legacy of Rome passed from Constantinople to Moscow, which, according to religious and political theorists, had become the Third Rome. As one historian has put it, "by the 1520s [this concept] meant that the first two Romes (Rome and Constantinople) had both fallen as God's punishment.... In other words, the Christian Russians were God's final chosen people."[13]

Despite such homegrown authenticities, many modern theoretical works deny these Eastern empires (as well as Byzantium itself) their Roman heritage. It may make sense for those whose interests are in European state formation to ignore civilizations that developed independently. Nevertheless, this justification does not work in the case of the Habsburgs, the Russians, or the Ottomans, all of whom remained in continuous contact with Western Europeans throughout the early modern era and all of whom claimed a legacy from Rome.

The early modern Ottoman Empire in particular looked exceptionally "European" for a number of reasons. First, unlike other empires that we usually exclude from the European standard, it in fact exercised control over one-third of that subcontinent during the crucial years of Europe's Renaissance and Reformation. It also is too often forgotten that during the 1400s, the Ottoman polity constituted the Italian city-states' principal antagonist and partner. It was this entity against which Genoa, Venice, and the Papal States had to test their military and diplomatic skills, and with which they ultimately had to cooperate in order to survive. It was this empire that not only distracted Catholic Europe from a nascent Protestant rebellion, but also provided a harbor for religiously oppressed minorities from both the Catholic south and the Protestant north.

Venetian cooperation with the Ottomans, for example, is seen most dramatically in that city-state's quick negotiations after the conquest of Constantinople in 1453. That moment was only the most spectacular of a string of accommodations, however, during which the Venetians compensated for an unrelenting Ottoman advance against their eastern Mediterranean colonies with commercial presences in these very same places. In other words, the Venetians replaced the corporal empire they had carved out of Byzantium after the Fourth Crusade with a commercial one that by the middle of the sixteenth century projected far into Ottoman domains.[14] The Ottoman Empire, meanwhile, provided refuge not only to Jews fleeing persecution in Catholic Europe, but also to Anglicans, Calvinists, and those very same Catholics from whom they were escaping.

While the Jewish and Calvinist instances of Ottoman acceptance may be the best known, the Catholic example is perhaps the more compelling and unexpected. In 1656, for example, the *şeyhülislam*, the highest Ottoman religious functionary, ordered his officials in Jerusalem to prevent members of the Greek community in that city from seizing control of the Virgin Mary's home, which had "been in the hands of Frankish monks in Jerusalem for 360 years."[15] It must have been infuriating to the Greek Orthodox Patriarch that these Catholic monks still retained holy sites that they had seized during the Crusades; it seems not to have bothered the Ottomans at all. Just as surprisingly, in the seventeenth century it became almost customary for the Ottoman government to issue travel documents to Catholic priests wishing to travel across the empire. One example occurred in 1644 when some French Jesuits obtained Ottoman consent to wander (and proselytize?) across Egypt and Syria, and visit the cities of Jerusalem, Aleppo, and Damascus.[16]

The Ottomans also straddled the transformation of empires that accompanied the development of mercantile structures. Before the British, French, and Dutch established their vast overseas empires in the eighteenth and nineteenth centuries, they first developed and tested their institutions of empire in Ottoman domains. The English did so at both the North African fringe of the empire (especially in the cities of Tangiers and Algiers) as well as in the eastern Mediterranean heartlands (particularly in Istanbul, Izmir, and Aleppo). In Tangiers especially, where high hopes were quickly dashed, the English began to learn about the dangers and vagaries as well as the opportunities of overseas settlement. In the Ottoman heartlands of the eastern Mediterranean, meanwhile, the early modern Englishmen quickly learned not even to try to control or conquer. Instead, they imitated, adapted, and learned.

In these and other ways, the Ottomans and other European states learned from and emulated each other. The Ottomans, for example, constituted Byzantium's geographic successor state, and ascertained much from that empire about how to weather dynastic succession and how to administer diverse territories. It subsequently expanded into the Mediterranean seas at the expense of Venice, and discovered from the overseas empire of that city-state how to fuse seaborne and land-based holdings into a single political entity, and how to exploit colonies overseas. Later European empires, including the British one, also learned from the Ottomans. After all, this empire was the very first non-Christian entity with which the English had to negotiate.[17] The English certainly feared Ottoman power and the religion that legitimized it, as countless plays, sermons, and political tracts verify.[18]

One example is "Selimus, Emperor of the Turks," an Elizabethan play published in 1594. In it, the playwright—probably Robert Greene—presents a Selim who was ruthless, tyrannical (that is, ruling without the guidance of either divine or natural law), and irreligious. In the soliloquy with which the play begins, Selim's father, Sultan Bayezid, muses that he has "three sons, all of inequal ages,/and all in diverse studies set their bliss:/Corcut, the eldest, a philosopher;/Acomat pompous, Selim a warrior."[19] He laments his own predicament and sets up a tension between father and sons as well as son and son that drives the plot and eventually leads Selim to poison his father and murder his siblings, even as he too doggedly (and no doubt shockingly for the play's English audience) repudiates his faith: "I count it sacrilege for to be holy/Or reverence this threadbare name of 'good.'/Leave to old men and babes that kind of folly;/Count it of equal value with the mud."[20]

The primary intent of this historical tragedy doubtlessly was to entertain and even to stun an English audience. It constituted more of a comment on the English than the Ottoman world, and the playwright, attuned to the passions of his London public, exhibits little interest in the historical context of his subjects. The Ottoman political use of fratricide as well as Bayezid's own struggle to win the throne over an older and competent brother, Cem, who then spent decades trying to overthrow him, remain unexplored (even unacknowledged), as does the religion, Islam, that legitimized Ottoman rule. We should not be surprised that this and other early modern English writings on the Ottoman world were disconnected from their distant heroes and scoundrels, who typically constituted little more than a trope for English mores and English concerns.

Nevertheless, the choice of the "Turk" as subject in this and other works suggests more than a deep-seated fear of and fascination with the growing empire to the East. The playwright's ability to represent the institutions (if not the behavior) of imperial son, vizier, pasha, and janissary with some accuracy also demonstrates an at least skeletal knowledge of their world. Such information derived in part from Ottoman captives and envoys, a few of whom found their ways to England.[21] Most of it, however, came from Greene's own compatriots, who already in the 1590s were beginning to explore the Ottoman world. Beginning in the 1570s, and in ever-increasing numbers, English merchants, diplomats, and captives visited and at times settled in Ottoman cities in North Africa and the eastern Mediterranean seaboard. Many even converted to Islam (and occasionally back again to Christianity). Even though their writings no less than Greene's and other fiction writers reflected the anxieties of their English audiences, their authors' personal experiences lent them an informed authenticity.

Those who ventured Eastward had to accommodate themselves to a vast, established, and resilient Ottoman society and government. Even more than misfortunes at Tangiers, experiences in the eastern Mediterranean taught the English how to establish trading factories in foreign realms.[22] The Genoese, the Venetians, the French, the Dutch, and the English all fashioned booming foreign districts in Ottoman cities such as Istanbul, Aleppo, and, later, Izmir before using what they had learned to expand Eastward into South and Southeast Asia, and Westward into the Americas.[23]

Perhaps it is not so revelatory that Western Europeans established proto-colonial port cities in the Ottoman Empire. More startling, however, is that they were not able to do so on their own terms, but instead had to adapt themselves to the powerful and sophisticated monarchy that the Ottomans had constructed. Most startling, perhaps, is the swift manner in which they incorporated Ottoman practices into the organization and culture of their small settlements within the empire. In most of early modern Western European society, there was little room for emotional or physical expressions of alien faiths. In Ottoman port cities, however, the Anglican English, the Catholic French, and other Christians quickly took as fixed their right not only to roam and worship freely but also to repair and even build chapels and churches.

To give a second example of Ottoman accommodation: whereas much of early modern Western Europe discouraged the employment of foreigners in political and commercial administration, the early modern Ottoman world was crowded with non-Ottoman administrators. Alvise Gritti, for one, was both the son of a Venetian doge and an Ottoman official who in the 1520s led an Ottoman army against the Hungarians and was a close friend of the Ottoman grand vizier. İbrahim Pasha.[24] Another example is Henry Hyde, who in the 1630s was the English consul of the Morea and simultaneously (that is, until English Levant Company officials found him out) served as an Ottoman collector of taxes who commanded a body of janissary guards.[25]

The early modern Ottoman world comprised a multitude of peoples—Christians, Jews, and Muslims; Greeks, Hungarians, Armenians, Turks, Arabs, and Kurds; pastoralists, guildsmen, and bureaucrats; freedmen and slaves.[26] In other words, unlike early modern England, Ottoman society was intensely heterogeneous. Also unlike England, few social or economic restrictions were put upon non-Muslim Ottomans. In this Islamic society, Christians and Jews lived where they wished and worked as farmers, textile workers, traders, shopkeepers, translators, moneychangers, and tax collectors (but not as soldiers and administrators). The ability of this society to organize itself so differently from the relatively homogeneous England derived in large part from its foundation. The Ottomans fashioned many of their institutions in the fourteenth-century frontier zone of western Anatolia, a middle ground, if you will, in which they had to negotiate with the civilizations of Islam, Persia, Byzantium, and others. The early Ottomans adeptly selected, adapted, and fused these traditions into a new civilization that was religiously flexible, disregarded ethnic and racial difference, and produced a body politic able to incorporate diverse religious, economic, and social groupings.

One principal device by which they did so was a selective mingling of Islamic and customary law. First, Islamic law allowed the incorporation of non-Muslim monotheists—such as Christians and Jews—into society. The Ottomans embraced a particularly liberal reading of this sanction in its treatment of its millions of Christian and Jewish subjects, the patriarchs and rabbis of whom, consequently, continued to collect communal taxes and to manage their communities according to their own laws and customs (at times even constructing new churches and synagogues in direct contradiction to the *sharia*). Second, the state dealt with the political and legal diversity of its realm by compiling a series of provincial law books that retained much of the local law (at times even at the expense of Islamic law) after each conquest.

In this and other ways, the Ottoman body politic manifested a protean quality that absorbed religious and other communities almost at will—even those of enemy aliens. The Ottoman state conceived of Venetian, Genoese, French, and English foreign settlements very much as they did their own subject ones—that is, according to a rather elastic rendering of several bodies of law. Under such laws, foreign infidels not only legally became *müste'min*—members of communities that were granted temporary rights of residence in the Ottoman domains— but also established their own political structures and administrations, worshiped as they pleased, and collected their own taxes.

Scholars often view these communities and administrations that the Dutch, English, French, and Venetians established in Ottoman port cities during the seventeenth century as imperial outposts that constituted little more than first steps toward the creation of empire. To imagine them in this way is not only anachronistic, but also eurocentric. The foreigners who lived in these communities understood how tenuous their positions were, and concentrated on adapting themselves in order to survive rather than transforming their hosts. Many Ottoman administrators, meanwhile, considered such "factories" or "nations" as legal first steps toward integration into their empire, and the state protected these settlements in much the same way and for many of the same reasons that it protected non-Muslim subjects.

Within the parameters of their ideology, the Ottomans defended foreigners from abuse by both subjects and rival foreigners. They did so in the area of finance and commerce as well as law and religion. In the first sphere, for example, Western Europeans set out to protect their compatriots from their rivals, as in 1620 when the Venetian consul in Izmir complained that the English community there was seizing a special tax (consulage) on Venetian goods that in the past had gone to pay for the running of the Venetian factories.[27] They also appealed to the Ottoman authorities for protection against Ottoman officials, as in the 1620s when the janissaries appointed to guard Venetian goods (*yasakçıs*) demanded exorbitant monies in order to do so.[28]

Such protection extended to freedom of worship. For example, when in 1622 the Venetian bailo in Istanbul accused Ottoman officials in Jerusalem of abetting Muslim subjects in their attempts to seize Venetian churches, monasteries, and other structures, the government declared that "this treatment is unlawful. Places that have long been Venetian possessions—churches, monasteries, orchards in Bethlehem, houses, rooms, . . . should remain theirs." Nor, the decree continues, should anyone "interfere in their pilgrimage to Mount Sinai, or any other places where the Venetian Frankish community customarily visits."[29]

Jerusalem, of course, was a place of pilgrimage, and consequently might be considered exceptional. Nevertheless, the Ottomans extended such protection to other settlements as well. For example, in February 1625 the government not only ordered officials in the Anatolian port town of Izmir to shield Venetian and other Europeans who wanted to worship in a church there, but also insisted that the community of foreigners be allowed to repair their place of worship.[30] In another case, in the summer of 1624, the consuls of the various European communities resident at Galipolli asked that local Ottoman subjects not prevent them from repairing crumbling churches.[31] In Jerusalem, Izmir, and Galipolli, Ottoman authorities perceived these foreigners not as temporary sojourners but as settlers who would eventually become integrated into Ottoman society (and consequently into the Islamic world).

There also is evidence of forces within the Ottoman administration that wanted to hurry this process of integration. Inherent in status as *müste'min* was exemption from payment of the *cizye*, a head tax to which non-Muslim subjects were liable, and various other dues. The *cizye* was not only remunerative; it also was the symbolic acknowledgment that a non-Muslim lived in the "Abode of Islam" (*dar al-islam*). Both residents and visitors understood the definitional centrality of this Islamic law. Consequently, local administrators (non-Muslim as well as Muslim) often looked for opportunities to impose this tax upon sojourners, and foreigners usually resisted the imposition by appealing to central authorities. In 1606, for example, the Ottoman government insisted that as long as Venetian shopkeepers in Istanbul paid their customs, they should not be put in the same category as non-Muslim Ottoman subjects in contradiction to the terms of their capitulations (*ahdname*).[32] Seventeen years later, it was the Venetian community on Chios who petitioned that a Jewish tax collector on the island wrongly insisted that their members pay the *cizye*.[33]

Situations also arose in which individuals as well as communities could exploit the flexible manner in which the Ottoman state tended to interpret its laws and traditions, and especially with regard to the integral situation of foreigners within these structures. One example concerns the slippery matter of who fit the category of *müste'min* and the rights and obligations inherent in that position. In the mid-seventeenth century, as *müste'min* the Ottoman government granted the French and Genoese the right to pay only three percent customs on goods exported from the Ottoman Empire, which was one percent less than subject Muslims and two percent less than subject non-Muslims paid. In 1676, however, five Jews who had settled in the city of Izmir some fifteen years previously, and who clearly were Ottoman subjects, claimed a "connection" with the French and Genoese, and that they should be liable to pay only three percent duty on goods.[34]

Such a manipulation may be considered an abuse. Nevertheless, it also was a reflection of Ottoman malleability. Indeed over time Ottoman subjects redoubled their efforts to lessen their customs charges. In 1684 a group of Armenians and Jews in Istanbul who traveled and shipped goods on French vessels insisted that "we came by the ship of a Frenchmen," and consequently should "give our customs as the community of Frenchmen give it."[35] Even though the consequence was a loss of revenue for the imperial treasury, the Ottoman government ordered local authorities to comply with the request.

Both the Ottoman government and many Ottoman subjects conceived of foreigners as a component integral to, rather than an appendage disconnected from, the Ottoman world. The Ottoman government considered Muslims, non-Muslim subjects, and foreigners residing in the empire as an inextricable part of the Ottoman whole. This vision not only helped the state integrate myriad peoples into its realm but also provided opportunities for subjects and foreigners to exploit the resultant fluidity of laws and relationships.

Scholars have long studied early modern states, whether conceived as empires, city-states, or nation-states, as precursors to the modern world. Singled out have been those aspects of the European monarchy that seem to forecast the bureaucratization, centralization, and increasing authority of the state. The idea of "composite monarchies," first proposed in the early 1980s, advances an alternative to this vision. It emphasized the persistence of personal loyalties, patronage, and loose organization, and the protagonists of this model had in mind chiefly the Spanish Habsburg and Stuart English cases. They were struggling to conceptualize monarchies "made up of different kingdoms and territories acquired by conquest or inheritance, and preserving their distinctive laws and traditions after their incorporation into a union of kingdoms subject to a single monarch."[36] In other words, these remained political entities that clearly constituted multiple peoples without common ethnicities, languages, or histories, although their religion was generally the same.

By the mid-seventeenth century, the era of composite monarchy in Western Europe essentially had come to an end. Nevertheless, even the so-called historical nations, which became so important for later advocates of nationalisms, were rarely if ever as homogeneous in the early modern period (or thereafter) as nationalists imagine them to have been. Even France, perhaps the archetypal nation state, was not nearly as uniform as often supposed, as proven in the fact that in 1789 more than fifty percent of Frenchmen did not speak French.[37] All European states may have remained more or less "composite," particularly in terms of language and ethnicity. Nevertheless, even the most ethnically and linguistically diverse monarchies of Western Europe were less "composite" than were the Ottomans, particularly when it came to religion.

The Ottoman Empire, in fact, fits this model at least as well as does any other early modern European state. It constituted many distinct peoples, it preserved myriad distinctive laws and political and social institutions, it encouraged patronage and personal loyalty, and its organizations remained remarkably loose and flexible. In other words, without espousing democratic, republican, or pluralistic notions, this realm still managed to be far more diverse, flexible, inclusive, and composite than was any contemporary Western European state. The early modern Ottomans were able to accommodate the English, the French, and others without compromising either their own or these interlopers' social, religious, and political integrity. They constituted a type of composite monarchy, the diverse fragments of which owed allegiance to the sultan even as they retained their own distinguishing laws and customs, and the experiences and observations of English men and women in the Ottoman world helped them establish their own (initially) composite empires in both the Americas and East Asia, helped condition the behavior of Britons in these places, and helped form British attitudes toward the multiple others that they encountered in these worlds.[38]

The Ottoman polity was also composite in at least two distinctive ways. First, its ruling class was as heterogeneous as were its subjects. In early modern Western Europe, the ruling class typically consisted of a nobility born into its rights. It was held together through bonds of blood and a belief in its natural right to lead, to have privileges, and to govern. The Ottoman elite was different. Its viziers and pashas, its janissaries and scribes derived from every region, both within the empire and beyond. Many of them began lives as non-Muslims, even non-Ottomans. They sometimes entered the Ottoman world as captives, as servants of the sultan, and rose within that household or, later, within the households of important officials. Consequently, it is unsound to define this group in terms of race, ethnicity, or even religion (it was a Muslim elite, but as often because of conversion as because of the rights of birth). What its members shared was a high culture, an education, a manner of speaking, and a vision of the world.

The empire was composite in a second distinctive way. Its subject peoples were not obliged to share the religion of their monarch. In the remainder of Europe, the fierce religious wars of the mid-sixteenth century had shattered the catholic ecumene and, in 1555 at the Treaty of Augsburg, had engendered the principal of *cuius regio eius religio* (by which each prince was to decide whether the inhabitants of her or his realm would be Catholic or Lutheran). The Ottoman world, however, was exempt from this shattering decision. In a radical (and, for the English and others, confounding) departure from the European norm, then, the Ottoman realm was a *religiously* as well as a geographically, linguistically, and politically composite state. Christian European composite monarchies never were able to overcome the problem of religious exclusivity, which quickened their demise. The Ottomans, however, managed to solve this conundrum; their composite empire remained in place until other European states replaced the composite state with the nation-state and carried to the Ottoman and other worlds their new political construct.

* * *

The picture we have drawn of the Ottoman world differs considerably from the one that early modern English, French, or German representations in popular literature suggests. A sampling of the plays, polemics, and sermons produced in the late sixteenth and seventeenth centuries reveals a relentlessly negative popular image of the "Turk," who is portrayed as rapacious, violent, dissolute, fiendish, and foul. For Luther, for Marlowe, for Shakespeare, and, as we have seen, for Greene and myriad lesser weavers of words, to "turn Turk" meant far more than to convert to a non-Christian faith; such descent into treacherous iniquity signified a cultural, even a character, transformation—a metamorphosis from goodness into evil.

One way to make sense of this apparent contradiction between these two renderings of the Ottoman and/or the Turk is to consider early modern representations of other notorious Others, such as the Jew. It was easy for the English or French to generate profoundly wrong stereotypes of the Jews, a people who shared with Islam a repudiation of the Christian faith, and who were only beginning to resettle in England after an almost three-century-long exile. It also was easy for the English or French to generate profoundly wrong stereotypes of the Ottomans, a people who never had settled among them. Most scholars consider, often quite explicitly, the acute disconnection between the Jewish world and English imaginings of that world in their readings of early modern English texts. Woven into their assessments of English representations of the Jews is sensitivity to the history of that community and its relations with Christian England.[39] It seems to us that such sensitivity to similar stereotyping, which can be mastered only by investigating the people being labeled, is often lacking in our treatments of English representations of the Ottomans.

A second way to consider this apparent contradiction is to compare it with post-9/11 views of Arabs or Islam. Imagine, if you will, a literary critic or historian 200 years from now who is studying representations of Islam or the Arab in early-twenty-first-century films, television, and the sound bites of news-show pundits. If such a critic took these representations at face value, the result would constitute a crude caricature. Nevertheless, they probably no less accurately reflect the popular American view of Arabs and Islam than do early modern plays and sermons replicate a popular English view of Turks and Ottomans. We think it is vital not only to recognize that the early modern English image of this mysterious and terrifying polity, as reflected through the prism of popular entertainment, was reductionist, extreme, and misshapen, but also to investigate why and how this prevalent image emerged. This task demands just as sophisticated and subtle a sense of the civilization that the early modern Ottomans had fabricated as we possess of the English one.

Notes

1. Eric J. Hobsbawm, *Nations and Nationalism since 1780: Programme, Myth, Reality* (Cambridge: Cambridge University Press, 1990), 70.

2. Including the term "imperialism" in this discussion would confuse our nomenclature in at least two ways. First, it denotes aggression in a manner that "empire" does not necessarily do. More critically, it is so embedded in theories of Western relations with the rest of the world, and especially in the specific case of capitalism, that it is difficult to apply to earlier or non-European cases. See Patrick Wolfe, "History and Imperialism: A Century of Theory, from Marx to Postcolonialism," *The American Historical Review* 102.2 (1997): 388–420 for both a survey of the theoretical underpinning of the word and an example of how it typically is applied specifically to the modern period.

3. The literature on nationalism and nation-states is immense. In addition to Hobsbawm, *Nations and Nationalism*, see Ernest Gellner, *Nations and Nationalism* (Ithaca: Cornell University Press, 1983); Benedict Anderson, *Imagined Communities: Reflections on the Origin and Spread of Nationalism* (New York: Verso Books, 1983); and Anthony D. Smith, *Nationalism and Modernism: A Critical Survey of Recent Theories of Nations and Nationalism* (London and New York: Routledge, 1998).

4. On which see the collection of essays, David Armitage, ed., *Theories of Empire, 1450–1800* (Aldershot: Ashgate, 1998).

5. On these terms and their slipperiness, see Daniel Power, "Frontiers: Terms, Concepts, and the Historians of Medieval and Early Modern Europe," in *Frontiers in Question: Eurasian Borderlands, 700–1700*, eds. Daniel Power and Naomi Standen (Houndmills, Basingstoke: Macmillan, 1999), 1–12.

6. A recent example, that seems persuasive in the North American context, but does not travel particularly well, is Jeremy Adelman and Stephan Aron, "From Borderlands to Borders: Empires, Nation States, and the Peoples in Between in North American History," *The American Historical Review* 104 (June 1999): 814–41.

7. Victor S. Mamatey, *The Rise of the Habsburg Empire, 1526–1815* (New York: Holt, Rinehart & Winston, 1971), iii–iv.

8. Georg Schmidt, *Geschichte des Alten Reiches: Staat und Nation in der Frühen Neuzeit, 1495–1806* (Munich: Beck, 1999), 191–92.

9. On which, see Daniel Goffman, *Britons in the Ottoman Empire, 1642–60* (Seattle: University of Washington Press, 1998), 212–21.

10. Armitage, *Theories of Empire*. The very title of the series in which this book appears, "An Expanding World: The European Impact on World History, 1450–1800," is problematic.

11. David Armitage, *The Ideological Origins of the British Empire* (Cambridge: Cambridge University Press, 2000), 33.

12. Franz Babinger, *Mehmed the Conqueror and His Time*, ed. William C. Hickman, trans. Ralph Manheim (Princeton: Princeton University Press, 1978), 417–18.

13. Walter G. Moss, *A History of Russia: Volume I, to 1917* (Boston: McGraw-Hill 1997), 100–01.

14. Daniel Goffman, *The Ottoman Empire and Early Modern Europe* (Cambridge: Cambridge University Press, 2002), 137–64.

15. Başbakanlık Arşivi, Ecnebi Defteri 26, p. 88, n. 1.

16. Ibid., 26, p. 38, n. 1.

17. On which see Linda Colley, *Captives: Britain, Empire, and the World, 1660–1850* (New York: Pantheon, 2002), 23–134.

18. Three examples are in Daniel J. Vitkus, ed., *Three Turk Plays from Early Modern England: Selimus, A Christian Turned Turk, The Renegado* (New York: Columbia University Press, 2000). The first, which concerns the Ottoman heartland, is more about the Ottomans than are the last two, which focus on a peripheral North Africa that was both more familiar to early-seventeenth-century England than was the eastern Mediterranean, and far less representative of the Ottoman world.

19. Vitkus, *Three Turk Plays*, 63–64.

20. Ibid., 69.

21. On whom, see Nabil Matar, *Turks, Moors and Englishmen in the Age of Discovery* (New York: Columbia University Press, 1999), chap. 1.

22. Goffman, *Britons*, especially chap. 2.

23. On which, see Edhem Eldem, Daniel Goffman, and Bruce Masters, eds., *The Ottoman City Between East and West: Aleppo, Izmir, and Istanbul* (Cambridge: Cambridge University Press, 1999).

24. Gülru Necipoğlu, "Süleyman the Magnificent and the Representation of Power in the Context of Ottoman-Hapsburg-Papal Rivalry," *Art Bulletin* 71.3 (1989): 401–27.

25. Goffman, *Britons*, 51–67.

26. All such terms are slippery both because of the vagaries of translation and because their meanings have shifted over time. Two examples: a "Turk" in early modern Ottoman meant something like a "country bumpkin" rather than suggesting a particular ethnic, linguistic, or

national identity; an Ottoman "slave" was as likely to be a high-ranking administrator or military man as a household or plantation slave in the American sense. Most of these other terms are equally problematic.

27. Başbakanlık Arşivi, Maliyeden Müdevver 6004, pp. 6 and 9.

28. Ibid., 10.

29. Ibid., 20, n. 1.

30. Ibid., 33.

31. Ibid., 102, n. 3.

32. Başbakanlık Arşivi, Ecnebi Defteri 13/1, p. 35, n. 5.

33. Başbakanlık Arşivi, Maliyeden Müdevver 6004, p. 51, n. 1.

34. Ibid., 2825, p. 93.

35. Ibid., 2947, p. 50.

36. J. H. Elliott, "Understanding the Past," www.balzan.it/english/ pb1999/elliott/paper.htm; J. H. Elliott, "A Europe of Composite Monarchies," *Past and Present* 137 (1992): 48–71.

37. Hobsbawm, *Nations and Nationalism*, 60.

38. For the argument that the English "triangulated" their experiences in the East and the West, see Matar, *Turks, Moors, and Englishmen*, especially chap. 3. The flexibility of English law in the "first" British Empire is explored in Eliga H. Gould, "Zones of Law, Zones of Violence: The Legal Geography of the British Atlantic, circa 1772," *William and Mary Quarterly* 60.3 (2003): 471–510.

39. A recent example is James Shapiro, *Shakespeare and the Jews* (New York: Columbia University Press, 1996), whose text covers such subjects as "What is a Jew?" and "Who is a Jew?" and whose bibliography reflects submersion into historiography on the Jews.

C H A P T E R   8

THE MALIKI IMPERIALISM OF AHMAD AL-MANSUR: THE MOROCCAN INVASION OF SUDAN, 1591

Nabil I. Matar

On February 28, 1591, a Moroccan army reached Niger across the Sahara, 135 days after leaving the capital Marrakesh. The musket-wielding combatants who survived the ordeal had been sent by the Moroccan ruler, Ahmad al-Mansur, to defeat the king of Songhay, Askiah Ishaq II, who had assembled an army of 80,000 footmen and horsemen, armed with lances and javelins (al-Gharbi, 207–08). The battle took place on March 13, 1591 and ended with the slaughter of the Songhay army by the superior weaponry and discipline of the Moroccans. The "Sudan" (land of the Blacks) subsequently submitted to Morocco and sent a tribute of 100,000 pieces of gold and 1,000 slaves to Marrakesh, while promising an annual *khiraj*/tribute too. So "deluged" was al-Mansur with gold that he was given the epithet, al-Dhahabi, the golden.[1]

This invasion is the only episode in early modern Islamic history in which an Arabic-speaking Muslim polity invaded another Muslim polity. Earlier in the century, there had been the invasion of the Mamluks by the Ottomans—both Muslims but both non-Arab with significant differences in jurisprudence and ideology.[2] Because Morocco was the only Arabic-speaking region that did not come under Ottoman hegemony, the 1591 invasion episode provides the opportunity to examine an Arab, as against Turko-Ottoman, act of conquest and to focus on the inception, interpretation, and justification of imperial ideology in the Arabic-speaking Maghreb of the early modern period.[3]

The 1590s witnessed a number of imperial thrusts in the western hemisphere. England began its conquest of Ireland; the Spaniards began their conquest of New Mexico (1595); and the Ottomans relaunched their armies into the Hungarian region (the Hungarian Wars, 1593–1606) after having completed their Eastward thrust into Persia. In similar fashion, al-Mansur launched his army against Sudan. But what was different for al-Mansur in the justification of his invasion was the absence of the religious excuse that served the other imperial ventures. The English were Anglicans—fighting Catholics; the Spaniards were Catholics conquering pagans; and the Ottomans were Muslims pushing into Christian territory. Al-Mansur had no such easy excuse because the Sudan was Muslim, Sunni by denomination, Arabic-speaking and Maliki by jurisprudence whose ruler had been pronounced a caliph in the line of the Prophet Muhammad. To justify his imperial design—and imperial it was in the sense that he sought to conquer, subjugate, and rule through military governors—al-Mansur had to resort to ideological arguments that drew on lineage, ethnicity, and race—arguments that are unique in the early modern history of the Arabic-speaking world. After all, the rest of the Arabic-speaking world had itself already been imperialized by the Ottomans.

The term "imperial" should be used carefully in the context of the Arab–Islamic argument. There were no words in Arabic that corresponded to "imperial," "empire," or "emperor" during the early modern period; their transliterations and introduction into the language came later. In the 1680s, the Tunisian historian, Ibn Abi Dinar, used the term in its transliterated form, but did not seem to be clear about its meaning:

> I said *al-imbarator* in that time was the ruler of Spain, may God destroy him. But the name is given to him because he reigns over most of the land of the Andalus. So he raised his nose and is called *imbarator*. None of his forefathers had that title since *imbarataor* is one of the names of the kings [muluk] of the Germans because their kingship is ancient. For them the *imbarator* is like the caliph among the Muslims.[4]

Without the kind of "imperial" vocabulary that gave legitimacy to conquest in the English, Spanish, and even Ottoman contexts, al-Mansur had to revert to his distinctive religious legacy for arguments and justifications for undertaking the subjugation of a coreligionist people. And these arguments he found in the Maliki school of jurisprudence—the school that prevailed in the Maghreb and whose followers distinguished themselves from the Ottoman followers of the school of Ibn Hanbal. This jurisprudential separation had also produced a linguistic and social separation between the Ottomans and the Arabs, the conquerors and the conquered. Each linguistic community identified and distinguished itself from the other by reference to its distinct jurisprudential school.

The Ottomans did not produce any records of the Moroccan invasion southward: despite the repercussions of the invasion around Western Europe, they ignored it, making only a few inaccurate references to it.[5] The record of this invasion survives in two kinds of Moroccan documents. First are the letters from al-Mansur to the Sudanese leaders in which he asked them to submit to his authority if they wanted to avoid invasion. And then, there are the contemporary justifications by the court scribe and apologist, al-Fishtali, and the analysis in the eighteenth century by al-Wufrani, who wrote in praise of al-Mansur. These sources are the chief material on which this essay relies.

*　*　*

The land of the Sudan was both fertile and rich, "one of the most favoured of the lands of God Most High in any direction," wrote the chronicler Al-Saadi;[6] the Marrakesh court scribe al-Fishtali was effusive about how God had enriched it "with the river of paradise and source of the water of mercy."[7] It is not surprising therefore that Mulay al-Mansur wanted the riches of Sudan and tried to find justifications/excuses for seizing them. Indeed, he was quoted by al-Fisthali[8] as saying that it was a land of beauty and urban growth, full of precious metals and slaves. Such desire for possessions had to convince the court jurists in Marrakesh who could not sanction war against another Muslim people and who presented a formidable obstacle for al-Mansur. The latter had gathered around him some of the finest jurists in the country, and "did not exclude any," as his scribe noted.[9] In their presence, he was punctilious in following religious codes: as the prince of the faithful, he reported to them on his leadership and protection of the Muslim community—including, of course, the Muslim Sudanese.

The jurists presented both practical and religious reasons against al-Mansur's decision to invade the Sudan. Initially, they warned that it was nearly impossible for the Moroccan army to cross the Sahara and carry out the invasion; it had, after all, been tried twice before in the early 1580s, with disastrous failure. Al-Mansur retorted that merchants crossed the Sahara all year round, and therefore the project was not impossible. Then, in a blunt admission of imperial realpolitik, he explained that the invasion of the Sudan was the only course of action left for him. He could not, he continued, fight the infidels in the Andalus because they had completely reconquered the peninsula; nor could he fight eastward into the principality of Tlemsan because it was in Ottoman hands. Meanwhile, the Sudanese army was weak, consisting of soldiers armed with spears and swords who could not defeat the "modern canons; fighting them is easy and doing battle with them is easier than anything else. The lands of the Sudan are the richest in Africa, and invading them is more profitable than confronting the Turks where there is much effort and little positive results."[10] The invasion was the best and only possible imperial choice.

The jurists reverted to religious arguments against invasion—that the Sudanese were fellow Muslims and no war was legally sanctioned against fellow believers. After all, the *Sahih* of Bukhari had mentioned only once the possibility of inter-Muslim warfare—and denounced it: if two Muslims fight each other with their swords, then both "of them are from the pole of the Hell Fire."[11] It was at this juncture that al-Mansur turned to Maliki jurisprudence in order to frame the enterprise within the legal codes of that school. Al-Mansur proclaimed to the jurists that he would abide by the Maliki formula for waging a *jihad*. The first part of the formula was the summons for war. This ritual/summons in Malik's *Kitab al-Jihad* entailed an initial announcement of hostile intent by sending a messenger to the enemy. "It is not permitted to fight the enemy," commented Ibn Rushd, the leading twelfth-century authority on Maliki jurisprudence, "until after they have received the summons" (*da'wa*) to Islam.[12] Such a call was inevitably problematic because the Sudanese enemy was already Muslim. Had the enemy been non-Muslim, the sheer difference in religion was itself the summons: Islam had been revealed, and the enemy had refused to embrace it: thus war or polltax/*jizya*. "Muslims concur that the reason for war is either converting the enemy to Islam or collecting the *jizya*," wrote Ibn Rushd.[13] Because the Sudanese were Muslim, it was going to be doubly necessary to announce the intent to invade; indeed, as the jurists reminded al-Mansur,[14] the Sudanese had converted to Islam willingly (and not as a result of defeat in battle) which illegitimized either *jihad* against, or the collecting of *jizya* from, them.

Sometime in December 1589, therefore, al-Mansur sent the summons to the Sudanese king not to war, but to submit to him an annual revenue from the rich salt mine at Taghaza, of one *mithqal* of gold per every loadful of salt. In order to appease the jurists, he urged the king to submit and spare himself military action: "We have dispatched this noble letter to you so that you might know what God has spared you through our swords";[15] a month later, the letter was sent again by his scribe al-Fishtali to confirm the summons.[16] The argument that al-Mansur used to justify his summons to a fellow Muslim ruler was as old as the Athenian argument to the Melians in Thucydides's account of the Peloponnesian War. In the debate, with which al-Mansur was very unlikely to be familiar, the Athenian told the Melians that they, the Athenians, had protected them from the Spartans and that the Spartans would soon attack their island and conquer it. The Athenians demanded that the Melians surrender to them in order to preclude their conquest by the Spartans. The Melians refused and the Athenians attacked and conquered the island, and then sold its inhabitants into slavery.

In his summons, al-Mansur explained that he was and has been the only barrier between the European Christians and Islamic Africa, "the blockade for [Muslims] against the unbelieving Christians."[17] He had fought the infidels and defeated them at Wadi al-Makhazen, he told the Sudanese, and had therefore shown his mettle in repelling invasions and conquests. In order to continue in his *jihad* against those Europeans who treated Morocco as the bridgehead to the conquest of the rest of the Islamic dominions in Africa, he needed resources to support the armies of Islam against the invaders. The Sudanese therefore needed to surrender/submit to him so he could continue to fight the Christians and protect them. This was the argument that in his view legitimized his request for *kharaj*/revenue:

> We have adopted, God willing, the sound opinion and the blessed and well-guided view, that we should impose upon it a *kharaj*, which, God willing, shall redound to the benefit of the Muslims, and to the discomfort of the infidel enemies of God ... Our intention is to spend what accrues from this—God willing—in pursuit of campaigning and *jihad*, and in stipends for those soldiers and armies who are under our exalted purview ... for defence of the authority (*kalima*) of Islam, and to protect the lands and people.[18]

By demanding *kharaj* rather than *jizya*, al-Mansur was avoiding a Maliki proscription. For Malik had insisted that *jizya* be taken only from polytheists without exception.[19] In his formulation of the *causus belli*—that the Sudanese should submit so he could continue to protect them and other Muslims—al-Mansur was appealing to *istislah*/extrapolation—a supplementary principle of law associated specifically with the Maliki school. The jurist, wishing to practise *istislah*, determines what is best for the (Muslim) community, which had not been clarified in Qur'anic or prophetic law, *shariah*. The *Sahih of al-Bukhari*, however, which was a fundamental text in Moroccan/Saadian ideology, had declared that a Muslim should fight not for booty, fame, or pride, but for the cause of God.[20] Al-Mansur explained that his justifications for fighting the infidels and protecting the lands of Islam from their repeated incursions situated his design on the Sudan within the context of fighting not for booty but for the cause of God. "Had not the soldiers of God [Morocco's] not stood between you and the idols of polytheism," he wrote to Askiya, the idols would have fallen upon you like a flood.[21]

Askiya presumably refused to submit to al-Mansur's terms (no letter survives from him) whereupon the Moroccan ruler became quite angry.[22] As he explained in a letter to some of "the Sudanese leaders": "we wrote to him," al-Mansur stated, "regarding the important welfare of the Muslims, and we called him to our obedience and fealty which God has commanded the Muslim umma," but he refused.[23] Al-Mansur now found himself in a legal quandary. How could he now "summon" the Muslim to war? After all, he had tried to appeal to Askiya before threatening him, and as he stated in his letter, "We follow God's book: we do not act before we warn, and warn repeatedly."[24] To justify the submission of Askiya, al-Mansur thus turned to another argument stemming from ethnic lineage. He stated that his descent from the Prophet Muhammad's tribe, Quraysh, gave him the right to claim the kingdom of Sudan. In a letter of August 1590, he explained the role that his Qurayshite lineage played in the legitimization of his claims:

> In the two *Sahihs* [it is reported] from the Messenger of God—May God bless him and grant him peace—that he said: "The imams are from Quraysh." He also said—peace be upon him ...: "This task [of the caliphate] is for Quraysh. If anyone should oppose them, God shall cast him down upon his face."... Since God appointed us to this Great Imamate (*al-imamam al-uzma*), through which we assumed the imamship of the [Muslim] community, and—Sublime is He—through it made unquestioning obedience to us binding upon people, and through it handed over to our noble regency inheritance of the earth and those upon it until the Hour strikes, we have not sheathed the sword of truth.[25]

To justify the invasion, al-Mansur brought in the ethnic superiority of the descendants from Quraysh. Indeed, in al-Wufrani's account of the invasion, al-Mansur is quoted as giving priority to his Qurayshite descent. It is because he is of Quraysh, and Askiya is not, that the latter loses legitimacy. "He is not a Qurayshite," al-Mansur said, "nor does he have the basic qualities of the great sultanate."[26]

Al-Mansur had repeatedly berated Askiya with this superiority, and long before the invasion,[27] he had written how he was "the prince of the faithful, successor of God on earth, descendent of the last of the prophets, inheritor of prophets and messengers, who is to be obeyed by all humanity and whose blessed imamate is to prevail over all the world."[28] He had subsequently written, inviting Askiya to submit to his "blessed imamate whose light has extended from the earth's east to its west," and "to obey his noble commands which had been ordained by God to this prophetic imamate."[29] Al-Mansur's claim to a pure Arab ethnicity, along with his appeal to a Qurayshite lineage, led him to proclaim himself the imam of the Muslims, which gave him legitimacy to conquer those Muslims who submitted to a king not of the tribe of the Prophet Muhammad, as he, Ahmad, was. Both al-Fishtali and al-Wufrani recorded the jurists' support of al-Mansur on the grounds that he was the imam, and the imam had the right to natural resources.[30] Al-Mansur thus bluntly wrote to Askiya to "enter into what the Muslim community has entered and support and approve our honorable imamate."[31]

Although he was really after Sudan's gold, al-Mansur had to justify his motives on other grounds—which led him to the argument from mahdism. Al-Mansur proclaimed his role as God's *khalifa* over the Muslims, the *imam* and prince of the faithful. Indeed, in some letters to the Sudanese princes, he went further and even suggested a prophetic status for himself.[32] No other Muslim ruler could lay claim to such divine authority: only he had the noble blood of the Prophet's family running in his veins and therefore only he was caliph with the right to take possession of Muslim wealth—in this case the wealth of the Sudan—and use it in the *jihad* against the infidels. In a convoluted argument, al-Mansur proclaimed himself the bulwark against Spanish invasion: without him, the Sudan would succumb to the infidels, as western parts of sub-Saharan Africa (and of Morocco) had already succumbed to the Portuguese and to other Europeans. The Sudan, by right of his mahdist mission, belonged to him.

Whether al-Mansur was a Maliki or not, he would have still pursued his goal of seizing the rich salt and gold mines of the Sudan. Religion served imperial justification. For the issue of the *khilafa*, which he adduced to justify invasion, was quite complicated and not as simple as al-Mansur made it up to be. The *khalifa*/prince of the faithful/ruler of the Muslim *umma* was always to be an Arab and descended from the Prophet's tribe of Quraysh. The last *khalifa* had been the Abbasid al-Mutawakkil in Egypt who had named Askiya Mohammad I (1492–1528) *khalifa* over the Sudan, during the latter's pilgrimage to Mecca. Al-Mutawakkil lost his caliphate to the Ottomans who conquered Egypt in 1516 and who, from Selim I (1512–20) on, assumed the title in their capital city of Istanbul. Meanwhile, Mohammad al-Sheikh (reg. 1541–57), had also assumed the title of *khalifa* upon his founding of the Saadian dynasty (claiming descent from Halima Al-Saadia, the Prophet's wetnurse).[33] Al-Mansur simply reaffirmed what his father had claimed. And in order to make doubly sure that the *shar'*/religious law supported him in his claim to the *khilafa*, he sought—and got—approval from jurists from as far away as Egypt.[34] Nothing now could stop the invasion.

On October 16, 1590, the Moroccan army left Marrakesh in great pomp. After about 2,000 kilometers, they reached Kabara, just near Timbuctoo,[35] and defeated the Sudanese army. Upon receiving the news, al-Mansur sent a generic letter to all the mosques in the kingdom proclaiming the happy victory.[36] His court scribe al-Fishtali, also registered his joy in the chronicle that he kept of the Saadian ruler. During the battle, the Sudanese screamed: "We are Muslims, we are your brothers in religion" as they were being massacred by the Moroccan troops. Such a scream, which was remembered down to the eighteenth century, reached al-Mansur necessitating thereby some retrospective justifications on his as well as his scribe's part.[37]

The victory convinced al-Mansur that he was no mere prince of the faithful, but had approached the status of a prophet, since from your forehead, wrote one poet in praise of him after the victory, "the light of prophethood beams."[38] But such sentiment was not shared by the Sudanese who found a spokesman in the figure of the scholar Ahmad Baba al-Tinbekti, whose library had been ransacked by the Moroccan troops and who had been hauled in chains, with members of his family, to Marrakesh. When the captive was brought before al-Mansur, he derided the ruler who had started presenting himself from behind a veil/hijab. Such a practice had been instituted by some of the Abbasid caliphs, who sought to separate themselves from their subjects, and in many respects, had pushed the caliph, now isolated from his people, into despotism and indifference. In the eyes of Tinbekti, al-Mansur was going beyond despotism to pretensions of divinity since it is God, and only God, who appears from behind the veil of His revelation of the Qur'an. The Sudanese scholar further taunted al-Mansur by asking him why he preferred to fight the Arabic-speaking Sudanese rather than the Turks. Al-Mansur of course did not reply with the reason he had given to his jurists before the invasion. Rather, he appealed to the *Hadith* and answered that "The Prophet, God's prayer and peace on him, had said: Leave the Turks so they will leave you"—a distant echo of Malik. (Malik had forbidden battle against the "Ethipoians" and the "Turks"; but when he had been asked about the authenticity of his statement of not fighting the Turks, he had prevaricated). Recalling al-Bukhari's *Sahih* where there are two prophetic hadiths about fighting the Turks,[39] al-Tinbekti replied to al-Mansur that while the Prophet's words had applied in the Prophet's own time, in present times, al-Mansur should "not leave the Turks even if they leave you."[40]

Al-Mansur realized that he needed a strong argument to refute al-Tinbekti. As he proclaimed the happy news around Morocco, he therefore introduced a new motif into his justification of the invasion— the matter of race. After all, the lands he conquered were defined by reference to the skin color of the inhabitants. He reiterated to his subjects his noble lineage, "Prophetic, Fatimid, Alawite, and Hashemite." It was with the Hashemite blades, he wrote, that "he had defeated the yellow skinned enemies [the Portuguese] as well as the black-skinned of Sudan; and it was by the prophetic light of the caliphate which upholds this dynasty that he chased the night away from the people where the crow has croaked since the days of Ham. God answered the prayer that this [Saadian] dynasty bring together the race of Sam with the race of Ham."[41]

The contrasts in the letter emphasize the racial if not the racist factors. Against the crow of the night there is the falcon of the dawn; against the black darkness, there is the light of prophecy; against the Sudan, there is the Maghreb.[42] Al-Mansur appealed to the racial difference between the Moroccans, the descendents of Sam, and the Sudanese, the descendents of Ham. He proclaimed that the conquest had served to bring the black-skinned inhabitants under the fold of the Qurayshite descendents of Sam. In that respect, therefore, it had been a *jihad* and the Moroccans had "*jahadoo fi al-Lahi haqqa jihadinin*"— earnestly struggled for God. The conquest was not just a war driven by the desire for possession but by religious zeal—to realize the "*fat-h*" of Sudan. Importantly, *fat-h* was the term used to describe the seventh-century Arabian conquests, suggesting thereby that al-Mansur viewed his imperialism in the light of the religio-military expansion of early Islam. So too did his court scribe, Ibn al-Qadi, call the invasion a *fat-h*, since the soldiers of al-Mansur had reached kingdoms never before reached.[43] Now that al-Mansur had conquered the kingdom of Sudan, he could prepare to fight the "infidel enemy"/the Christians on their own turf—presumably Spain.

Al-Mansur confirmed the goal he had earlier proclaimed to his jurists: by conquering the Sudan, he would acquire resources to enable him to invade Spain. But then he added a racially based, but not a racist, justification for the preponderance of the race of Sam over the race of Ham. Such an appeal to race drew on sources that were of major importance to al-Mansur—the *Sahih of al-Bukhari* and the history of al-Tabari, which had discussed the question of the black race. Al-Tabari (A.D. 839–923.) confirmed that Ham's descendants were "black with hardly any whiteness." To Ham, Noah had given "the part (of the earth) west of the Nile and regions beyond to the region from where the west wind blows."[44] Al-Tabari continued: Canaan, the son of Ham, "married Arsal ... and she bore him the Blacks, the Nubians, Fezzan, Zanj, Zaghawah, and all the peoples of the Sudan." His offspring "reside[d] in the coastlands of the East and West." The reason why Ham had black descendants was because of his father's curse on him: he saw his father's genitals but did not cover them. "Cursed is Cannan b. Ham," declaimed Noah, "Slaves will they be to his brothers." Although Noah later regretted the curse that had changed the color of Ham's descendents, and prayed that the black color be removed, he still maintained that Ham's children would be slaves to his brothers' descendents—but also prayed that they be treated compassionately.[45] Other writers, such as al-Jahiz, Ibn Marziban, and al-Sayuti, wrote in praise of the Blacks.[46]

There is no racism here; rather a punishment that Noah later regretted, and expressed more in a social status than in a racial denigration. Al-Mansur armed himself with the socio-ethnic rather than a racist justification for the invasion of Sudan. Whether he subscribed to the racist anti-Black views that had been sounded by Ibn Khaldun is not clear in this passage although his scribe al-Fishtali knew the writings of the Tunisian historiographer. Ibn Khaldun had stated: "The Negro nations are, as a rule, submissive to slavery, because (Negroes) have little that is essentially human and possess attributes that are quite similar to those of dumb animals, as we have stated."[47] As Abdallah Ibrahim has shown, the Arabs did not know much about the history of sub-Saharan Africans, except from what they had found in Greek sources—sources that had degraded the Africans and confined them in images of subhuman racism.[48]

Al-Mansur claimed that the invasion had served as a blessing to the sons of Ham brought to them by an *imam* descended from Quraysh and of the *jins*/race of Sam. In a note to a letter sent to his victorious army general in Sudan, al-Mansur declared that the conquest was nothing other than a "gift of God": for God was on the side of Sam against Ham and the Qurayshite against the non-Qurayshite who had deviated from the path of Islam. In this context, he justified the enslavement of the Blacks by appealing to racial stereotypes and sanctimoniously claiming that by enslaving and then employing the Sudanese in his army, he saved their souls and obtained "divine reward for himself."[49] In the eighteenth century, al-Wufrani added another argument in justification not only of the conquest but of the subsequent enslavement of the Sudanese:[50] the founder of the Sudanese ruling dynasty, Daoud Askiya, 1549–82, had been righteous and true to the teaching of Islam, leaning toward the Arab character. Similarly, his successor, Al-Hajj Muhammad II, 1582–86, and successor's successor, Muhammad Bani, 1586–88, had both been devout Muslims; only the last ruler, Ishaq Askiya, had deviated from the straight path of the law. As a result, he lost his right to rule the land. A *fatwa*/legal judgment by one of al-Mansur's jurists, Mohammad al-Arabi al-Fasi, stated that since the unbelievers/Portuguese had settled near the Muslim regions of the Sudan (on the western coast of Africa) and were intent on attacking the Muslims, and since Askiya had strayed from the path of Islam and failed to protect "the cities of the Muslims" against them, then he, Askiya, was in disobedience to the laws of God. Another ruler should therefore take over responsibility for protecting and fighting for the Muslims.[51] Al-Mansur had the right to conquer Askiya's dominion because Askiya had failed to protect his Muslim subjects from the incursions of the infidels. As al-Fishtali confirmed, al-Mansur had been ready since "the year ninety-seven to fight the polytheists and to position his imamate troops in their land in the south."[52]

* * *

Morocco was perhaps the closest country in the Islamic world to the culture and civilization of European Christendom. Not only did geographical proximity make interaction frequent and inevitable, but more importantly, Morocco accommodated a large number of the expelled Moriscos who arrived on its shores throughout the end of the sixteenth century and the first decades of the seventeenth century. These émigrés brought with them the intellectual legacy of Europe: while being Muslim by faith, they were "Christian" by heritage and training, more proficient in Spanish than in Arabic, more versed in continental thought than in Islamic jurisprudence and history. It is therefore quite possible that they brought with them some of the influences of the conquistador culture that characterized early modern Spanish imagination. Although there is no evidence to show that al-Mansur read European works (he knew Arabic and Turkish only), some of his advisors and jurists were multilingual and well informed about European military discourse and imperial strategy. Was the racial bias in the argument that al-Mansur developed after the conquest an echo of the same racial argument that had been developed in Spain just a few decades earlier? Or is it inherent in all religiously based arguments for empire?

From within the Maliki argument, al-Mansur devised a justification for initiating the conquest. Imperialism was disguised as service to the Muslim *umma* against possible future depredations of the Christians. After the conquest, the appeal to national security or, in al-Mansur's terminology, the security of the Islamic *umma* in Africa, gave way to more visceral as well as noble explanations: the purpose of the invasion had been for an inferior race to be religiously enlightened under the benevolent rule of the one and only ethnically legitimated imam in all Islamdom. The invasion had been a civilizing mission— to remove a corrupt king who was degrading his people and proving incapable of protecting them against possible future attacks by Christians. The invasion was a preemptive measure intended to secure for the Sudanese a leader who would march them into battle against the Christians—should the Christians attack. What gave further legitimacy to the preemptive invasion was the Qurayshite lineage of the invader: he was God-chosen to lead a *jihad*—not only against the infidels in the future, but, as his post-victory letter bluntly showed, first and foremost against a people whose only fault was having a corrupt ruler—and rich natural resources.

Some historians have treated al-Mansur's invasion favorably[53] and viewed it as rendering a great service to Islam.[54] But there is no better epitaph to the violence of Moroccan imperialism than the words of the nineteenth-century Moroccan historian, al-Nasiri:

> The Sudanese were of the best of Muslim peoples, seeking learning with dedication and mahabba, and pursuing orthodoxy in their religion. All the Sudanese whose kingdoms were adjacent to Morocco were like this. [Their religious piety] exposes the ugliness of what occurred in the lands of Morocco of enslaving the inhabitants of Sudan, and bringing many groups of them every year and selling them in the markets of Morocco, both in the cities and the desert, bargaining over them as if they were beasts, and much worse. The Moroccans have become so accustomed

to this enslavement of the Suadanese; indeed so many generations have become used to it that the common people now believe that the criteria for enslavement are black color and origin from that region. This, by God, is the worst of what religion has prohibited and the foulest.[55]

NOTES

1. Muhammad al-Sahgir Al-Wufrani, *Nuzhat al-Hadi*, ed. Abd al-Latif al-Shadli ([Casablanca: s.n.], 1998), 168–69.

2. I am grateful to Dr. Daniel Goffman for discussing this episode with me.

3. Although there have been numerous studies of the invasion, there has been no discussion of its ideological construction: see, Dahiru Yahya, *Morocco in the Sixteenth Century: Problems and Patterns in African Foreign Policy* (New Jersey: Humanities Press, 1981), chap. 7, and the various articles in *Le Maroc et L'Afrique subsaharienne au debuts des temps modernes* (Rabat: Université Mohammed V-Souissi, Institut des études africaines, 1995).

4. Ibn Abi Dinar, *Al-Munis fi Akhbar Ifiqiya wa Tunis* (Tunis, 1968), 154.

5. Abd al-Rahman Al-Mouden, "Tasa'ulat hawl mawqif al-Uthmaniyyeen min al-ghazu al-Sa'adi lil-Sudan," in *Le Maroc et L'Afrique subsahari-enne au debuts des temps modernes* (Rabat: Muhammad V University, 1995), 11–19, the Arabic section.

6. Abd al-Rahman Al-Saadi, *Tarikh al-Sudan*, ed. and trans. O. Houdas (rep. Paris: Leroux, 1964), 192.

7. Abu Faris Abd al-Aziz Al-Fishtali, *Manahil al-Safa*, ed. Abd al-Karim Karim (Rabat: Matbu'at Wizarat al-Awquaf, 1972), 117.

8. Ibid., 64–65.

9. Ibid., 126.

10. Al-Wufrani, *Nuzhat*, 164.

11. Al-Bukhari, in Muhammad Muhsin Khan, *The Translation of the Meanings of Sahih al-Bukhari*, (Medina, 1981), 9:158.

12. Ibn Rushd, *Bidayat al-Mujtahid wa nihayat al-Muqtasid*, ed. Ali Muhammad Mu'awwad and Adil Ahmad Abd al-Mawujud (Beirut, Dar ibn al-Hazm, 1995), 3:433.

13. Ibid., 3:442.

14. Muhammad Al-Gharbi, *Bidayat al-Hukm al-Maghribi fi al-Sudan al-Gharbi* (Kuwait: Mu'assast al-khalıj, 1982), 273.

15. J. O. Hunwick, *Timubktu and the Songhay Empire* (Leiden: Brill, 1999), 295.

16. Georges Pianel, "Les Préliminaires de la conquête du Soudan par Mulay Ahmad al-Mansur," *Hesberis* 40 (1953): 185–99.

17. Hunwick, *Timubktu*, 187.

18. Ibid., 295.

19. Ibn Rushd, *Bidayat*, 3:443; Rudolph Peters, *Jihad in Mediaeval and Modern Islam* (Leiden: Brill, 1977), 39.

20. Al-Bukhari, *Translation*, 4:50.

21. Abdallah Guennun, *Rasail Saadiya* (Tetuan: Instituto Muley el-Hasan, 1954), 133–35.

22. Al-Nasiri, *Kitab al-Istiqsaa* (Dar al-Bayda', 1955), 5:112.

23. Guennun, *Rasail*, 128–29.

24. Ibid., 137.

25. Hunwick, *Timubktu*, 299–300.

26. Al-Wufrani, *Nuzhat*, 163.

27. For a history of preconquest relations, see the summary in appendix I of E. Ann McDougall, "The Question of Tegaza' and the Conquest of Songhay: Some Saharan Considerations," in *Le Maroc et L'Afrique Subsaharienne*, 273–78.

28. Al-Fisthali, *Manahil*, 69.

29. Al-Ghrabi, *Bidayat*, 666.

30. Al-Wufrani, *Nuzhat*, 159.

31. Guennun, *Rasail*, 136–38.

32. Ibid., 83–84.

33. Zakari Dramani-Issifou, *L'Afrique noire dans les relations internationals au XVIe siècle* (Paris: Centre de Recherches Africaines, 1982), 76.

34. Nicola Ziadeh, *Afrikiyat* (London: Riad al-Rayyes, 1991), 377.

35. H. de Castries, "La Conquêt du Soudan Par el-Mansour (1591)," *Hesperis* 3 (1921): 449.

36. A generic letter meant that a blank replaced a specific place name. The letter produced by al-Gharbi shows that the address was to the "people of so-and-so" (675); the same letter produced by de Castries addresses the "people of Fez."

37. Al-Wufrani, *Nuzhat*, 167.

38. Ibid., 169.

39. Al-Bukhari, *Translation*, 4:110–11.

40. Al-Wufrani, *Nuzhat*, 172; Hunwick, "Ahmad Baba and the Moroccan Invasion of the Sudan (1591)," *Journal of the Historical Society of Nigeria* 2 (1957): 311–28.

41. De Castries, "Conquêt," 479.

42. Abd al-Majid Qadduri and Al-Hussein Mujahid, "Surat al-Sudan fi al-Khitab al-Tarikhi al-Maghribi," in *Al-Tarikh wal-Lisaniyyat*, ed. Abd al-Ahad al-Sabti (Rabat: Mohammad V University, 1992), 34.

43. Ahmad Ibn al-Qadi, *Al-Muntaqa al-Maqsur ala Maathir al-Khalifa al-Mansur*, ed. M. Razzouk, 2 vols. (Rabat: Maktabat al-Ma'arif, 1986), 2:833.

44. Tabari, *The History of al-Tabari*, trans. and annot. Franz Rosenthal, Vol. 1 (New York: SUNY Press, 1989), 1:368, 370.

45. Tabari, *The History of al-Tabari*, trans. William M. Brinner, 39 vols. (New York: SUNY, 1987), 2:11, 16, 12, 214.

46. Aziz Al-Azmeh, *Al-Arab wa-al Barabira* (London: Riad El-Reyyes Books, 1991), chap. 2.

47. Ibn Khaldun, *The Muqaddimah,* trans. Franz Rosenthal, ed. N. J. Dawood (Princeton: Princeton University Press, 1967), 117.

48. Abdallah Ibrahim, *Almarkaziyyah al-Islamiyya* (Beirut: Al-Markiz al-Thaqafi, 2001), 169.

49. J. O. Hunwick, "Islamic Law and Polemics over Race and Slavery in North and West Africa (16th–19th Century)," in *Slavery in the Islamic Middle East,* ed. Shaun E. Marmoh (Princeton: Markus Wiener Publishers, 1999), 43–69.

50. Al-Wufrani, *Nuzhat,* 162.

51. Al-Gharbi, *Bidayat,* 148–49.

52. Al-Fishtali, *Manahil al-Safa,* 81.

53. Abd al-Karim Karim, *Al-Maghrib fi ahd al-dawla al-saadiyya* (Rabat: Sharikat al-Tab' wal Nashr, 1977), 145–73.

54. Muqallid al-Ghunaymi *Tarikh al-Maghrib al-Arabi* (Cairo: d'alam al-Kitab, 1994), 6:226.

55. Al-Nasiri, *Kitab,* 5:131.

CHAPTER 9

COLONIAL BENEDICTIONS: WORLDLY CATHOLICS AND SECULAR PRIESTS IN FRENCH INDOCHINA

Patricia M. Pelley

In the 1890s Adrien Launay published a massive (approximately 1,800 pages!), three-volume history of the French Society of Foreign Missions, which was created in the mid-seventeenth century in response to the Propaganda, issued by Pope Gregory XV in 1622.[1] Founding members of the Society of Foreign Missions solicited the help of French entrepreneurs; together, they organized the East Indies Company. In this way, Launay explains, missionaries and merchants were able to serve God and, at the same time, promote the interests of France. Given the densely detailed quality of Launay's work, it is often regarded as the most comprehensive survey of precolonial contacts between Indochina and France. To be sure, no other author has commented more thoroughly on the Society's administrative decisions and financial concerns or on its position vis-à-vis the East Indies Company, France, and the Catholic Church. Moreover, the level of detail concerning popes, emperors, kings, and military men is truly impressive. Launay also clarifies why, when other orders were already competing for access to the "pagan nations" of Asia, "Providence called forth a new evangelical order" (I: v, 11). In short, his work has attained a canonical status. Because this monumental piece is structured in a linear fashion, readers are prepared to find a narrative of how, over the course of two centuries, the Society of Foreign Missions and the French East Indies Company succeeded in expanding the reach of the Catholic Church and in protecting French interests in areas once considered remote. Despite the profusion of details, however, and the neat chronological framework Launay deploys, his work does not function in the way one expects.

Claiming to represent the attitude of Catholic authorities who agreed to create a new missionary order, Launay makes his own sense of outrage clear. Even though other missionary groups had engaged in evangelical work for more than a hundred years, in all of Asia there existed but one archbishop and three bishops (I: 37). These deficiencies were fatal, he believed, because only bishops could ordain indigenous priests, and these were essential: only they understood the errors, impieties, and abominable mysteries of the local religion. From Launay's perspective, these abominations included the cult of ancestors; astrology; Buddhism; Daoism; what he regarded as a highly corrupt form of Confucianism; and the worship of tutelary spirits, forests, and waterfalls (I: 90). Indigenous priests, Launay remarked, in addition to knowing the perversity of local traditions, could also more easily hide during times of persecution (I: 7). Therefore, unlike their feckless predecessors, French missionaries would cultivate an indigenous clergy; to free converts from their dependence on Europeans, the new missionary order would also localize Catholic institutions. By "calling forth" the Society of Foreign Missions, Launay also observed, Providence could make use of the qualities that were specifically French—devotion, generosity, the evangelical spirit, and the joyous heroism of the soldier (I: 12).

Although Launay often repeats the Society's principal goal, he doesn't describe the process through which the local clergy evolved. He offers few insights into the missionaries' methods and says next to nothing about their liturgical rituals and texts. Nor does he address other critical concerns: What did Catholicism mean to Vietnamese and why did they convert to a faith that, more often than not, was officially banned? Rather than investigate these issues in a thorough and compelling way, Launay glibly mentions that conversions were "miracles"; they were the "work of God" (II: 182). In a similarly evasive way, he also notes that the conversion of "pagan adults" was not the only way to "fill heaven with the elect" (II: 197): The baptism of orphans and children on the verge of death and the recitation of last rites for the newly deceased were also "admirable and relatively easy ways to save souls" (II: 202–03). As for the missionaries' progress in gaining adherents to what Launay regarded as the only legitimate faith, he reduces their accomplishments to a series of bland statistical portraits appended to Volume III. Although he doesn't acknowledge it, Launay is mostly interested in the factors that impeded the missionaries' progress; his chronological narrative, therefore, is governed by the sequence of obstacles that the missionaries were forced to overcome.

First of all, once it was established in the seventeenth century, the Society of Foreign Missions continually struggled against rival missionary orders. Launay takes part in this competition by depicting the evangelical work carried out before French missionaries arrived as a dangerous failure. However, the evidence he uses to condemn rival orders—Jesuits from Portugal above all, but Dominicans, Augustinians, Franciscans, and Barnabites as well—actually attests to their success. In Tonkin and Cochinchina, he notes, 200,000 Christians (a considerable number, in other words) risked "eternal damnation" because local priests were lacking (I: 19).[2] Like his contemporaries, Launay also undoubtedly knew that in the mid-1600s, on the eve of the Society's funding, there were in Cochinchina alone more than 300 Catholic churches.[3] In fact, the association between Portugal and Catholicism was so great that in Asia, Christianity was known as the "Portuguese faith" (II: 141). The competition among missionary orders was not a static, monolithic struggle. When the Jesuit order was suppressed in the 1770s, the Society's most troublesome opponents disappeared (II: 100). But just as it prepared to annex former Jesuit territories in Vietnam, Franciscans and Dominicans submitted petitions to do the same. In the 1780s the Vatican resolved this problem: in the north, Spanish Dominicans and the Society of Foreign Missions would share control; in the south, the Society would continue to be the dominant power; only small groups of Portuguese Franciscans would remain (II: 102–05). In the early nineteenth century, when the Jesuit order was reinstated, the earlier form of competition reemerged (III: 5). At the same time, not only rival Catholic orders created problems for the Society, but Protestant missionaries, including Lutherans, Unitarians, and the Bible Society of London, also joined the fray (III: 2). Their presence was even more destructive than that of rival Catholic orders, for their goal, according to Launay, was to "destroy Catholicism" (III: 4). Furthermore, the conflicts between Catholic and Protestant doctrine and conflicts among the missionaries themselves confused potential converts. If both Protestants and Catholics believed in the same god, how could one explain the animosity each group felt for the other (III: 4)?

Second, as French missionaries tried to compensate for the incompetence and even corruption of other missionary orders, they also attempted to circumvent the obstacles put in place by rival nations. Unlike the French, whose motives were pure, the Portuguese and Dutch habitually intertwined missionary goals with mercantile designs. Because the twin institutions of France—the Society of Foreign Missions and the East Indies Company—seemed to convey the same sort of confusion, Launay carefully explains that the commercial component of French evangelism resulted from the intransigence of others. In the mid-seventeenth century, he points out, the Portuguese objected to the creation of a new missionary order and managed to delay its establishment (I: 15). Nevertheless, the founding members of the Society of Foreign Missions, figures such as Monsignor François Pallu, still expected that Portuguese and Dutch ships would provide French missionaries with free passage to Asia, Africa, and the Americas. Because these two powers were motivated by mercantile more than missionary concerns, they refused. In this specific set of circumstances, Launay explains, Pallu and the wider community of missionaries collaborated with French entrepreneurs to create the East Indies Company (I: 56–58). Still, the Portuguese continued to subvert French endeavors. When the first group of missionaries reached Cochinchina, the Portuguese begged local authorities to expel them (I: 123). Furthermore, two French missionaries (Hainques and Brindeau) died when their domestics, goaded by Portuguese, poisoned them (I: 146). In yet another instance of betrayal, a Portuguese merchant deliberately mistranslated the words of Vietnamese officials from whom the French sought permission to build a church. Because of their own innocence, the missionaries had no reason to suspect foul play. Wrongly believing that their project had been approved, they started to build the church (I: 197). This action was disastrous because the French were openly defying local officials—even though they had no intention of doing so. Worse still, because of its intended size, the church alerted officials to the great number of French missionaries who had illegally entered Vietnam and suggested that many more Vietnamese than suspected were receptive to the alien faith. This information, revealed because of the Portuguese merchant's deceit, provoked a new round of persecutions.

In fact, the theme of subterfuge figures prominently in Launay's discussion of missionary work. Although Launay censures the Dutch and Portuguese because they were so dishonest, he seems to admire the deceit and cunning of the French. Clarifying the hidden benefits of the joint missionary/mercantile venture, Launay notes that

French missionaries, once they boarded the company's ships, could conceal themselves under the "cloak of commerce" (I: 169). In the seventeenth century, when Monsignor Lambert de la Motte reached Tonkin for the first time, he was introduced to Vietnamese officials as the chaplain who served crewman on board the company's ships. What would have been an effective misrepresentation was spoiled, however, when the nefarious Dutch and Portuguese denounced it (I: 139). As French missionaries continued to battle their enemies (specifically the Portuguese, in this case), two seminarians disguised as merchants presented themselves to officials in Hanoi. Thanks to this ruse, they gained permission to build a "lodge," which they envisioned as a future gathering place for Christians (I: 188, 199). Launay also recounts the episode in which two French missionaries, Deydier and Bouges, assumed false identities by wearing merchants' clothes and by disguising their Vietnamese catechists as domestics (I: 201). In the turmoil of the late eighteenth century, Launay points out, when other Europeans had been imprisoned or expelled, Vietnamese priests disguised as fishermen, merchants, and soldiers were able to travel from north to south (I: 568). To escape the continuing persecutions in Tonkin, two Vietnamese priests, vaguely identified by Launay as "Father Chieu" and "Father Hanh," disguised themselves, one as a merchant of betel quids, the other as a physician (II: 325).[4]

Repeatedly Launay condemns the confusion of this-worldly and other-worldly interests among the Portuguese and Dutch, but he reserves special praise for Monsignor Pallu precisely because he advocated this dual sense of mission—promoting national power, on the one hand, and extending the reach of Catholicism, on the other. To express their gratitude to the East Indies Company, Pallu predicted, missionaries would disseminate "love and knowledge of France" (I: 170). Initially, Vietnamese converts would be attached to France through their new faith; but later, when circumstances allowed, commercial and political ties would bind them (I: 170). Pallu believed that the France of Louis XIV, "tranquil within and respected abroad," could easily make "rich and solid establishments" in lands the missionaries "opened up"—if "colonial operations" were carried out in a systematic way (I: 170). Thanks to the work of missionaries, the lands would be "open" not only to the commercial enterprises of France, but to her "civilizing genius" as well (I: 170). Because Pallu more than anyone else understood that evangelical, mercantile, and nationalist ambitions were mutually reinforcing, Launay rewarded him with the "double dignity" of being the quasi-official ambassador of Louis XIV and Clement IX (I: 181, 186–87). In an attempt to clarify Pallu's double vision, Launay emphasizes that he never intended for the French government to conquer the lands "opened" by missionaries. On the contrary, Launay affirms, Pallu only hoped for "peaceful relations" and for treaties that were advantageous to France and other countries and contributed to the "good of souls and the glory of the Church" (I: 188). Missionaries were not "political agents of France," Pallu insisted; they had no intention of helping their compatriots conquer newly Christianized lands (I: 188). Therefore, in the eighteenth century, when a French missionary reached Cochinchina, kissed the ground, and declared: "Let us take possession of this kingdom, since God called us to its conquest," he had only spiritual, not commercial or political, concerns in mind (I: 509). Still, when Launay summarizes the Society's accomplishments, he mentions, in addition to evangelical work, its success in making French literary works more widely known, its role in disseminating French scientific thought, its contributions to the East Indies Company, and its determination to protect French commercial enterprises in Asia (II: 267).

Until the eighteenth century, the Portuguese and Dutch, and Spaniards to a lesser degree, were the major antagonists of France. By mid-century, following the siege of Quebec and the Seven Years' War, France was forced to cede its North American territories to the "English race," the new "enemies of France" (II: 22, 121). In a brief deviation from his main narrative, Launay derides Voltaire in particular for having criticized French imperial efforts in Canada, but he also implicates Louis XV's disastrous tactics (II: 22). The critics of empire and the muddled thinking of royal officials, Launay argues, caused France to fall from the first to second tier of colonizing nations (II: 22). He also points out that, determined to restore the glory of France, the Society of Foreign Missions decided to focus its attention on Asia (II: 40). In addition to fortifying its missions in India, Thailand, Cochinchina, Tonkin, China, and Macao, the Society also more vigorously explored evangelical possibilities in Cambodia and Laos (II: 69). Late in the eighteenth century, Launay emphasizes, as social and political tensions in France were about to erupt, the Society was in top form. Even if other institutions collapsed, the Society would expand its Asian territories to an unprecedented level, and, as before, it would stabilize the essential link between France and the Church (II: 93–94).

In identifying the major obstacles to French evangelical work, Launay also dwells on the malfeasance of Vietnamese. To appreciate the significance of his accusations, it is essential to understand the various contexts in which the French tried to bring their missionary and mercantile enterprises to fruition. Possibly the most important factor is that by the mid-seventeenth century, when the Society's missionaries first arrived, north–south divisions had already emerged. For centuries, Vietnamese had immigrated from the heartland in the Red River delta to the south, defeating other kingdoms (especially the Cham and Khmer) along the way and colonizing newly conquered lands. In the mid-1500s, however, this process accelerated to a new degree. As the borders of Vietnam continually expanded, the Le dynasty (1428–1788), with its capital in Hanoi, still claimed authority over the entire realm. At the same time, two rival clans, the Trinh in the north and the Nguyen in the south, presented themselves as the only legitimate executors of the imperial will. Unavoidably, political and emotional attachments to the tradition and power of the north conflicted with the sense of belonging to a more vibrant, autonomous, and pioneering south. For Vietnamese, this dynamic was tremendously destabilizing all on its own; but its effects were made more calamitous by the Europeans' skill in exploiting tensions between north and south. In exchange for commercial privileges, for instance, they supplied the Trinh and Nguyen clans with weapons. Competing missionary orders and missionaries within a single order also used local conflicts to their advantage. If they were expelled from one part of the country, and this was frequently the case, missionaries quickly resurfaced in the other. When the evangelical work of individual missionaries was interrupted, in other words, the missions themselves maintained their stability and, as always, the number of converts increased.

The proliferation of anti-Catholic edicts underscores the inability of both the northern and southern courts to control the Christian phenomenon. Many decrees indirectly addressed the question of missionaries and Vietnamese converts, but in the years mentioned below, specifically anti-Catholic prohibitions were announced: 1630, 1644, 1658, 1663, 1664, 1665, 1688, 1696, 1700, 1710, 1712, 1737, 1744, 1750, 1754, 1761, 1765, 1773, and 1785.[5] Some acts specified that Catholics would pay taxes at a rate three times higher than non-Catholics and perform three times the amount of uncompensated labor, such as building roads, maintaining dikes, and dredging canals, levees, and reservoirs. Other edicts decreed that the property of Catholics would be confiscated, churches razed, sacred texts destroyed, and the houses of missionaries burned to the ground. At various moments in the seventeenth and eighteenth centuries, Catholics could be detained, sent into exile, expelled, or sentenced to a lifetime in prison. Converts could be tattooed on their foreheads and cheeks—a penalty earlier reserved for garden-variety criminals and the most wicked sociopaths as well (I: 95, 122, 403, 406–07; II: 141). And in some truly gruesome incidents, Catholics were skinned alive, trampled to death by elephants and horses, strangled, decapitated, or hanged. Initially, Launay depicts the Vietnamese as an essentially "civilized" people but damned nonetheless because their religious life was "filled with error" (I: 87, 90). Gradually, as he converts this story into a drama of evil and overcoming, the Vietnamese become increasingly vile. They are "appallingly corrupt," he notes (I: 170). In pagan nations where the Devil has reigned, not only the pagans themselves, but the blood, the atmosphere, the soil—in short everything, including nature—has been infected. The Devil burdened pagans with a *two-fold* original sin (II: 172–73). Missionary work, meaning the battle between Paganism and Christianity, Launay asserts, revolves around the combat between law inspired by the Devil and law revealed by God (III: 22–23).

From 1770 to 1850, the precolonial and colonial histories of Vietnam most evidently overlapped. In 1771, the Tay Son rebellion erupted in a small coastal town of southern Vietnam. By 1788, after years of warfare that involved China, Laos, Cambodia, Thailand, France, and the two Vietnams, the Le dynasty collapsed and a new dynasty—the Tay Son—assumed the throne. Until the early 1800s, the northern and southern clans continued to fight against each other and against the Tay Son. In 1802, another new dynasty, the Nguyen, which was based on remnants of the Nguyen clan of the south, came to power. Nominally, the Nguyen kings (including Gia Long, Minh Mang, Thieu Tri, Tu Duc, and Bao Dai) ruled until 1945, when Bao Dai (the "Great Protector") surrendered the imperial seal and sword to Viet Minh revolutionaries. In fact, beginning in the mid-nineteenth century, Vietnam, Cambodia, and Laos were reconstituted as Indochina and governed by France. From all points of the political spectrum, the Tay Son rebellion appears as a transforming moment in the history of Vietnam, but disagreements about how it should be understood are profound. Unless they were aligned with the French Society of Foreign Missions, missionaries who witnessed the rebellion tended to regard it with sympathy; they saw it as a failed but still defensible uprising against the greed and corruption of officials. Developing this idea to a much greater degree, postcolonial historians have reconfigured the Tay Son rebellion as the Tay Son Revolution that would have radically changed the course of Vietnamese history—had the French not intervened.[6] This interpretation of the eighteenth century is essential to postcolonial constructions of twentieth-century events. Whereas the distinguished French historian Paul Mus depicted post–World War II events in Vietnam as a series of unmotivated and purely contingent reactions to Japan's surrender, postcolonial historians celebrate the great August Revolution of 1945 as the completion of a process begun by Tay Son revolutionaries nearly two centuries before. On the other hand, for Vietnamese partial to southern visions of the national past, for colonial historians generally, and particularly for defenders of the Society of Foreign Missions, the Tay Son rebels were simply a "gang of bandits" (II: 132). This version of events hinges on the efforts of Pierre Pigneau de Béhaine, a member of the Society of Foreign Missions who is highly revered in some sources and much reviled in others.

Pigneau de Béhaine reached Cochinchina in the 1780s in the midst of the chaos that then engulfed Vietnam. His brief encounters with Nguyen Anh, the leader of the Nguyen clan, convinced him that he had met the "New Constantine" who, once enthroned, would Christianize a pagan realm (II: 252). He emphasized that the Portuguese in Macao, the Dutch in Indonesia, and the English had all promised to protect Nguyen Anh but, righteously, he had refused their offers. In recriminatory tones, Launay notes that France, who had proposed nothing, risked losing "what she already possessed" (II: 229–30). To convince the court of Louis XVI to "rescue" Cochinchina, Pigneau de Béhaine underscored its proximity to Dutch, Spanish, and Portuguese colonies. He also affirmed that Cochinchina's central position in the South China Sea would allow France to dominate regional and even international trade. Moreover, he argued, the presence of France in Cochinchina would balance English power in India (II: 237). The king and his officials, however, greeted this proposal with indifference (II: 245). When he turned to the East Indies Company, Pigneau de Béhaine received an even harsher response. Expressing not just indifference to his idea but real disdain, a prominent official dismissively remarked that France still had enough time to abandon Cochinchina and leave it to the English, "who would take from it what they could" (II: 244). Undeterred and indefatigable, Pigneau de Béhaine returned to Cochinchina, where he enlisted the support of the French navy (II: 234). Launay acknowledges that the missionary he most favored had manipulated politics in France and Vietnam, devised military tactics, and directly engaged in combat, but he excuses this behavior because Pigneau de Béhaine was trying to realize admirable goals: he sought only to develop Christianity in Indochina, expand the influence of France, and restore Nguyen Anh to the throne (II: 138, 340). Here a critical gap arises. Had Launay praised him for restoring Nguyen Anh to his rightful place as head of the Nguyen clan, no one could fault him. Instead, he makes a gigantic and, one suspects, deliberately disingenuous leap when he credits Pigneau de Béhaine, the Society of Foreign Missions, the power of Catholic France, and the French navy for having restored Nguyen Anh to the throne—because there was no Nguyen dynasty to "restore" (II: 242).

With Nguyen Anh "restored" to the throne as king Gia Long (1802–20), French missionaries expected to be treated with gratitude and respect. Although Gia Long's court did not enact any specifically anti-Catholic legislation, the political climate was not what missionaries anticipated. First, they continued to encounter serious misunderstandings about their faith. According to some, Christians made a poisonous infusion out of the pulverized bones of people they killed. Then, they "watered" the heads of unsuspecting villagers who, in turn, were bewitched. According to others, missionaries made holy water not from pulverized bones but from the eyes of those who were ill (II: 331; III: 178–79).[7] Second, the pervasive distrust of missionaries also stemmed from their own deceitful practices, such as wearing disguises, and the regularity with which they violated national laws. Although they were prohibited from entering the country, they did so with total nonchalance; if they were expelled, they devised more furtive ways to return. Third, no one knew more than Nguyen officials how extensively Christian missionaries could meddle in politics. Consequently, their claims to be concerned only with the gospel resonated in unintended ways. Nevertheless, when signs of hostility toward converts and missionaries appeared, Launay traces them to the demonic superstitions of ordinary Vietnamese and to the venality of officials.

Although Gia Long was billed as the Vietnamese Constantine, none of his gestures suggested his Christianizing potential. Some of his high-ranking officials were baptized, it is true, but the king himself did not convert. Nevertheless, he abandoned the openly anti-Catholic attitudes of his predecessors, at least initially (II: 137). Whereas many writers portray the laws he promulgated in 1804 as a betrayal of the Christians who brought him to power, Launay has a more nuanced view—as he must. He explains that Gia Long's legislation was meant to regulate the structure, organization, and practice of all religions—Confucianism, Buddhism, Daoism, ancestor worship, and Christianity—in a period that followed decades of turmoil. To conserve economic resources, Gia Long's code prohibited villagers from making donations to local temples, community halls, churches, and pagodas. Village notables, on the other hand, were allowed to contribute, but to a very precise and limited degree. The new laws also established which festivals were legitimate (II: 390, 394). Launay acknowledges, though, that the new legal code characterized Christianity in ways that troubled converts and missionaries alike. It depicted the faith as a "foreign superstition" that, having entered the kingdom illegally, threatened the simpleminded with hell and promised paradise to the naïve (II: 390). If Gia Long was the new Constantine, his successor, Minh Mang (1820–40), was the Vietnamese version of Nero (III: 28). Because the rise of the Nguyen dynasty depended entirely on Christian missionaries and Vietnamese converts, Minh Mang, like Gia Long, should have recognized his debt. Instead, encouraged by "jealous" officials who were also "infantile" and "cruel" and collectively "revealed the stupidity of men who were incompletely civilized," Minh Mang authorized violent anti-Catholic persecution (II: 330). In edicts issued in 1831 and 1832, he ordered officials to keep Christians under surveillance, but his edict of 1833 required all Christians to denounce their faith. To hasten this process, officials burned crosses and razed the houses of priests (II: 544–45). Minh Mang's immediate successor, Thieu Tri (1841–47), was less aggressive, but during the reign of Tu Duc (1847–83), persecution increased. Using the persecution of Christians as a pretext to attack, the French navy launched the first of several expeditions against the Vietnamese. Ultimately, these assaults resulted in total French control (II: 493–94).

By taking a glance at Southeast Asia overall, circa 1850, it is possible to appreciate events in Vietnam more fully. At this point, the Spanish occupied the Philippines; the Dutch controlled the East Indies; and the British were consolidating their conquest of the Malay peninsula (including Singapore), parts of Borneo, and Burma. A more comprehensive portrait of Asia reveals that the British also occupied India and that, as Launay points out, in the aftermath of the first Opium War (1839–42), British imperialists thoroughly undermined the sovereignty of China (III: 155–56). Japan, in the process of "escaping Asia," was transforming itself into an imperial power—precisely to avoid the fate of other Asian nations. A still broader perspective includes the invasion of Algeria in 1830 because difficulties the French encountered there led them to contemplate more seriously the idea of an empire in Asia (III: 156). The problem, though, was that few unconquered territories remained. According to Launay, French colonialists imagined the Sulu archipelago (between Indonesia and the Philippines) as the ideal center of their empire; but Spanish officials would have protested (III: 156). As the possibilities of empire in Asia seemed to evaporate, French officials, including King Louis Philippe, looked anew at the anti-Catholic persecution in Vietnam. They warned Minh Mang, who was as "irrational as he was cruel," that persecution of missionaries would be avenged (III: 82–83). Soon thereafter, when a French commercial ship seeking trade relations reached the Vietnamese port of Danang, the captain inadvertently learned that the Nguyen court had recently sentenced five missionaries to death (III: 93–94). As if these violations alone didn't justify French retaliation, Britain, the "new enemy of France," Launay indignantly insists, also offered to protect French missionaries (III: 181). Surely, he asserts, this was merely a ploy; the British would have used this opportunity to control the country—which (by the 1890s) had become one of the "most beautiful colonies" of France (III: 183). Like other apologists for evangelism and empire, Launay frames the military conquest of Vietnam as an essential and shamefully delayed response to centuries of Vietnamese provocations. In other words, the savagery of Vietnamese—excepting Nguyen Anh—forced French naval commanders to attack. Unlike postcolonial historians who emphasize the phenomenon of global capitalism and the military dimensions of conquest (the bombardments of Danang in the 1840s and 1850s), colonial historians underscore its diplomatic origins: Indochina, the new child of France, was brought to life in 1862 by the Treaty of Saigon.

Launay presents his three-volume monolith as a straightforward history of the Society of Foreign Missions. By reading between the lines, however, it is possible to decipher his implicit agenda. First, Launay indicts the Church. In the seventeenth century, when the Church should have unambiguously expressed its support for the Society of Foreign Missions, it hesitated to do so and, instead, allowed itself to be manipulated by Portugal and Spain. Furthermore, by retaining the fifteenth-century *padroado* system even though the conditions that inspired it had vanished, the Church continued to privilege the evangelical projects of Portugal and Spain—even when they conflicted with the more effective endeavors of France. Moreover, when great luminous figures like François Pallu and the Society of Foreign Missions more generally were accused of Jansenism, the Church failed to dismiss these baseless allegations (I: 182, 492–93). When the Church should have been internally united and devoting its resources to evangelical work, it was at war with itself. The rites controversy was particularly disruptive (I: 499). Finally, in the late eighteenth and early nineteenth centuries, at a time when other European Christians had abandoned the missionary ideal, the evangelical spirit of French missionaries was vibrant and alive. The Church should have affirmed, but did not, a special rapport with the Society of Foreign Missions (II: 206–07). On the contrary, the Propaganda didn't bother to reply to Pigneau de Béhaine's desperate missives (II: 234). In short, rather than consolidating its existing missions and promoting new ones, the Church squandered what it already had—while Protestant contamination spread across the globe.

Launay fixes his narrative gaze on the phenomenon of suffering—barbarous executions, deprivations of every sort, and hideous forms of torture. For Launay, these details are essential because they allow him to describe the missionaries' persistent, even unreasonable devotion to God. Had he concentrated on their efficiency, had he emphasized the deliberate and methodical manner in which they carried out God's plan, or had he dwelled on their success, he would have outlined the rationale that motivated them. For Launay, however, part of Christianity's appeal, especially in its Catholic form, was that it transcended mere reason. Martyrdom, when welcomed with grace, spread the gospel more surely than reasonable plans or practical gestures. As the missionaries' bones were crushed, as blood dripped from their veins, their covenant with God was continually renewed—even when the Church itself was in disarray (I: 579). More critically, Launay's fascination with the missionaries' suffering makes the Society's marginalization during colonial times appear glaringly unjust.

Launay, it's worth recalling, published his history of the Society of Foreign Missions in the 1890s, after the conquest of Indochina was complete and at a time when civilian government had displaced military rule. Because missionaries were responsible for "opening up" Indochina and "rescuing" it for France, they naturally expected to play a significant role in colonial administration. But colonial officials failed to recognize the true origins of French Indochina. Therefore, throughout this three-volume opus, Launay continually insists on its genuine lineage: the Society of Foreign Missions and the genius of Pierre Pigneau de Béhaine, who intervened, who saved Cochinchina when republican France was ready to discard it (II: 248). Condemning his contemporaries and contemporary times, Launay remarks: "In the past, those most devoted to the glory of France were true friends of missionaries" (II: 468). Highlighting his sense of betrayal, he quotes the pagan governor general Paul Bert: "I will not make use of missionaries and they will not make use of me" (II: 469). The suffering of missionaries created the pretext for French military action; but once civilian, republican government was in place, missionaries were pushed to the side. Instead, colonial administrators elaborated new notions of salvation. Modernity itself, not Christian superstition, provided the pathway to salvation.

NOTES

I would like to thank Emmanuelle Affidi, Antonio Butardo, Hoang Thi Yen, Huynh Boi Tran, Nguyen Thi Bac, Nguyen Thi Huong Giang, Nguyen Thi Thu Trang, Nguyen Van Tai, and Vo Van Sen for their friendship and assistance while I was in Vietnam conducting research for this piece.

1. Adrien Launay, *Histoire de la Société des Missions Étrangères*, 3 vols. (Paris: Téqui, 1894). Subsequent references are cited parenthetically in the text.

2. There is no reason to identify all the names by which Vietnam has been known, but I should clarify some basic dynamics. As Vietnamese from the Red River delta migrated to the south, regional identities developed more keenly. The designations Dang Ngoai (the "outside") for the north and Dang Trong (the "inside") for the south encapsulated this increasing sense of difference. When Europeans and especially Portuguese arrived, they referred to the south as "Cochinchina" and to the north as "Tonkin." Later, the French in particular but other Europeans as well used the term "Annam" to identify the central part of Vietnam *and* the collectivity composed of the three regions. The name "Vietnam" was first used by the Nguyen dynasty early in the nineteenth century.

3. Mac Duong, "Nguoi Viet Nam Thien chua giao o mien Nam nuoc ta tu the ky XVII den the ky XIX," in *Lich su dao Thien chua trong lich su dan toc Viet Nam*, ed. Ban Ton giao (Ho Chi Minh City: Khoa hoc Xa hoi, 1988), 69.

4. Because Launay uses the priests' first names only, it is probably impossible to trace their identities. Incidentally, betel quids, which consist of acorns from areca palms wrapped in a leaf and dipped in lime, are now mostly consumed by elderly people in the countryside, but in earlier times they were widely enjoyed.

5. Do Duc Hung et al., *Viet Nam: Nhung su kien lich su (Tu khoi thuy den 1858)* (Hanoi: Giao duc, 2001), 297–98, 309, 313, 318, 325, 338, 341, 345, and 352; and Huynh Lua, "Do dau ma co viec dam dao Thien chua trong cac the ky XVII, XVIII, va XIV?" in Ban Ton giao, *Lich su dao Thien chua trong lich su dan toc Viet Nam*, 174.

6. See, for example, Vien Su hoc, *Lich su Viet Nam* (Hanoi: Khoa hoc Xa hoi, 1971 and 1985); Le Thanh Khoi, *Histoire du Viet Nam des origines à 1858* (Paris: Sudestasie, 1981); Ban Ton giao, *Lich su dao Thien chua trong lich su dan toc Viet Nam*; and Nguyen Van Kiem, *Su du nhap cua dao Thien chua giao vao Viet Nam tu the ky XVII den the ky XIX* (Hanoi: Hoi Khoa hoc Lich su Viet Nam, 2001).

7. See also A. Delvaux, trans., *Lettres de missionnaires de la Cochinchine et du Tonkin au commencement du XVIII siècle* (n.p., n.d.), 6, 32.

A Note on "Further India"

Balachandra Rajan

To say that "Further India" is in need of further study may be to offer a pun of the utmost feebleness. The pun is justified by the extraordinary neglect of an international cultural coalescence that is unusual to the point of being unique. Romila Thapar's widely read *History of Ancient India* has two pages on "Greater India." She objects quite rightly to the phrase and consequently omits if from her index. Histories of India, ancient or modern, tend to be histories of North India, but Nilakanta Sastri's *History of South India* improves even on Thapar in its lack of attention to this topic. Perhaps it does so because Sastri published a book in 1949 on *South Indian Influences in the Far East*.[2] K. M. Pannikar's five pages in his brief *History of India* (unfortunately long out of print) are valuable and indeed aroused my own interest in the subject.[3] But five pages can only indicate how much more needs to be said. The same observation can be make of John Keay's two densely packed pages on the South Indian presence overseas.[4]

Art historians do better with "Further India." Heinrich Zimmer's *The Art of Indian Asia* is easily the most distinguished work in this genre.[5] "Further India," according to one scholar, is a phrase of French or Dutch coinage.[6] It attempts to meet Thapar's objections well before Thapar made them. Zimmer in using the phrase is well aware of its implicit balance of cohesion and autonomy. He sees India as "the creating hearth" but is also sensitive to the originality and aptness of regional realizations. "Out of various ethnological and biological requirements, self-contained styles were formed that were the peers in originality, nobility, and delicacy of the Indian."[7]

Standing together with Zimmer's work is J. P. Singhal's *India and World Civilization*. Singhal's monumental two-volume study has been set aside to much the same extent as Further India itself. Writing as a cultural historian, Singhal is able to take in literature and philosophy as well as the visual arts. His seventy-eight pages on "The Asianization of Indian Culture" are richly descriptive but limited by the conventions of his day.[8] He draws lines of transmission and makes clear how much was transmitted. Zimmer studies tradition and individuality. Neither study places itself in the context of imperialism or explores the possibility of "empires" that may not be imperialist, that are open to otherness or indifferent to othering.[9] Twenty-five years after Said's work, it is desirable to ask if Oriental empires practiced Orientalism with anything like the same zeal as their Western counterparts. Are the imperatives of otherness fundamentalist rather than imperialist? Has fundamentalist rhetoric, particularly that of militant Christianity, simply combined with the exploitativeness of certain forms of economic growth to produce the shapes of imperialism with which we are familiar? A study of Further India may not provide an answer to these inquiries, but it should be part of an educated response to them.

Commercial relationships between India and Southeast Asia probably existed before the Christian era but the storybook beginnings of Further India take place in the first century. The foremost archer of the Kaundinya clan landed in Funan (the lower valley of the Mekong), overcame hostile forces, and married the local princess. Her name was Lien-Ye, which translates as "Willow Leaf." Keay describes her as "ill-clad".[10] An inscription of the period suggests that she may have needed guidance in her attire.

The Mekong estuary was the scene of another and quite different cultural encounter when the Portuguese poet, Luis Vaz de Camões, was rescued from its waters with the manuscript of The Lusiads clutched to his heart. Camões authenticates the incident in his epic and a Portuguese coin was struck to commemorate it. An era of intercultural innocence ended with Vasco da Gama's voyage, as Southeast Asia came under Western dominance. The voice of religion was no longer the meditative voice of curiosity and wonder, seeking enlightenment. It was replaced by the more assertive voices documented in Patricia Pelley's essay (chapter 9).

Lien-Ye's marriage to her Indian suitor was in keeping with the norms of innocence. It was not greeted with the consternation which mixed marriages have caused in orthodox empires. It exhibited none of the constrictions of caste or anxieties of hybridity. India's presence in the region remained unmarked by the accoutrements of conquest. Settlement was restricted to what was necessary for commerce. No attempt was made to improve the condition of the natives.

The dynasty that Lien-Ye and her husband established is said to have been overthrown about A.D. 200. Nevertheless, Indian rule over the province continued until about A.D. 540. when it fell to the neighboring kingdom of Chenla. The conquest was not anti-Indian. On the contrary, the Kambuja royalty that ruled over Chenla traced its descent from the *Apsara*, Mera, and a rishi, Kambu Svayambhuva, who was Aryadesa's (India's) king. This is a foundation myth that is both rooted in India and follows Indian models.

The Khmer kingdom that emerged from the fusion of Funan and Chenla flourished for seven centuries. After the death of Jayavarman VII in 1220, it fell to the Thais. The ruins of Angkor are its unforgettable statement.

Rivalling Khmer in architectural splendour was the Sailendra empire centered at Pelambang in Java. The Sri Vijaya empire based in Sumatra which antedated it has indications of an Indian presence dating back to the pre-Christian era. Twenty thousand Indian families are said to have come to Java from Kalinga in the second century. These numbers seem exaggerated but indicate a migration of some importance. A Chinese traveller Fa-hsien who visited the island in 414, described it as a stronghold of Hinduism. Yet two and a half centuries later, it had become a stronghold of Buddhism with Buddhist monks in the territory numbering more than a thousand. Sanskrit was the language of enlightenment for both religions, which existed without friction side by side.

China's interest in Buddhism was intense at this time. Because of that interest, source materials no longer to be found in India are preserved in Chinese repositories. For Buddhist scholars from China, India was the climax of a pilgrimage. One such scholar, I-Tsing learned Sanskrit at Pelambang before proceeding to India. He recommended Pelambang to his colleagues as a site for preliminary study. His advice seems to have been followed with alacrity. Visiting scholars from Indonesia to Nalanda, India's centre of Buddhist learning, became so numerous that a separate monastery had to be built to lodge them.

Sri Vijaya's relationship with the Sailendra kingdom is far from clear. A Sailendra prince became the ruler of Sri Vijaya in the ninth century. His dynasty lasted for 400 years. He may have taken over Sri Vijaya because his prospects at home were limited, or to establish a protectorate, or to cement power-sharing through a dynastic alliance.

Borobodur's huge structure is the Sailendra civilization's maximum statement. Buddhism is not a religion that makes much of its majesty, so the statement is obviously nationalist as well as religious. Sacred triumphalism can be eloquent in conveying the insignificance of the human before the divine. Indian temple architecture reinstates the human by its dedication to plenitude, by its insistence that the pull of life be recognized, that it be quietened rather than erased. Borobodur and Angkor implement and reconsider the Indian balance in declarations that are impressively original, that seem to take India slightly beyond itself, justifying the appellation, "Further India."

Sacred architecture is not simply an education in the supremacy of the sacred. At York, the main cathedral window comprises the entire history of the human race. Narrative form is both admitted and evaded as the viewer's imagination wanders among the panels. Borobodur is carved out of a mountain top into nine terraces, increasing in height as one ascends, as if to suggest the growing arduousness of each step taken toward the divine. The four ascending galleries of the lower terraces contain 1,500 sculptural panels depicting the lives of the Buddha in his various incarnations. The entire structure is as Singhal observes, an example of iconological symbolism at its finest, the reworking of a vocabulary that India had articulated and refined.[11] It is also deeply expressive of a specific terrain and the distinctive genius of its people. Close to Borobodur are six Hindu temples not on the same scale, but modelled with the same devout intricacy. The juxtaposition is a reproach to current intolerance.

Angkor Thom, the capital city of the dynasty that built Angkor Wat, is laid out in the form of the world as discerned from Mount Meru. The causeway across the moat that surrounds the city displays the churning of the cosmic ocean, with the primeval snake, Vasuki, providing the rope that enabled the mythic mountain to be used as a churn. Angkor Wat itself has an outer wall half a mile in length adorned with 1,750 sculptures of Apsaras in elaborate headdresses nearly all of which are different from each other. Indian sculpture provides no precedent for the more lavish of these headdresses, some of which are nearly as tall as the wearer. Within the temple edifice itself, panel after sculptured panel presents scenes from the *Mahabharata*, the *Ramayana*, and the *Harivamsa*, which attest not simply to the mimetic skill but also to the emotional involvement of the craftsmen translating these episodes into stone.

Borobodur and Angkor are spectacular statements of an Indian cultural presence that was persuasive rather than prescriptive. That presence expresses itself in many ways. The Indian system of numbers travelled East before it travelled West to become the basis of Western mathematics. The Devanagiri script was brought to Indonesia by the Sailendra dynasty. India's presence in the performing arts lives on in the Indonesian shadow-play and is intimately woven into the culture of Bali. The names of Thai kings until recently bore the suffix, "Rama," and Thai state-ceremonies were conducted by Brahmin priests. India's presence in Southeast Asia is at least as pervasive and enduring as Rome's surviving presence in the empire it governed.

India's first links with Southeast Asia were commercial. Fourteen centuries before Columbus and Vasco da Gama, voyages across the cyclone-ridden seas that separated India from Indochina were not only undertaken but routine. India was not the only and may not even have been the most important destination for the freight that Indian vessels carried from the East. Much of the freight went to Rome across the Northern part of that ocean where Vasco da Gama was to make a voyage still widely treated as pioneering. As the Roman empire declined, India's trade with Southeast Asia fell off. Commercial links gave way to cultural bonds that proved to be more important and enduring.

How was this cultural bonding constituted? The culture that commerce carries today is typified by MacDonald's rather than by the *Mahabharata*. One might argue that since the ancient world lacked a MacDonald's, the *Mahabharata* was the best available substitute. If this view is conceded, laments should be in order. But we must also reflect on the character of societies that allowed not merely material goods but works of the mind such as philosophy, religion, and literature to pass so persuasively from one country to another. We then have to recognize that even persuasion needs ambassadors and an audience seeking to listen and to learn. Who were these ambassadors? Scholars and priests made the journey but only after the gates had been opened by others and after a demand had been established for their teachings. The first persuasion had to be artistic. It had to be not merely the voice but the ardently communicative voice of memory and longing.

Arthur Waley suggests and it may seem necessary to infer that travellers of the time were versed in metaphysics.[12] Today's sailors and longshoremen are more given to four-letter words than to unifying thoughts. In the absence of documentation, there is much on which to speculate, but Waley may be making too much of the mystery. Travellers may simply have carried the myths and stories of their homeland in their hearts and remembered them with sufficient passion to make them live again before a receptive audience. The ancient world was hospitable to travellers rather than suspicious of their antecedents. Those who made hazardous journeys required no passports.

Nevertheless it is one thing to listen to a guest with sympathy and quite another to adopt his culture. To achieve this spontaneous adoption, both the donating and receiving cultures have to be remarkably openminded and extraordinarily relaxed in their parameters of identity. If classical India approached these requirements, it could only have done so by pursuing with conviction the disinterested search for understanding implicit in its texts. More specifically, the relationship between Hinduism and Buddhism that classical India brought to Further India must have been amicable rather than contentious. As already pointed out, six Hindu temples lie in proximity to the impassive splendour of Borobodur. Angkor is replete with sculptural renderings of Hindu epics and Puranic mythology. It was built by Suryavarman II, a devout Buddhist.

The relationship between South India and Further India seems to have been unencumbered by the tyranny of center–circumference distinctions. In fact the "circumference" having received what the "center" had to offer, made its own spectacular harvest of that offering. Built in the eighth century, Borobodur surpasses in ambitiousness any Buddhist shrine in India. It encounters difficulties in the nature of its success. Proclaiming the world as will in order to demonstrate the will's limitations is a paradox that scared architecture cannot easily negotiate. The limitations can be lost in the splendour of the willing. Sanchi's modest structures may be as effective in leading us to the peace of thought that comes from disengagement. They instruct us by quietening the imagination. Borobodur instructs us by arousing it.

Angkor Wat is a further surpassing of the source. Built in the same century as Notre Dame, it lies in time between the temple complex at Khajuraho, fortunately not "discovered" by those who ravaged Northern India, and the resolutely symbolic structure of Konarak. Konarak stands in abandoned isolation on the coast of that Kalinga (now Orissa) from which thousands of Indians set out on Eastern journeys. The Portuguese used the tower of Konarak as a lighthouse for their own voyages. Both Angkor and Konarak are impressively assertive structures in which the telos of world-relinquishment is not denied but held within limits that allow a return to the "life of significant soil," to civilization, even with its vanities. Delineating the pull of the real against the phenomenal may be as much as sacred architecture should do. Recognizing the pull and living within its balances, or proceeding to an ultimacy free from its constraints, are responsibilities to be worked out by the seeker, rather than part of the instruction offered by the edifice.

Cultural movement between inner and further India seems to have been in only one direction. Two-way traffic might have provided us with the intimidation of a model to emulate. It is preferable to have a precedent on which to improve. As the "circumference" came into its own, it should have been difficult to stand before its achievements and not conclude that there was something to be learned from them. The failure to learn though unfortunate, is understandable. Teachers are reluctant to be instructed by their pupils.

To describe Further India as an empire may be to take the word beyond its limits. The closest equivalent is Macaulay's "imperishable empire of arts and letters" in which erstwhile imperial relationships are foreseen as fading away into cultural connections.[13] The commonwealth may even reveal the same cultural overtaking of the center by the circumference that we find in the late history of Further India. Nevertheless it remains a construction built on the centrality of English that emerging nationalisms find it necessary to resist. Englishness is now giving way to English speakingness, a global concept centred in the United States of America and based on the dominance of English as the language of world business. World business is fortified and to some degree given its patterns of transmission by American dominance in the export of cultural capital and in the means of production of that capital. The result, we are assured, will be an empire that is not imperialist. Further India may have been closer to this dream. But Further India may not have been an empire. It was not the administrative, legal, and fiscal entity for which the word "empire" once stood, a unity not inherently imperialist but deeply corroded by a history that suggests its extreme difficulty in being other than imperialist. Further India may only have been a community of shared understandings that grew from commerce and eventually left commerce behind, that mysteriously offered cohesion without coercion. As a precedent for the future, it may have something to tell us about the possibilities of bonding held away from bondage. If we are to progress in the science of sharing we need to do more than make the bottom line transcendent: we need to bring about not merely the sum but the synergy of the best that has been globally known and thought. Further India points us in this direction indicating how "thought's empire over thought" can both extend itself and submit to its own reinvention. We should call upon its meaning, not its name.

NOTES

1. Romila Thapar, *A History of India: Volume One* (London: Penguin Books, 1996), 164–65.
2. Nilakanta Sastri, *A History of South India from Prehistoric Times to the Fall of Vijayanagar*, 3rd ed. (Madras: Oxford University Press,

1966); Sastri, *South Indian Influences in the Far East* (Bombay, 1949).

3. K. M. Pannikar, *A Survey of Indian History* (Bombay: The National Information and Publications Ltd., 1947), 116–20.

4. John Keay, *India: A History* (London: Harper Collins, 2000; pbk ed. 2001), 177–78.

5. Heinrich Zimmer, *The Art of Indian Asia*, ed. Joseph Campbell (Princeton: Princeton University Press, 1988).

6. D. P. Singhal, *India and World Civilization* (Ann Arbor: Michigan State University Press, 1969), 320,n. 1. I have drawn heavily on this work.

7. Zimmer, *The Art of India Asia*, 1:363. For a more problematized account, see K. N. Chaudhuri, *Asia Before Europe: Economy and Civilization of the Indian Ocean from the Rise of Islam to 1750* (Cambridge: Cambridge University Press, 1990), 58–61.

8. Singhal, *India and World Civilization*, 80–157.

9. The Ottoman Empire's lack of interest in othering is dwelt on elsewhere in this book. See also Nabil Matar, *Islam in Britain 1558–1685* (Cambridge: Cambridge University Press, 1998).

10. Keay, *India*, 177.

11. Singhal, *India and World Civilization*, 152–53.

12. Arthur Waley, *The Way and Its Power* (London, 1942), quoted in Singhal, *India and World Civilization*, 85.

13. Macaulay made this prophesy in 1833 as a member of Parliament for Leeds. He left for India a year later. See *Macaulay: Prose and Poetry*, ed. G. M. Young (Cambridge, Mass.: Harvard University Press, 1967), 718.

PART IV

ENGLISH AND FRENCH IMPERIALISMS: EIGHTEENTH AND NINETEENTH CENTURIES

CHAPTER 10

"English" and French Imperial Designs in Canada and in a Larger Context

Jonathan Hart

The textual underpinnings of English (later British) and French expansion to the New World, with a particular interest in Canada but in a comparative context within the Americas and imperial frameworks generally, suggest a significant context for an understanding of comparative imperialism. From the fifteenth-century, the English and the French (centered in London and Paris respectively) were expanding their domain over the peoples adjacent to them while attempting to centralize their power in the Crown. Concerns at home and in Europe regularly affected and even nullified this effort to establish colonies or trading posts in the Western Atlantic. England and France, often using Italian mariners like Giovanni Caboto and Giovanni da Verrazanno early on, were sometimes rivals in colonization and at other times friends. The rivalry is well known, but the cooperation, particularly between Huguenots and the English in the late sixteenth century, is something often occluded in both national and imperial historiographies.

The textual background, rhetorical as well as legal, should complicate widespread notions of these imperial powers in Canada and the Americas. The meetings of cultures and "multiculturalism" in the Grand Banks, slavery in the West Indies, French efforts in "Florida," and alliances with, and representations of, Native and other groups all qualify notions of monological empires. Comparison helps to effect revisions of the views of the English and French empires in Canada and the New World. While the French lost Canada in 1763 and sold Louisiana in 1803, they left cultural and political traces as well as still maintaining some colonies in the Western Atlantic while Britain, once colonized by the Normans, lost its most populous colonies in North America in 1783. Canada and the West Indies then became part of a new kind of empire for France and Britain and their place in the imperial frameworks changed ineluctably with the American and French Revolutions.

I

From the 1490s into the 1520s, France was fighting to keep its Italian possessions.[1] England, which had lost most of its French territories under Henry VI, got off to a good start in the exploration of the New World but began to lag behind Spain. The papacy continued to play a role in legitimizing exploration after Columbus's landfall in the New World. The English and French opposed the papal donation to Spain and Portugal even while they imitated these leading colonial powers. England preceded France in voyages that successfully reached the New World.[2] In the first letters patent granted to Cabot, citizen of Venice, and his sons, on March 5, 1496, Henry VII gave them and their heirs and deputies the right to sail to any foreign parts in the eastern, western, and northern sea at their own expense.[3] In *Divers Voyages*, Verrazzano, a Florentine, would make the first official French voyage across the North Atlantic in 1524.[4]

The Portuguese thought that the land Cabot encountered was quite possibly in their sphere as set out in the Treaty of Tordesillas (370 leagues west of the Cape Verde Islands). On October 28, 1499, King Manuel of Portugal issued letters patent to João Fernandez to make a voyage to discover new islands in the North Atlantic.[5] The Portuguese king issued similar patents to Gaspar Corte Real on May 12, 1500, and for a second voyage in 1501; to Miguel Corte Real in January 1502; for a fourth voyage in 1503. In 1501, from Bristol, merchants from the Azores and England joined together to petition for a patent to seek out the new lands in the northwestern Atlantic.[6] The Company of Adventurers to the New Found Lands was to serve as a model for later companies that helped to extend English trade and settlement to new lands. Newfoundland itself became a figure for the rivalry, cooperation, claims, and counterclaims of the European powers. Perhaps the most tenacious heirs to the elder Cabot were the French fishermen, later the men of the French shore in Newfoundland and of St. Pierre and Miquelon. Two decades before official French voyages to North America, French fishermen were involved in the fisheries near Newfoundland. This commercial fishing as a response to Spain and England was something France maintained by keeping St. Pierre and Miquelon at the end of the Seven Years War (1756–63). In some ways the fishermen kept up contact with and interest in North America for the French between Jacques Cartier and Samuel de Champlain.[7]

II

France was more active than England was in exploring the northern reaches of North America from the 1520s to the 1570s. Even still, during the sixteenth century the French produced a small number of narratives compared to the Spanish and Portuguese.[8] Paulmier de Gonneville and Giovanni da Verrazzano were key figures in French expansion. Gonneville's relation of the voyage to Brazil in 1504 is the oldest account in French concerning an eyewitness report of the New World.[9] As much as François I seemed on one occasion to ignore the papal donation dividing the "unknown" world between the Iberian powers, he sought to avoid the condemnation of Rome. On his behalf, through his relations with Cardinal Hippolyte de Médicis, the archbishop of Montréal and nephew to the pope, Jean Le Veneur, bishop of Lisieux, approached Clement VII, who declared in 1533 that the bulls of 1493 applied to lands known to the Spanish and Portuguese before that date. The year before, when the French king had come on a pilgrimage to Mont-Saint-Michel, where Le Veneur was also the abbot, Le Veneur had proposed to the king that he back a voyage of discovery and presented Cartier, whose relative was a manager of the finances of the abbey, as his choice to lead it. Apparently, the success of that mission helped to make Le Veneur a cardinal. Similarly, Paul III (1534–49), Clement's successor, did not intervene in the French colonization of America, a policy that troubled Charles V.[10] One of the most important aspects of the Cartier voyages was that they were official and financed by the Crown. The goals set for Cartier were to find new lands full of riches, particularly gold, and to discover a passage to Cathay by the west.[11] Chief Donnacona's description of gold, according to Marcel Trudel, became the true motivation for French exploration, and this religious motive was a necessary façade to circumvent Portugal and Spain without offending the pope.[12]

In the course of discussions with the ambassadors of Charles V and John III of Portugal, François elaborated a new policy toward colonization. The doctrine was as elegant as it was simple: permanent occupation rather than discovery created possession.[13] He turned the Portuguese doctrine of *terra nullius*, begun in their exploration of Africa in the fifteenth century, against Portugal and Spain. In the fifteenth century the Portuguese had posts instead of colonies in Africa, so that the exact nature of this claim to possession there is not entirely clear, but allowed for an argument for the Portuguese precedence in the use of *terra nullius* in Africa.[14] This legal doctrine of *terra nullius* came to affect the English colonies as much as those of the French: for instance, as late as 1971 Justice Richard Blackburn had confirmed *terra nullius* in Australia, and it took until 1992 for the High Court of Australia to reject it.[15] The French king issued formal orders to French seamen not to go to places in the New World occupied by the Portuguese and Spanish. The primary aim of France in Canada, besides the demonstrative one of religion and the underlying one of riches, shifted to settlement. Roberval's commission of January 15, 1541 identified settlement as part of the French policy for the New World, for in it François said that his deputy should not encroach on the property of any other prince, including those of Spain and Portugal.[16]

III

Humphrey Gilbert was an important figure in the renewed strategy of exploring a northwest passage as a route to China in order to challenge Spain. Composed in 1566 but printed in 1576, Gilbert's *Discourse of a Discoverie for a New Passage to Cataia* was an attempt to have the queen give him permission to sail in search of this passage and to exercise a monopoly over it. His efforts to that end were unsuccessful. When in 1572 he met Frobisher, a new scheme began when this sailor—taken with the learning of Gilbert and Michael Lok, a member of the Muscovy Company, which generally opposed the route to the northwest and preferred the one to the northeast—found favor with the earl of Warwick, who in turn was able to gain the approval of privy council for the plan.[17] Gilbert himself thought a northwest passage would lead the English to "ye East in much shorter time, than either the Spaniard or the Portingale doth." In arguing for a great ocean in the north between Asia and America, he called on Jacques Cartier, Verrazzano, and Sebastian Cabot as well as Portuguese and Spanish sources, including the report of Salvaterra, a Spaniard who said the

Natives in America thought there was a passage and who offered to accompany Gilbert on the search for it.[18]

In the meantime, England was attempting to circumvent the Portuguese and Spanish monopoly of the New World. Elizabeth I was also pursuing a policy initiated under Henry VII but which François I had begun in earnest in France—discovery, conquest, and settlement meant possession. Before Martin Frobisher's first voyage, the state papers included a document, a brief summa *avant la lettre* of Richard Hakluyt's "Discourse" that set out an English colonial policy, sanctioning the discovery of lands that were unoccupied, the use of the commodities found there, and the spread of the Christian faith in that territory, all without offering "any offence of amitie."[19] This document suggested that the queen take up the lands toward the South Pole, which no other countries had possessed or subdued, so that providence, which had given the Spanish the west, the Portuguese the east, and the English the south would allow England to bring "in grete tresure of gold, sylver and perle into this relme from those countries, as other Princes haue oute of the lyke regions."[20] The riches of Spanish America still lured the English. One benefit of this enterprise would be to bring down the price of Spanish and Portuguese spices and commodities and to create a surplus in the English treasury.[21] England must have its place among the European colonial powers: "The Ffrenche have their portion to the northwarde directlie contrarie to that which we seke."[22] The queen did not act on these plans, but on June 11, 1578, she granted Gilbert letters patent of such scope that in Samuel Eliot Morison's words, they "deserve the title of the first English colonial charter."[23]

The letter patent of June 1578 allowed Gilbert "to discover, finde, searche out, and view such remote, heathen and barbarous lands, countreys and territories not actually possessed of any Christian prince or people."[24] This legal ground was consistent with the attitudes of England in Henry VII's time and of France at least since François I: do and do not recognize the papal donation to Spain and Portugal. On June 11, 1583, Gilbert sailed from Plymouth and, on August 5, took possession of Newfoundland for England, something Cabot had done in 1497. Edward Haie described how in St. John's harbor the fishermen greeted them in ships from Spain, Portugal, France, and England; how they all fired a salute of honor after Gilbert displayed his commission, and acknowledged that they were now under English sovereignty.[25] This scene is a reminder at the commercial and unofficial level, that the cosmopolitan nature of European exploration of the New World, so evident before the Reformation, persisted in the Newfoundland fishery.

IV

In the first decade of the seventeenth century, France and England established permanent colonies in North America. From the aftermath of the Spanish Armada of 1588 to the founding of Montréal in New France in 1642, France and England, no matter how tentative their exploration and the establishment of permanent settlements would be, were transforming themselves from explorers and pirates to settlers and neighbors.[26] Paradoxically, at the peak of Spanish power, the English and French established their first permanent colonies, at Jamestown in 1607 and at Quebec in 1608.

In France, the Crown's interest in New France lapsed after the completion of the last voyage of Cartier in 1544, although the fishery and the fur trade continued to grow. By 1578, the French ports that profited from the fish and fur trade in New France asked for the protection of Henri III, who appointed Mesgouez de La Roche, a Breton noble, governor of the lands in the New World.[27] Although this commission achieved little, it did show a renewed royal interest in New France. In 1603, Pierre du Gua, sieur de Monts, was granted a monopoly in Acadia for ten years and his main goal was to find rich mineral deposits. In 1607 the French merchants who had opposed these monopolies in the New World, succeeded in challenging the exclusive rights of de Monts and others.[28] What distinguishes Marc Lescarbot from Hakluyt is that he used the language of Christian republicanism and of a French preoccupation, which probably reached its greatest intensity under Louis XIV: "la gloire."[29] Paradoxically, Spain caused France to be defensive, but, in Lescarbot's rendition, the French should reclaim their past glory and go into the New World as the Spanish had but in a manner that was inimitable.[30] Gabriel Sagard, a contemporary historian of New France, recorded that for Port Royal, where some of the settlers were Catholic and some Protestant, sieur de Monts, the leader of the colony, had provided a Huguenot minister and a Catholic priest. The men squabbled and came to blows until scurvy claimed them. They were then buried in one grave to see whether they could in death rest in peace as they could not when alive.[31] As W. J. Eccles says, "In America they [the orders] had the example of the Spanish and Portuguese to challenge them."[32]

V

After the Glorious Revolution of 1688, France found that its ambitions in Europe and America met with a more sustained English opposition. French religious writing in and about the New World was also indebted to Spanish influences even as, in some instances, the writers resisted Spain or felt ambivalent about its colonization, particularly in its treatment of the Natives. In France, collections also helped to promote colonies in the New World, and between 1632 and 1672, the Jesuits published their annual relations, partly in order to promote their mission to the Natives to patrons from the upper class. Whereas accounts of America in French in the sixteenth century had been overwhelmingly Protestant, in the seventeenth century they were Catholic.

John Oldmixon's *The British Empire in America* (1708) took up the continuing importance of the trope of *translatio imperii* in the context of the preoccupation with Spain, the origins of European settlement in the Americas, the developing rivalry with the Netherlands, and the advantage of "our *American* Plantations."[33] Between 1713 and 1744, France and England, exhausted from war and attending to political problems, pursued peace at home and in North America. Observers from Europe, such as Peter Kalm, a professor of botany from Sweden who visited New France in 1749—the year the British founded Halifax in Nova Scotia—could not avoid seeing Canada stereoscopically, that is with one eye on the colony and another on Europe.[34] These comparisons continued until the fall of New France and its life under British rule in 1763 onward. Louis-Antoine de Bougainville, a colonel serving under Montcalm in 1757, engaged in the now familiar typology of Old World and New World, when he compared the independence of the *habitants* or farmers in New France with dependence of the peasants in France.[35] Toward the end of French rule in Canada, some Canadians, as W. J. Eccles has pointed out, made significant contributions to the French empire in the royal administration: for instance, François-Joseph Chaussegros de Léry, son of a Canadian officer, was commander of the engineers in the Grande Armée and one of Napoleon's generals whose name is engraved on the Arc de Triomphe.

The peace allowed the French to expand their overseas trade considerably and in particular France's trade with its colonies increased over five times between 1710 and 1741. France's trade in sugar in the Caribbean, in fish in the north Atlantic, and in all sorts of goods through Cadiz to the Spanish colonies and with Turkey made the

British nervous, particularly as Britain's overseas trade was stagnating in the 1730s and its contraband trade with the Spanish colonies was actively curbed by Spain. War began with Spain in 1739 and with France in 1743 over the Austrian succession. Throughout the war, the trade between the French West Indies and the British colonies on the American mainland flourished—the one exchanging sugar, molasses, and African slaves for lumber, flour, meat, and fish from the other. Although the Royal Navy and forces from New England took Louisbourg in 1745, there was little lost in this war because the Treaty of Aix-la-Chapelle more or less maintained the status quo from the Peace of Utrecht. The French gave up their gains in the Netherlands and exchanged Madras for Louisbourg. France feared the loss of its slave and sugar trade in the West Indies above all. But the clash of the imperial powers resumed soon after. George Washington was sent to drive the French out of the region between Lake Erie and the Ohio River, where he ambushed a French party.[36]

VI

In 1763 the French and British empires ceased to coexist in the territory that is now Canada, so in one sense that is the actual end of comparative imperialism in this territory. From that date onward, however, I will concentrate on a few of many comparative strands, not simply between European powers now, but between British North America as Canada (including Acadia and New France) came to be known and the United States (thirteen former colonies of British America). The Royal Proclamation of 1763 seemed to mark the beginning of a British hold over much of eastern North America and the triumph of British institutions, but this was not to be. The Quebec Act of 1774 restored French civil law and gave Roman Catholics religious and political equality but it also appeared to confine the expansion of the English colonies to Native territories in the west. This act contributed to conditions that led to the American War of Independence. The great break in British North America had come with the American Revolution. This division—after the defeat of France in North America but only possible with the military help of France (perhaps owing much to Benjamin Franklin's prestige and powers of persuasion after he had shifted from staying the course with Britain to choosing a way separate from the mother country)—has persisted through more than two centuries.

Within Canada itself there were lingering tensions between French- and English-speaking inhabitants, including divided loyalties to France and Britain and to Catholicism and Protestantism generally, although minorities in both linguistic groups, despite their relative neglect traditionally in school and official histories, did make Canada their home early on. In 1762, a year before the Royal Proclamation, John Gibson published a map of the British Empire in North America, an area that reached from Labrador beyond Lake Superior in the west and to Florida in the south. There was no officially recognized national border between Canada and the United States until twenty-one years after this map.[37]

On August 25, 1775, Thomas Jefferson wrote a letter to John Randolph in which he placed in a wider context the conflict between some in the British colonies and Britain: "Looking with fondness towards a reconciliation with Great Britain, I cannot help hoping you may be able to contribute towards expediting this good work. I am sincerely one of those, and would rather be in dependence on Great Britain, properly limited, than on any nation upon earth, or than on no nation."[38] Within weeks, however, the bond with Britain seemed not as secure, for George Washington, "Commander in Chief of the Army of the United Provinces of North America," appealed on September 7, 1775 in French and English to the inhabitants of Canada—as a result of "The unnatural Conflict between the English Colonies, & Great Brittain"—to throw off tyranny and to take up "The Cause of America, and of Liberty."[39]

The leaders of the American rebellion enlisted the help of Spain and France. In Paris on October 6, 1778, Arthur Lee wrote to Gardoqui, saying that if driving Britain from North America and dismembering the British empire is an advantage to Spain, then "this is the moment for its monarch to decide and enforce these events by an immediate declaration of our independency and a union of force which must be irresistible."[40] Spain, as well as Portugal and later the Netherlands, were leading factors in the relations between France and Britain in the Americas. Now an independent United States would affect that rivalry and connection. After victory and independence, the American leaders kept up their relations with continental powers. Tensions with Spain arose over the western expansion of the United States in the region of the Mississippi, something James Madison noted concerning the debates of Congress in late 1786 and early 1787 and that also involved negotiations with Gardoqui [Guardoqui].[41] Writing from Mount Vernon to the Marquis de Lafayette on March 25, 1787, George Washington acknowledged his contribution and, by implication, that of France to the United States: "Your endeavors my dear Marquis to serve this Country are unremitted."[42] France had lost New

France from its empire but had helped the Americans in the thirteen colonies to defeat Britain and win their independence. France and Britain had weakened each other and had suffered losses that would transform their empires, shifting their principal interests away from the Americas.

The Constitutional Act of 1791 followed on the Royal Proclamation of 1763 and the Quebec Act of 1774. An unfortunate consequence of this act was it gave the governor and his appointed council control over revenues from Crown lands and so made them fiscally independent from the elected assemblies, something that helped in Lower Canada to divide the English minority from the French majority. This division began in earnest when in 1809–10 the governor, Sir James Henry Craig, imprisoned members of the Parti Canadien because he thought they were sympathetic to Napoleon, who was at this time expanding France and its empire. This tension would build until Louis-Joseph Papineau, having won a convincing electoral victory in 1834, led a rebellion in 1837. The War of 1812, despite President Thomas Jefferson's assumption that Canada would be absorbed, ended with most French and English Canadians supporting the British connection or at least maintaining the status quo of their lives. Tecumseh and other Native leaders helped to preserve Canada for Britain. The American invasions failed and the Treaty of Ghent, signed as Christmas approached in 1814, returned boundaries to 1811.[43] In 1891, Martin J. Griffin wrote an extensive memorial for *The Atlantic Monthly* on John A. Macdonald, who had recently died. This article discussed Macdonald in terms of Canadian, North American, and imperial history. After describing the "wave of emotion" in Canada at the death of Macdonald, Griffin established a historical background: "Among the possessions of the British crown, Canada holds a peculiar place. For Canada, the empire made a great and costly struggle against France and against the United States. For the empire, Canada has thrice resorted to arms in 1775, in 1812, and in 1866 and turned the tide of invasion from the walls of Quebec and from the frontiers of Ontario."[44] In the wake of the American Civil War (where British commercial interests sometimes favored the defeated South) and the Fenian threat, Macdonald helped to unite British North America into Canada.

Other events, besides the American Revolution and the War of 1812, affected the survival and making of Canada. William Lyon Mackenzie, writing in Upper Canada in the 1830s, sounded like some British American writers, such as Franklin and Jefferson, in the 1760s and early 1770s. Mackenzie asserted that the British nation would not wish to perpetuate such a difficult situation in Upper Canada.[45]

His appeal to equal rights with the mother country and to the constitutional tradition and liberties granted in Britain was not unlike that made before the revolution that many in British North America had fled. Papineau led a rebellion the same year in Lower Canada and the legacy of the Rouges has informed Canadian politics, most especially among liberals and separatists in Quebec, although the latter also took up a nationalist strain owing much to leaders like Henri Bourassa. In two brief years a power shift occurred in the rhetoric of Mackenzie and his allies. On December 12, 1837, a group, chaired by Mackenzie, wrote a declaration on Navy Island, in which they praised the aid that General Van Renselaer and other Americans had provided, seeing what the citizens of Buffalo had done as support in proving "the enduring principles of the Revolution of 1776" and hoping that "emancipation will be speedily won for a new and gallant nation, hitherto held in Egyptian thraldom by the aristocracy of England."[46] In Nova Scotia, Thomas Haliburton could represent a satirical agon between the Yankee clockmaker, Sam Slick, and a Nova Scotian squire, the one upholding Jefferson and the Declaration of Independence as examples for the world, the other defending the British abolition of slavery and criticizing the American institution of racial inequality: " 'Jefferson forgot to insert one little word,' said I. 'He should have said 'All white men,' for, as it now stands, it is a practical untruth in a country that tolerates domestic slavery in its worst and most forbidding form. It is a declaration of *shame*, and not of *independence.*' "[47] Joseph Howe, like Mackenzie, believed strongly in responsible government and was an advocate of Lord Durham's report in Nova Scotia and elsewhere. Writing an open letter to Lord John Russell on September 18, 1839, Howe set out the remedy for problems of government in Nova Scotia and other colonies: "Lord Durham has stated it distinctly; the Colonial Governors must be commanded to govern by the aid of those who possess the confidence of the people and are supported by a majority of the representative branch. Where is the danger?"[48] The place of democracy in the debate on empire and colony is central from the 1760s onward in the thirteen colonies and in the remnant of British North America that became known as Canada in 1867 and after.

VII

In the twentieth century Canada has moved from the ideology of two founding nations, British and French, to multiculturalism. Its French-speaking minority has produced four prime ministers, some of them among the longest serving in British parliamentary history, so the legacy of French and British imperialism has melded into a new hybrid state that has opened its doors to immigrants from every corner of the world.

Canada has shared the languages of three great powers—France, England (Britain), and the United States—whose leaders have had ambivalent attitudes toward empire, expansion, and contraction—and it has sometimes been separated from these powers by a common culture and language—similar but not the same. Whereas some in those centers of power might have dismissed Canada over the centuries, others have not. However marginal or not to European and American expansion, since 1497, Canada (with all its names until 1949 when Newfoundland joined it) has been—in empire—a crossroads, a buffer, a beneficiary, a victim, a byproduct, an aid, an ambivalent representation, and a collection of peoples. It has been comparative and multiple since the beginning—with the meeting of Natives and Europeans, the rivalry and cooperation of Europeans, and immigration from probably every country. The Death of Wolfe—as Benjamin West's various versions of the scene and the myth of the young general attest—and the Quebec conference of 1864, the meeting of Churchill, Roosevelt, and King there during the Second World War, and the Quebec Referenda of 1980 and 1995 all show that the ancient center of the French Empire in America played and still plays a central role in the making and translation of empire as well as the building of nations and their possible fracture. In Voltaire's "quelques arpentes de neige" [a few acres of snow], those waves of peoples have found the apparently inhospitable habitable and even, despite its very real flaws, a generous space, one kind of example to other countries, comparatively distinct despite its role in the imperial past, present, and future.

Notes

1. See Raymonde Litalien, *Les Explorateurs de l'Amérique du Nord 1492–1795* (Sillery: Québec : Septentrion, 1993), 52.

2. Original ms. (Latin) of William of Worcester's *Itinerarium* is at Corpus Christi College, Cambridge; printed in James Naismith, *Itineraria Symonis Simeonis et Willelmi de Worcestre* (Cambridge, 1778), 267, in James A. Williamson, *The Voyages of the Cabots and the Discovery of North America under Henry VII and Henry VIII* (London: Argonaut Press, 1929), 18–19.

3. The Second Letters Patent Granted to John Cabot, March 5, 1496 and February 3, 1498 respectively in H. P. Biggar, *The precursors of Jacques Cartier, 1497–1534* (Ottawa, 1911), 7–9 and 22–24.

4. See, for instance, *The Italians and the Creation of America: An Exhibition at the John Carter Brown Library*, ed. Samuel J. Hough (Providence: Brown University, 1980).

5. For a detailed discussion of the Cabots and the Portuguese, see H. P. Biggar, *Voyages of the Cabots and of the Corte-Reals and Greenland, 1497–1503* (Paris: [Macon, Protat], 1903) and also Williamson, *Voyages*, 119 ff., esp. 200–03. For treatments of the Cabots, see Henry Harrisse, *Jean et Sébastien Cabot: leur origine et leurs voyages* (Paris: Ernest Leroux, 1882) and John T. Juricek, "John Cabot's First Voyage, 1497," *Smithsonian Journal of History* 2 (1967): 1–22.

6. Williamson, *Voyages*, 204. For a study of the Corte Reals, including documents, see Henry Harrisse, *Les Corte-Real et leurs voyages au Nouveau-monde* (Paris: E. Leroux, 1883).

7. See Selma Barkham, "The Basques: Filling a Gap in Our History between Jacques Cartier and Champlain," *Canadian Geographical Journal* 96 (1978): 8–19.

8. See Jean-Paul Duviols, *Voyageurs français en Amérique (colonies espagnoles et portugaises)* (Paris: Bordas, 1978), 3–4.

9. Julien cites many French historians who agree with the claim that he makes: "The *Authentic Relation* of Gonneville represents the oldest testimony of the contact of the French with a territory and the American indigenes"; ibid., 5; my translation. For Michel de Certeau's interest in this topic from Gonneville onward, a project he never completed, see his "Travel Narratives of the French to Brazil: Sixteenth to Eighteenth Centuries," *New World Encounters*, ed. Stephen Greenblatt (Berkeley: University of California Press, 1993), 323–28.

10. Charles-André Julien, *Les Voyages de découvertes et les premiers établissements* (Paris: Presses Universitaires de France, 1948), 115–17, 135–38; David B. Quinn and Alison M. Quinn, "Commentary," in Richard Hakluyt, *Discourse of Western Planting*, ed. D. B. and A. M. Quinn (London: Hakluyt Society, 1993), 187. In *Les Français* Julien outlines Le Veneur's principal part in the Cartier expedition and the family connections and friendships behind this; see Julien, "Introduction," *Les Français en Amérique pendant la première moitié du XVIe siècle : textes des voyages de Gonneville, Verrazano, J. Cartier et Roberval*, ed. Ch.-A. Julien, R. Herval, Th. Beauchesne; introduction by Ch.-A. Julien (Paris: Presses Universitaires de France, 1946), I, 11. Also see Baron de La Chapelle, "Jean Le Veneur et le Canada," *Nova Francia* 6 (1931): 341–43.

11. See Julien, *Les Français* (1946), I, II and Julien, *Les Voyages* (1948), 2, 115–17, 135–38.

12. See M. Trudel, "Section One: Introduction to the New World," in *Canada: Unity in Diversity*, ed. Paul G. Cornell et al. (Toronto: Holt, Rinehart and Winston, 1967), 9.

13. Julien, *Les Français* (1946), I, 14.

14. See Keller et al., *Creation of Rights of Sovereignty*, 23–25, cited in Olive Patricia Dickason, "Concepts of Sovereignty at the Time of First Contacts," in *The Law of Nations and the New World*, ed. L. C. Green and Olive Dickason (Edmonton: University of Alberta Press, 1989; rpt. 1993), 221, 287.

15. Tim Rowse, *After Mabo: Interpreting Native Indigenous Traditions* (Melbourne: University of Melbourne Press, 1993), 8, 21.

16. See "Roberval's Commission," January 15, 1540/1, in *A Collection of Documents Relating to Jacques Cartier and the Sieur de Roberval* (Ottawa : Public Archives of Canada, 1930), 180; my translation.

17. Humphrey Gilbert, *Discourse of a Discoverie for a New Passage to Cataia* (London, 1576), j ii recto–j ii verso.

18. Ibid., B iii verso–B iiii recto, D ii recto, F iii recto.

19. Anon., "A Discovery of Lands Beyond the Equinoctial," in *The Three Voyages of Martin Frobisher: In Search of a New Passage to Cathaia and India by the North-West, A.D. 1576–8*, ed. Richard Collinson (London: Hakluyt Society, 1867), 4. Whereas Hakluyt would look to North America, this advisor and promoter of colonization was apparently thinking about the southern end of South America.

20. Ibid., 5.

21. Ibid., 6.

22. Ibid., 7.

23. Ibid., 566.

24. "June 11, 1578. Patent granted to Sir Humphrey Gilbert by Elizabeth I," in *New American World: A Documentary History of North America to 1612*, ed. David B. Quinn, 5 vols. (New York: Arno Press 1979), III: 186.

25. Samuel Eliot Morison, *The European Discovery of America: The Northern Voyages, A.D.500–1600* (New York: Oxford University Press, 1971), 574–75.

26. On relations between France and Spain, what Philip II called "the principal thing" in 1589, see J. H. Elliott, *Europe Divided 1559–1598* (London: Fontana/Collins, 1968; rpt. Glasgow, 1974), 339–50 and for Spain's crisis in the 1590s, see J. H. Elliott, *Imperial Spain 1469–1716* (1963; Harmondsworth: Penguin, 1990), 285–300.

27. For an account of Acadia, see Marcel Trudel, *Histoire de la Nouvelle-France*, Vol. 1, *Les vaines tentatives, 1524–1603* (Montréal: Fides, 1963). My discussion of New France is indebted to W. J. Eccles, *France in America* (Vancouver: Fitzhenry & Whiteside, 1972), 12–15.

28. Marcel Trudel, *Histoire de la Nouvelle-France*, Vol. 2, *Le Comptoir, 1604–1627* (Montréal: Fides, 1966), 9–15. See Eccles, *France in America*, 14–15.

29. Marc Lescarbot, *Histoire* (1609), b iv-verso. In his address to Pierre Jeannin in the 1612 edition, Lescarbot used this language of

republicanism; see Marc Lescarbot, *Histoire de la Novvelle-France* ...
(Paris, 1612), jx.

30. Lescarbot, *Histoire* (1609), b iiij-verso.

31. Sagard, quoted in W. J. Eccles, *The Ordeal of New France* (Toronto:
Canadian Broadcasting Corp, 1967), 21–22.

32. Eccles, *France in America*, 24.

33. John Oldmixon, *The British Empire in America* (London, 1708), xxxv.

34. Peter Kalm, *The America of 1750: Peter Kalm's Travels in North
America*, rev. from the original Swedish and ed. Adolph B. Benson
(1937; 2 vols., New York: Dover Publications, 1966), II: 374–76.
Also see Martii Kerkkonnen, *Peter Kalm's North American Journey:
Its Ideological Background and Results, Studia Historica, Vol. I, Finnish
Historical Society* (Helsinki, 1959), 109–10 and Eccles, *France in
America*, 134.

35. *Rapport de L'Archiviste de la Province de Québec, 1923–1924, 58*,
quoted in Eccles, *France in America*, 127; see 126.

36. Eccles, *France in America*, 133–34, 138–39, 146–47, 172–77, 181–
82 here and above.

37. J. Gibson, "An Accurate of the British Empire in North America as
Settled by the Preliminaries in 1762," *The Gentleman's Magazine*,
Vol. 32 (London, 1762), 602–03. See also *Library of Congress
Geography and Maps of North America, 1750–1789*, 92.

38. Thomas Jefferson to John Randolph, August 25, 1775, *Thomas
Jefferson Papers Series 1, General Correspondence, 1651–1827, Library
of Congress*.

39. George Washington to Canadian Citizens, September 7, 1775, *George
Washington Papers at the Library of Congress, 1741–1799: Series 4,
General Correspondence, 1697–1799*.

40. Arthur Lee wrote to Gardoqui, Paris, October 6, 1778, *1 Sparks' Dip.
Rev. Corr., 518. The Revolutionary Diplomatic Correspondence of the
United States, Volume 2, A Century of Lawmaking for a New Nation:
U.S. Congressional Documents and Debates, 1774–1875, Library of
Congress*.

41. James Madison's Notes of Debates, March 13, 1787, *Letters of
Delegates to Congress, 1774–1789: Volume 24, November 6, 1786–
February 29, 1788, A Century of Lawmaking*, ed. Paul H. Smith
(Washington: Library of Congress, 1976)

42. George Washington to Marie Joseph Paul Yves Roch Gilbert du
Motier, Marquis de Layfayette, March 25, 1787, *The Writings of
George Washington from the Original Manuscript Sources, 1745–1799*,
ed. *John C. Fitzpatrick in The George Washington Papers at the Library
of Congress, 1741–1799*.

43. See Graeme Wynn, "On the Margins of Empire," *The Illustrated History of Canada*, ed. Craig Brown (1987; Toronto: Lester Publishing,
1991), 209–17.

44. Martin J. Griffin, "The Late Sir John Macdonald," *The Atlantic Monthly*, 68.408 (October 1891): 52.

45. William Lyon Mackenzie, *Province of Upper Canada, Assembly, Committee on Grievances, Seventh Report*, April 10, 1835, quoted in *The Colonial Century: English-Canadian Writing Before Confederation*, ed. A. J. M. Smith (1973; Toronto: Tecumseh Press Limited, 1986), 1:152.

46. Mackenzie (chairman) et al., quoted in Smith. *The Colonial Century*, 155.

47. Haliburton in Smith, *The Colonial Century*, 185.

48. Howe in Smith, *The Colonial Century*, 211. For more on wider contexts, see Jonathan Hart, *Comparing Empires: European Colonialism from Portuguese Expansion to the Spanish-American War* (New York: Palgrave Macmillan, 2003).

C H A P T E R 11

DISPLACEMENT AND ANXIETY: EMPIRE AND OPERA

Linda Hutcheon and
Michael Hutcheon

Despite Edward Said's extensive analysis of the manifestations of Orientalism in European culture, music receives little of his attention. Yet he had a strong interest in the art form and frequently used musical imagery in his critical language.[1] His formal treatment of empire and opera, for instance, was confined to a discussion of the genesis—and not the music or narrative—of Verdi's *Aida* in *Culture and Imperialism*.[2] Like him, many have written about nineteenth-century Paris as the hub of Orientalist study and even more specifically about the French Romantic taste for the exotic and the Orientalist in literature (Nerval's *Voyage en Orient* or Hugo's *Les Orientales*) and in the visual arts (the paintings of Delacroix or Ingres). Ralph Locke and Susan McClary, among others, have discussed the nature and politics of the exotic in French music in general.[3] Many have made the obvious generalizations about the link between colonialism and Orientalism, but few have tied the overt operatic explorations of imperialism directly and concretely to the historical fact that France was an active colonial power in North Africa and the Islamic Middle East in the middle and late nineteenth century.[4]

The Battle of the Nile in 1798 not only had brought to France's attention the very real risks of imperialism, but it was also a blow to their imperialist desires. Yet, it did set the stage, so to speak, for a form of aesthetic colonization through the theatrical and musical discourses of opera. And the country to be colonized in this way was India, one the French had already lost to the British—a fact that may explain why it was invested with such great imaginative desire. In her study *Widows, Pariahs, and Bayadères: India as Spectacle*, Binita Mehta argues that it is precisely because of the French loss of colonies to the British in 1763 that India "continued to hold such a sway in the imagination of French dramatists," in particular, in the nineteenth century.[5] Opera librettists were no exception.

Opera may not appear at first to be quite the same as those other Western means, explored by Said, of "dominating, restructuring, and having authority over the Orient."[6] But it is important to recall that opera was a powerful discursive practice in nineteenth-century Europe, one that created, by repetition, national stereotypes that, we argue, are used to appropriate *culturally* what France could not always conquer *militarily*. France's history of colonization was not without significant difficulties and considerable opposition at home (especially as the nineteenth century wore on). Because of the loss of both lives and money, anxiety was arguably as powerful a motivator of Orientalism as what Ali Behdad has dubbed "Orientalist desire": "the historical urge to 'capture' the Other through the official discourse that the speaking subject has at his disposal."[7] In this case, that official discourse was opera. Like advertising or commercial theater today, successful opera (always an expensive art form) has always had to target its audience carefully and it often does so not only through the spectators' desires but through their anxieties and fears as well.

With tongue firmly in cheek, Ralph Locke once described the Orientalist operatic paradigm in this way: "Young, tolerant, brave, possibly naïve, white-European tenor-hero intrudes, at risk of disloyalty to his own people and colonialist ethic, into mysterious, dark-skinned, colonized territory represented by alluring dancing girls and deeply affectionate, sensitive lyric soprano, incurring wrath of brutal, intransigent tribal chieftain (bass or bass-baritone) and blindly obedient chorus of male savages."[8] Ironic and postcolonialist as it is in its ethos and tone, this is more a description of what Orientalism *should* look like in opera than a depiction of actual works. Of the ones he lists—*La Perle du Brésil, Madama Butterfly, Samson et Dalila, L'Africaine* and *Lakmé*—none actually fits the description precisely. In fact, there are very few of these "colonial contact" operas at all;[9] instead, the real paradigmatic theme of Orientalist opera involves an overlapping of interest in the *femme fatale* and the exoticized Other. French Romantic grand opera was arguably more fascinated with depicting the female exotic Other—transferred in time, of course, to ancient eras—than it was with exploring the actual (and fraught) encounter between imperialist and colonized: Adolphe Adam's *Si j'étais roi* (1852), Charles François Gounod's *La Reine de Saba* (1862), Georges Bizet's *Les Pêcheurs de perles* (1863) and *Djamileh* (1871), Jules Massenet's *Le Roi de Lahore* (1877) and *Thaïs* (1894), Ambroise Thomas's *Le Caïd* (1894) take us to the mysterious "Orient," but without staging the actual presence of empire.[10] But the French operas that did venture into the more dangerous cross-cultural contact zones did so in most intriguing ways.

Giacomo Meyerbeer's opera *L'Africaine*, which opened in Paris in 1865, and Clément Philibert Léo Delibes's *Lakmé*, which premiered in 1883 at the Opéra-Comique, differ from the many Orientalist operas that were for the most part set in the Americas or in the Islamic Middle East and North Africa (the site of actual French colonization). Here, instead, the arena of empire is the world of Hindu India, but the imperial forces are not French at all, but rather France's imperial rival—both historical (Portugal) and contemporary (Britain). Perhaps as a post-Napoleonic response to the French debacle in Spain, the French at this time preferred to show the Portuguese on stage, as in *L'Africaine*, rather than the Spanish conquistadors;[11] but it is also the case that France had been competing with Portugal commercially almost since Vasco da Gama sailed around the Cape of Good Hope and into the Indian Ocean. By the time of *Lakmé*, the French and the British, on the other hand, had been fighting each other militarily over India and other overseas territories for more than a century. Said is no doubt right that "European intellectuals were prone to attack the abuses of rival empires, while either mitigating or excusing the practices of their own,"[12] but here something else seems to have been going on: it is as if the French were seeking ways to explore other aspects of imperialism by means of the safety afforded by distance and displacement. In other words, European nations did not define themselves only against their Oriental Other; their rivals for empire also served as defining entities. Empires too compared imperialisms.

Unlike most Orientalist operas, these two are about Indians and their Hindu religion, not about the Moslem Turks who had been so visible and audible on European operatic stages in the eighteenth century. (As the actual Ottoman threat receded from Europe, the Turks became the subject of operatic comedies, most commonly using an "abduction from the seraglio" plot, best known today in Mozart's version.) But the links between religion and imperialism are early and extensive.[13] The reasons for building an empire were not only economic, political, and military; they also included religious evangelization. The other important point about India, however, is that, while it had never been a threat to Europe, it had become a major source of intra-European rivalry.[14] Hence the displacement: once again, what France lost militarily, it could appropriate culturally.[15]

The Orientalist aspects of the music and drama of both *L'Africaine* and *Lakmé* are not hard to hear and see. Both certainly contain examples of what Locke calls "musical exoticism" in their instrument-ation, harmonies, rhythms, and melodic patterns.[16] These are most evident in *Lakmé*, where they are restricted, however, to the Hindu prayers, dances, and marketplace scenes, as if used for local color[17] or as a symbol of the conflict of cultures, to offer a more politicized read-ing. And the narratives of both, while not fitting Locke's ironic plot outline precisely, are clearly Orientalist. Despite its title, *L'Africaine* is about the encounter of the Portuguese and the Indians. Its extended genesis over a twenty-five-year period explains some of the more con-fusing aspects of its plot and setting,[18] while offering an interesting lesson in imperial thinking.

When Eugène Scribe first signed a contract with Meyerbeer in 1837, this was supposed to be an opera based on a poem about a girl, sit-ting under a tree that has a poisonous fragrance and being rescued by her lover. Not surprisingly, perhaps, given the paucity of inter-esting plot possibilities here, it soon became a historical opera set in Philip III's Spain, in which an obscure naval officer purchases a woman, Gunima (later Sélika), on the slave market and, in Act III, sails for Mexico with her. A storm drives them onto the African coast—and right into the woman's kingdom. Hence the title, *L'Africaine*. A decade or so later, when the French were actually active in both Mexico and Africa, it became an opera about Portugese exploration and was renamed *Vasco da Gama*.[19] Meyerbeer died before the opera could be staged, and the Belgian musicologist François-Joseph Fétis, who was in charge of revising it for production, changed the title back to *L'Africaine* because he decided Sélika was (or should be) the main character, despite the fact that she was not African any-more, but Indian. Leaving in the text specific and indeed pointed references to her Indian—that is, non-European and non-African—physiognomy and not excising the frequent prayers to Hindu gods, Fétis nonetheless moved the action of the last two acts to Africa, or, more precisely, Madagascar. This island historically, we should recall, had a Malayo-Polynesian and African multiethnic popula-tion with various indigenous religions (none of which was Hindu). The opera's islanders, however, remain Hindu and Indian, as in the previous version. It does not seem to matter *which* indigenous

Other the opera evokes, as long as it is sufficiently exotic and different.

The opera, as it is known today, takes considerable liberties with actual history. It tells the story of Vasco da Gama, here presented as an impetuous, defiant, not to say arrogant explorer. In this version (if not in fact), he brings home something important from Africa, following the total destruction of Bartolomeu Diaz's fleet in an unsuccessful expedition around the Cape: physical proof of the existence of unknown peoples, here in the form of two slaves he purchased on the slave market, a woman and a man who are said to be neither African nor European. We quickly learn that the woman, Sélika, is in love with Vasco—who, in turn, is in love with Inès, his childhood sweetheart. Vasco demands ships from the Royal Council, explicitly to "discover" and "conquer" the new rich lands he now knows exist (thanks to the woman's testimony). His request is refused, but what is interesting in an opera is that the Council does debate the possible economic and political benefits and dangers of such exploration for Portugal. In *Under Western Eyes: India from Milton to Macaulay*, Balachandra Rajan offers a concise version of the general economic and political context the opera too evokes: "The purpose of da Gama's voyage was to open a passage to the Orient that would destroy both the Venetian monopoly of the spice trade and the Arab monopoly of the trade routes between the East and Europe. Lisbon would become Europe's richest city, and the blow dealt to the Moslem Infidel would felicitously serve both commerce and religion."[20] Da Gama's story was most famously told in Luis Vaz de Camões's *Os Lusiadas* (1572). Even if Paris audiences at the time might not have known this text,[21] Meyerbeer himself had read it,[22] though he appears to have ignored many of the actual historical details in the interests of his more flamboyant operatic narrative.

To make a long and complex story a bit shorter if not much less complex, the opera's Vasco eventually does get his ship and does make it around the Cape (as he did historically in 1497), but he and his compatriots—including Inès—are wrecked on an island and captured by Indians, who are shown singing praise to Brahma. Sélika turns out to be their queen and uses her power to save Vasco's life by claiming he is her husband. Although their "marriage" is consecrated in a Hindu ceremony, Sélika then allows Vasco to leave with Inès, his European beloved. For a brief moment—provoked by a sacred potion and a belated sense of duty—Vasco appears to return the queen's love at last, but then he takes advantage of her offer and leaves. Accompanied by "mysterious, ethereal" music,[23] Sélika retires to a grove of manchineel trees, a plant whose perfume, if inhaled, is here said to be fatal. (It only grows in the Caribbean, just to confuse realists even further.) There she dies, with Nélusko, the faithful but vengeful man who had been enslaved with her and who loved her. He is also the one whose deliberate treachery (or righteous revenge) had caused the shipwreck and ruin of the "Christians," as he always pointedly called them.

Lakmé is set in 1883, the time of its performance, in British-occupied India.[24] Its tale of intercultural love (requited, this time) is not historical, but current. Gérald, a young British army officer engaged to be married to the governor's daughter, Miss Ellen, falls in love with Lakmé, the daughter of a Hindu priest who has sworn vengeance for the desecration of the sacred grounds where he and his daughter live and where the couple meet. The entire narrative is framed by the anger of this Brahmin, Nilakantha, against the "hateful conquerors." But the English people on stage (who have indeed ventured heedlessly into the sacred grounds) seem more concerned with discussing the difference between the kinds of love felt by Indian and English women than in subjugating a religion and a race. But always in the background is the threat of Indian insurrection; the British soldiers are set to leave to quell a rebellion.

The next act offers an exotic Hindu festival—exotic, that is, for the British on stage and for the French in the audience. Today it is tempting to read this as a site of assertion of Indian cultural identity and survival, but at the time, the staging of exoticism was likely its main function. In the confusion of the festival, Nilakantha stabs Gérald and leaves him for dead. Lakmé saves him, taking him to a secret place in the forest and healing his wound. As the two lovers fantasize about a secret life alone and are about to consecrate their devotion with water from a holy spring, Gérald hesitates, hearing military music. When Lakmé can't get his attention, she realizes that he will indeed rejoin his regiment and not stay with her. She smiles and takes a leaf from the datura tree and chews it. Earlier in the opera this plant was said to be fatal in India, though not in England. As Gérald realizes, with despair, what she has done, she thanks him for his tender words, for the joys she could never have known "as a Hindu," and then offers herself to her father in expiation for their transgressive love; she dies ecstatically, bound to her lover at least in death.

It is striking that both colonial encounters end in the suicide of the Indian woman, who through death remains faithful to her religion and society, though she does die for her ill-fated love. In both, of course, the European man's loyalty is to his people, and to his own ego, perhaps. Yet both women come to stand for their nations in at least one way: the feminizing of India has a long and well-documented history, from Virgil to the present, and with this intersection of gender and empire, as Rajan memorably puts it, "An ambivalent construction of the Orient becomes necessary, in which Western morality can denounce what Western cupidity continues to desire."[25]

While Lakmé fits the description of the "deeply affectionate, sensitive lyric soprano" from Locke's ironic plot outline, Sélika does not. Like many other exotic women in nineteenth-century French opera, from Bizet's Carmen to Saint-Saens's Dalila, Sélika is a mezzo-soprano whose low voice range suggests worldliness, independence, and, frankly, sensuality. Yet both Indian women are also infantalized by the men they love: Gérald calls Lakmé a child and believes his fellow officer when he assures him that he can leave the Hindu priestess with impunity, since "Ces enfants-là ne savent pas souffrir" (These children don't know how to suffer). In the discourse of French imperialism, "peuples enfants" was a common positive term for the colonized—seen as simple, capricious but capable of devotion and loyalty.[26]

It is not hard to imagine how a twenty-first-century audience, imbued with postcolonial sympathies, might respond to these operas. But what about the original spectators? What precisely was going on in France when these operas premiered that would help explain how an audience of the time would have reacted to these stories and this kind of language, for both operas were immense successes on stage?[27] When L'Africaine opened in 1865, the Second Empire was managing an aggressive but not terribly well-conceived policy of colonial expansion as a "maritime empire,"[28] that is, wanting not to subjugate the colonies, but to operate with minimal cost and maximal benefit. Until then, as Said explains, "empire had a less secure identity and presence in French culture" than in English culture.[29] But the real ideological purpose of expansion was to unite a divided people at home in France through the glue of patriotic pride.[30] North Africa and the Middle East were the sites of action, but Africa and, especially, Madagascar were seen as the first steps to India and the recovery of trade there.[31] But the actual French experience of colonialization thus far had never matched the promises of glories and riches that L'Africaine's Vasco da Gama promises the Portuguese court. This financial disappointment may explain France's move to cultural rather than military or economic imperialism: not only these operas' creators, but (as Said and Girardet explore at length) French geographers, journalists, teachers, and writers actively went about constructing a discourse of colonization. Why? Because the real motive for empire after Napoleon was not commerce or conquest, but rather a matter of restoring prestige.

The purpose of the colonies "was partly to dispute Britain's claim to be mistress of the seas and partly to make the whole world conscious of the presence, the grandeur and the radiance of France"[32]—a message that it clearly wanted heard at home too.

French nationalism had to be reasserted again after the humiliating defeat of the French in the Franco-Prussian War in 1871. The renewed fervor for expansion and the belief in the "mission civilisatrice" of France abroad were the Third Republic's forms of national ego-compensation, for sure, but both were also directly connected to the presence of an historical rival. As Said puts it: "France seemed literally haunted by Britain, anxious in all things connected to the Orient to catch up with and emulate the British."[33] Raoul Girardet argues that it is in the 1870s (in other words, in the years leading up to *Lakmé*) that France develops a moral, economic, and political doctrine and discourse of imperialism.[34] This is in spite of (or because of?) considerable anticolonial feelings in France, especially among economists (who felt others—like the British—benefited, while France paid the bills). Perhaps by contemplating the difficult situation of the imperial British in India, French audiences could consider, with greater distance, the tensions involved in their own colonial efforts somewhat more easily. In other words, the eager Paris reception of this opera may have "reflected some (mostly unspoken) discomfort with the costs and risks of French colonizings, notably in Algeria."[35] If so, what other anxieties might also be displaced in this shifting of imperial focus? After all, in imperial historian John MacKenzie's words, "Empire was traumatic as well as triumphal, as productive of apprehension as much as comprehension, fear as well as fantasy."[36]

Some of the more obvious risks and dangers encountered by imperialists are represented "up-front", so to speak, in the operas' dramatic plots: for instance, the economic and human loss when European ships are wrecked on foreign reefs or captured by hostile indigenous peoples. The Indians who board the Portuguese ships in *L'Africaine* are said to be dangerous and death-dealing; Nélusko, the ex-slave who has brought the Europeans to their end by deception, is portrayed as fiercely proud and fiercely vengeful, much in keeping with versions of this stereotype in the literature of the time. Nelikantha, the intransigent Hindu priest in *Lakmé*, is very much of the same type.

Both men, significantly, are Hindus and pray to their gods often, explicitly for revenge against the Europeans. In these operas, it is the men who act (violently) to protect their religion, but it is the women who articulate the immensity of the religious and cultural differences. Sélika releases Vasco from his marriage vows because they were sworn to her god, not his; Lakmé reminds her British lover that his heaven is not hers, that the god who protects her is not the one he knows ("Mon ciel n'est pas le tien. Le Dieu qui me protège/N'est pas celui que tu connais"). This divide would have resonated for the Parisian audience of the time: in a Europe whose missionaries had made their way into all parts of the known world, religious differences were more than cultural differences. (In neither opera, however, is *language* a cultural issue: the Portuguese, English and Indians all speak that universal diplomatic language—French.)

The setting in the tropics—either in Madagascar or in India itself—is central to both operas, and in both it is constructed as dangerous. French audiences of this time would have associated the colonies not only with the exotic and opulent Orient, but also with disease and the loss of European lives: from yellow fever in Saint Domingue, plague in Napoleon's Syrian campaign, malaria and cholera in Vietnam. It was said that the cemeteries were "the only colonies that continually prosper[ed] in Algeria."[37] When cholera arrived in Europe in the 1830s, military medical personnel recognized it, for they had already treated it earlier in India (where it was endemic). This history helped alter Europeans' associations with India from fantasy and exoticism to danger and disease.[38] While no one dies of disease in these works, the operatic language of love—a conventionalized language of fevers and intoxication—takes on a different set of connotations (dangerous ones) in the tropical context.

As the cultural cliché would have it, the hot sun of this part of the world symbolically inflames the passions. But it also appears to intensify both the beauty and the danger of India's women and its flora. Botanical inquiry was very much a part of European exploration, and so this linking of plants and people is not accidental. These Indian women cause men to lose their senses, to abandon reason for the intoxication of love. But in these operas Indian women also commit suicide using local flora, the manchineel tree whose perfume kills and the "*datura stramonium*," said to be very inoffensive in England, but "under this beautiful Indian sky" ("sous ce beau ciel indien") fatal to ingest. (Perhaps the datura is intended as a metaphor for the British themselves: harmless at home, dangerous in India.) Both Sélika and Lakmé are Hindu women who kill themselves for the love of a European man. In Binita Mehta's terms, "the sacrifice of the (subject) woman is the formulation upon which the colonial (male) ideology of temptation and duty are resolved."[39] But this does not account for the fact that the women appear to die ecstatic, as if in unification with the universal soul or Brahman. Therefore, neither ending is set up to be conventionally tragic, in operatic terms: the men live on (with their European beloveds) and, although the Indian women die, they do so within a culture and religion that are explicitly said to valorize their sacrifice. Is this the consoling, if evasive, closure offered Parisian audiences? Does the need to translate Hindu theology into recognizably Christian terms explain the imagery used to describe their particular visions of death: as ascension into heaven accompanied by a heavenly chorus? Paris audiences could feel sympathy for the abandoned women and yet absolve the departing European men, off to do their imperial duty.

In other words, are these operas about the colonial encounter—safely displaced to rival empires as they are—incredibly canny in how they appealed to their audiences? The anti-expansionist discourses of the time spoke of the waste of French gold and blood ("L'or et le sang de France").[40] Were these operas, with their representation of the dangers faced by imperial forces, astute responses to precisely these objections? The immense success of both on stage would suggest that this could be the case, for they fed at once into anticolonial anxieties (once again, safely displaced) and into the continuing colonizing urge, the "mission civilisatrice."

Like Verdi's *Aida*, these can actually be read as anticolonialist operas in which the custodians of the values of the colonized voice their opposition to empire. When Vasco da Gama asks (but only after drinking a sacred potion) how he could have missed the fact that Sélika loved him, she offers him a succinct and accurate answer: "Le mépris," his imperial scorn. The frame of *Lakmé*, similarly, is one of the British willful destruction of a religion and a culture. The victimized and colonized in both works are very aware of their Otherness: when Sélika first sees her Portuguese rival, Inès, she comments on how white she is ("Qu'elle est blanche!"). Audiences at the time may well have seen her love for Vasco as a sign of her taste and sense of nobility, as Herbert Lindenberger has argued.[41] But they might also have seen her death as religiously acceptable or as culturally explicable, and therefore not conventionally tragic.

This convenient consolation, combined with the distancing allowed by displacement to rival empires (British and Portuguese), could explain not only the success of these operas in the nineteenth century, but their relative invisibility today.[42] The postcolonial perspective is different—not least in its knowledge of the consequences of exploitation—from that of a France at the moment in history when it had to redefine its sense of nationhood and national pride, and had chosen to do so in part by expanding its empire. And, however odd it may seem today, opera turns out to be one of the many discourses that allowed France to explain and perhaps even excuse the risks and costs of such a policy, allowing doubt to sit alongside glorification. Today audiences are much more likely to read Vasco da Gama, in his desire for immortality above all, as a kind of "organization man" for empire, rather than as the heroic explorer Scribe and Meyerbeer meant him to be. But the precise historical moment and its complexities of response and intricacies of judgment demand a reconsideration of this all too easy response.

NOTES

This essay is dedicated to Balachandra Rajan, who first started us thinking about operatic India and comparing imperialisms. We'd also like to thank Eric Jennings for keeping our colonial history in order.

1. See Pegram Harrison, "Music and Imperialism," *Repercussions* 4.1 (1995): 53–84.
2. Edward W. Said, *Culture and Imperialism* (New York: Knopf, 1993), 111–32.
3. See Ralph P. Locke, "Exoticism and Orientalism in Music: Problems for the Worldly Critic," *Edward Said and the Work of the Critic: Speaking Truth to Power*, ed. Paul Bové (Durham, N.C.: Duke University Press, 2000), 257–81; Susan McClary, *Feminine Endings: Music, Gender and Sexuality* (Minneapolis: University of Minnesota Press, 1991); Danièle Pistone, "Les conditions historiques de l'exotisme musical français," *Revue internationale de musique française* 6 (1981): 14–15 especially, on Romanticism and its relation to musical exoticism in general.
4. A historian of imperialism does note that the musical exoticism of French operas might be seen "as the cultural analogue of developing French political power in North Africa." See John M. MacKenzie, *Orientalism: History, Theory, and the Arts* (Manchester: University of Manchester Press, 1995), 150. Albert Gier also argues a generalized colonial ideology at work in the music of the time. See his "*L'Africaine* und die Ideologie des Kolonialismus," *Meyerbeer und das europäische Musiktheater*, ed. Sieghart Döhring and Arnold Jacobshagen (Laaber: Laaber Verlag, 1998), 134–47.
5. (Lewisberg: Bucknell University Press, 2002), 14. Her argument differs from the one we develop here because she sees the absence of French power in India as allowing writers to "freely exercise their imagination and create an India based on a remembered reality, or on a reality that had perhaps never really existed at all" (20). We see the dynamics of appropriation in more fraught terms, as is clear shortly.

6. Edward W. Said, *Orientalism* (New York: Vintage, 1978), 3.

7. Ali Behdad, "Orientalist Desire, Desire of the Orient," *French Forum* 15 (1990): 39.

8. Ralph P. Locke, "Constructing the Oriental 'Other': Saint-Saëns's *Samson et Dalila*," *Cambridge Opera Journal* 3.3 (1991): 263.

9. In "The Soldier and the Exotic: Operatic Variations on a Theme of Racial Encounter," *Opera Quarterly* 10.2 (1993–94): 33–56, James Parakilas argues for a distinction between "Age of Discovery" operas (like *L'Africaine*) and "Soldier and the Exotic" operas (as in *Lakmé*). But *L'Africaine* does not really fit in his first category—in which he claims that there is allegedly no difference of an "inalienable nature" between explorer and exotic. Instead, in the opera, both race and religion actually figure as significant dividing differences.

10. See János Kárpáti, "Non-European Influences on Occidental Music (A Historical Survey)," *The World of Music* 22.2 (1980): 25.

11. James Parakilas, "How Spain Got a Soul," in *The Exotic in Western Music*, ed. Jonathan Bellman (Boston: Northeastern University Press, 1998), 137–93.

12. Said, *Culture*, 241.

13. See Anthony Pagden, *Peoples and Empires* (New York: Modern Library, 2001), 63–65.

14. Said, *Orientalism*, 75. For more on the French/British imperial competition, see Christopher M. Andrew and A. S. Kanya-Forstner, *The Climax of French Imperial Expansion, 1914–1924* (Stanford: Stanford University Press, 1981); H. C. Darby, "The Anglo-French Struggle, 1689–1789," in *A Short History of France: From Early Times to 1972*, ed. Hampden J. Jackson, second ed. (Cambridge: Cambridge University Press, 1974), 92–95 especially; Mehta, *Widows*, 16–19.

15. For a general look at operas about India, see Robert J. Del Bontà, "Song of India," *Opera Quarterly* 2.1 (1984): 5–14; Mehta, *Widows*, 53–54. On the French lack of knowledge of and interest in Indian music, see Jann Pasler, "India and its Music in the French Imagination before 1913," *Journal of the Indian Musicological Society* 27 (1996): 27–51. On Heidi Holder's work on the representation of India on the British stage in the same period (especially in melodramas, operas, and spectacles), see MacKenzie, *Orientialism*, 186–96.

16. For more details on techniques and modes of musical Orientalism, see Locke, "Exoticism," 276; Carl Dahlhaus, *Nineteenth-Century Music*, trans. J. Bradford Robinson (Berkeley: University of California Press, 1989), 306; McClary, *Feminine Endings*, 53; MacKenzie, *Orientalism*, 141–46; Ramón Pelinski, "Orientalische Kolorit in der Musik des 19. Jahrhunderts," *Weltkulturen und moderne Kunst* (Munich: Bruckmann, 1972), 153.

17. Hugh Macdonald, "*Lakmé*," in *The New Grove Dictionary of Opera*, ed. Stanley Sadie (London: Macmillan, 1992), 2:1083.

18. See Steven Huebner, "*L'Africaine*," in Sadie, *New Grove*, 1:31–33; John Roberts, "The Genesis of Meyerbeer's *L'Africaine*," Ph.D. dissertation, University of California, 1977; Robert I. Letellier, "History, Myth and Music on a Theme of Exploration: Some Reflections on the Musico-Dramatic Language of *L'Africaine*," in Döhring and Jacobshagen, *Meyerbeer*, 188–89; Heinz Becker, *Meyerbeer* (Hamburg: Rowohlt, 1980), 122–30; Reiner Zimmermann, *Giacomo Meyerbeer: Eine Biographie nach Dokumenten* (Berlin: Parthas, 1998), 312–19; Christhard Frese, *Dramaturgie der grossen Opern Giacomo Meyerbeers* (Berlin: Robert Lienau, 1970), 218–67.

19. Another possible influence on the change to a Portuguese setting is the German success in 1823 of Louis Spohr's opera *Jessonda*, based on a French eighteenth-century play, *La veuve de Malabar*, by A. M. Lemierre. Set in Goa in the early sixteenth century, the opera is about the encounter of Brahmins and the Portuguese army under General Tristan d'Acunha—and about the love of the general and Jessonda, the widow of the rajah. Gier argues that a black heroine would not have been an ideal of beauty for Meyerbeer's audience and that this is why he changed her to an Indian/Aryan ("*L'Africaine*," 137). For theories about the impact of other books Meyerbeer was reading at the time, see Zimmermann, *Giacomo Meyerbeer*, 313.

20. Balachandra Rajan, *Under Western Eyes: India from Milton to Macaulay* (Durham, N.C.: Duke University Press, 1999), 35–36.

21. Gier, "*L'Africaine*," 138.

22. Letellier, "History," 155.

23. Ibid., 155.

24. The source usually claimed for the story is *Le mariage de Loti* by Pierre Loti, but too many important details differ: its setting is Tahiti; its romance is not only requited, but set up by the queen and most definitely consummated; the death of the abandoned young woman is from consumption. Both do have English protagonists, but that seems a slim reason for claiming this as a source.

25. Rajan, *Under Western Eyes*, 43.

26. Raoul Girardet, *L'idée coloniale en France de 1871 à 1962* (Paris: La Table Ronde, 1972), 91.

27. On the success of the Meyerbeer opera, see Sergio Segalini, *Diable ou prophète: Meyerbeer* (Paris: Beba, 1985), 111; Henri DeCurzon, *Meyerbeer* (Paris: Librairie Renouard, 1970), 87. For Delibes's opera's success, see Coquis, *Léo Delibes*, 114 and 126–27; Henri DeCurzon, *Léo Delibes: sa vie et ses oeuvres* (Paris: Legouix, 1926), 197.

28. Pagden, *Peoples*, 88.

29. Said, *Culture*, 63.

30. Frederick Quinn, *The French Oversees Empire* (Westport and London: Praeger, 2000), 109; Pagden, *Peoples*, 136–37.

31. Henri Froidevaux, "Du XVIe siècle à 1720," in *Histoire des colonies françaises et de l'expansion de la France dans le monde*, Vol. 5, *L'Inde*, ed. Gabriel Hanotaux and Alfred Martineau (Paris: Société de l'histoire nationale; Librairie Plon, 1932), 8.

32. Henri Brunschwig, *French Colonialism 1871–1914: Myths and Realities*, trans. William Glanville Brown (London: Pall Mall Press, 1964), 18.

33. Said, *Orientalism*, 218.

34. Girardet, *L'idée*, 39: 8–9.

35. Locke, "Exoticism," 279.

36. MacKenzie, *Orientalism*, 12.

37. Quinn, *The French*, 7.

38. See Alan Bewell, *Romanticism and Colonial Disease* (Baltimore: Johns Hopkins University Press, 1999), 242–76.

39. Mehta, *Widows*, 52.

40. Girardet, *L'idée*, 60.

41. Lindenberger, *Opera in History: From Monteverdi to Cage* (Stanford: Stanford University Press, 1998), 184.

42. For an example, see Martin Cooper's review of the 1979 Covent Garden revival, " 'L'Africaine' Revived and Re-Assessed," *Opera* 30 (1979): 14–17. The change in ideology may also explain why Daniel-François-Esprit Auber's big success of 1868, *Le premier jour de bonheur* is no longer part of the repertoire. The story takes place during the British siege of the French holding called Pondicherry, in India. However, somehow, despite the obvious obstacles, a French officer and the daughter of the British governor of Madras end up living happily ever after. Indian colonial politics enter the story in the form of the temple priestesses who are imprisoned in the temple by French troops and released by the officer.

PART V

GERMAN IMPERIAL PHILOSOPHIES AND PRACTICES

Germany's "Orient": Discursive Alliances of the Philosopher, Historian, and Fiction Writer

Kamakshi P. Murti

In his incisive work *La Renaissance Orientale* Raymond Schwab presents us with a view of Orient and Occident not as mere bipolar opposites caught up in an embittered polemics, but rather as productively entangled in a web of multiple tensions. As the late Edward Said remarks in his foreword to the English translation of Schwab's work, "Dualities, opposition, polarities—as between Orient and Occident, one writer and another, one time and another—are converted in his writing into lines that criss-cross, it is true, but that also draw a vast human portrait."[1] Schwab's analysis reveals the rich intertextuality of English, French, and German writings about the Orient:

> ... while England was the native land of Indic studies, the native land of the Indic Renaissance was Germany [...]. During the 1790s the impact of oriental studies in Germany was like a rapid-fire series of explosions. [...] The publications of the Indic scholars at Calcutta ignited a kind of fervid intensity in certain young Germans. [...] And among the great innovators of the new ideas that were to become Romanticism, a certain Herder passed the word to a certain Friedrich Schlegel.[2]

This "certain Friedrich Schlegel"—aesthetician, literary critic, poet, and publisher—had high expectations that India would provide him with the ultimate truth about his own historical origins. According to Sheldon Pollock, Schlegel's encounter in Paris (1802–04) with Alexander Hamilton was "[o]ne of the critical moments in the academization of Sanskrit studies."[3] Schlegel learned Sanskrit from Hamilton who, marooned in Paris during the Napoleonic wars, was spending his considerable leisure time in cataloguing the "Oriental" contents of the Bibliothèque Nationale. He was later to become a professor of Sanskrit at Haileybury College where East India operatives were trained with Malthus as a lecturer and James Mill's *History of British India* was a prescribed book. Schlegel is the classical representative of—to use a term coined by Pollock—"romanticism"—*Wissenschaft* [romanticism-science]" within the context of the German Romantic's search for self-definition. Schwab observes that "Sanskrit was the providential answer—suddenly provided by luck on the part of the searchers—to the German Romantics' long appeals for the light of the Orient. ... Through Sanskrit came the material destined to fill in the preliminary outlines of the philosophy of history."[4] Going back to roots hitherto unknown, to original sources of knowledge, an "Urwelt," Europe would transform itself and be rejuvenated.

How did the German discourse differ, if at all, from that of Britain, France, and other European colonizers? Is there any reason to believe that German participation could in fact be perceived as collusion with the British imperialist administration inasmuch as it provided the latter with a justification for existing colonial rule and anticipated colonial activity? The exclusion of Germany in debates about Orientalism as an integral part of colonialist aggrandizement needs to be addressed. I propose that German Orientalism shared intellectual authority with Anglo-French and later American Orientalism, as Said reminds us.[5] Suzanne Zantop contends:

> German colonial fantasies were different even when they imitated or rewrote those of other European nations. By virtue of existing in the "pure" realm of the imagination, "untainted" by praxis, German fantasies were not only differently motivated, but had a different function: to serve not so much as ideological smokescreen or cover-up for colonial atrocities or transgressive desires, but as *Handlungsersatz*, as substitute for the real thing, as imaginary testing ground for colonial action.[6]

It is true that Germany did not act as colonizer until very late in the nineteenth century. However, German fantasies were not a mere

Handlungsersatz. Within the historically specific framework of nineteenth-century territorial aggrandizement imagination was an integral part of imperialism. Hence a divide between thought and action, as Zantop calls them, is purely artificial and detracts from the actual issue. As Zantop herself notes, the "ubiquity and interchangeability [of colonialism and imperialism], their common basis in sexuality, in a universe experienced and represented as gendered, divided, and potentially violent, blurs the distinctions."[7] The fact that Britain and France beat Germany in the scramble for India, forcing the latter to resort to other strategies of domination, has not yet been accepted widely, even among scholars. The general belief is that Germany was solely interested in the originary connections to India. Even a scholar of Pollock's stature seems to echo this general belief:

> In the case of the Germans who continued, however subliminally, to hold the nineteenth-century conviction that the origin of European civilization was to be found in India (or at least that India constituted a genetically related sibling), and who at the same time had *none of the requisite political needs*, Orientalism as an ideological formation on the model of Said simply could not arise.[8] (Emphasis added)

This essay argues that although German imperialism cannot be said to have overtly entertained ambitions of territorial aggrandizement, the Germans contributed to an emerging Orientalist discourse about the "other." Comparative studies were in their infancy at that time and provided the means to dichotomize and create hierarchies of knowledge and power. There was a renewed opportunity for Germany to lead the way to new power and knowledge through Sanskrit studies. The Germans would acquire this ancient treasure/wisdom and make it an integral part of European knowledge. In fact, Germany would be a focal point of Europe, radiating its newly found wisdom from the Orient to other European nations, becoming "der Orient Europas," As the Orient of Europe, Germany would speak for the Orient most effectively, a gesture that has continued into the early twenty-first century.

When Schlegel began his studies of Sanskrit in Paris, he sought the origin of his nation's history through language. As Gary Handwerk mentions, "[h]is direct experiences with French culture were fundamental, for instance, in shaping his political and cultural conceptions of Germany as a nation."[9] For him, every word revealed the history of its people. The root of a word was equivalent to the root of a concept. Consequently, he believed in the possibility of constructing entire family trees of genetically related languages, similar to those in comparative anatomical studies. This led him to assume that such structural parallels could not be merely coincidental—they pointed to a common origin.

In the preface to *Über die Sprache und Weisheit der Indier*, Schlegel discusses the reasons underlying the composition of this text. He wishes to acquaint his people with "the Asian spirit," signifying that there is a singular immutable Asian spirit, rather than a multitude of nations, belief systems, and languages that would belie such an attempt at homogeneity:

> If only the study of India were to find builders and patrons similar to those who appeared suddenly in Italy and Germany in the fifteenth and sixteenth centuries for the study of Greek and who achieved greatness in the shortest time; since the form of all sciences, one can even say of the whole world, has been transformed and rejuvenated by the reawakened knowledge of the classical age, we can dare to hope for the same effect from the study of India, if only it were attacked with the same vigor and introduced into the sphere of European knowledge.[10]

Returning to an "Urwelt," Europe would be reborn. After all, Germany and Italy had initiated a similar transformation in the fifteenth and sixteenth centuries through Hellenistic studies. Schwab remarks that Schlegel made India "into the cradle of all primitive purity, especially religious purity, and at the same reanimated the idea of relationship between Asia and Germany."[11] This remark is typical of what Said calls "[T]he avoidance of ethno- and anthropocentric attitudes" that "dictates an interest in Oriental literature for its own sake," an attitude that Said finds sympathetic.[12] However, it obfuscates rather than clarifies the nature of this "relationship" as a hierarchy, where "primitive purity" connoted an origin, a prehistory.

In his judicious reading of Schlegel's *Über die Sprache und Weisheit der Indier*, Handwerk states:

> . . . this idea of an originary revelation does not really provide a simple or inevitable model of historical decline and fall. For there is a potential continuity among historical moments of revelatory insight that makes it possible for subsequent revelations (the appearance of Christ, for instance) to restore the integrity of the original vision. Indeed, the force behind Schlegel's effort at recovering the Indian past was his implicit belief that such revelations can be sparked by an immersion in those earlier breakthrough moments.[13]

Handwerk mentions Said's sharp criticism of Schlegel's functionalist perspective. But, he adds, "... it is not immediately clear that some sort of study ostensibly for its own sake would have been a more desirable alternative, or that study of the other for the sake of that other would have implied less pretension."[14] I am not sure, however, that the alternative to a functionalist perspective is "some sort of study ostensibly for its own sake." My own postcolonial reading of Schlegel's text does not see as viable alternatives either a "study ... for its own sake" or a "study of the other for the sake of that other." It would rather be a study that, although differentiating self and the other, treats both as viable intellectual entities engaged in a new-historical debate. In Schlegel's text, India as a dialogic force is absent. By selecting an India that is blatantly ahistorical or at any rate rooted in an immutably ancient past, Schlegel ignores a "desirable altern-ative." Although Schlegel describes his key ideas as "the foundation of the Indian constitution and legislation, one could say of Indian life, and just as unmistakably the fundamental thread uniting Indian legend and mythology, their ruling spirit,"[15] the words "Indian" and "Indian life" belong to a static past, not a present that is dynamic-ally comprehending, developing, and changing these very same ideas. Ironically Schlegel mentions "Indian legend and mythology" in the same sentence, for it is precisely the legendary and mythological that he appropriates for his own needs. Handwerk might argue that this is acceptable. However, Schlegel is not working in a vacuum. The ambi-guity of the word "impact" in Handwerk's argument that "[M]uch depends upon the specific dynamics that a writer like Schlegel saw gov-erning the potential impact of Asia upon Europe" parallels the more deliberate ambiguity of words like "ancient," "pure," "childlike," or "original" used for the purposes of imperialism. Handwerk might wish to vindicate Schlegel from the accusation of imperialism, when he says:

It is clear, for instance, that [Schlegel's] picture of an exception-ally enlightened, historically ancient Indian culture undercuts the Enlightenment or Romantic myths of primitivism. These ancestors may clearly have been noble, but were not in any sense pre-civilized. Schlegel's 1805–06 lectures on universal history ... insist upon the highly developed nature of Indian civilization and its priority in this sphere over the West, along with his insistence that historical devel-opment must be measured in moral terms (where ancient India ranks highly) rather than in technological terms (where it would not) undercut any simplistic, historicist claims of European superiority ... He reserves for India an absolutely crucial role in disseminating to the rest of the world the "wisdom" that he evokes in his title. "[Indian philosophy] is the first system that steps into the place of truth."[16]

Schlegel and the philosopher, Georg Wilhelm Friedrich Hegel, expanding on Johann Gottfried Herder's understanding of India as the cradle of civilization, see India, however, as the original home of their own language and ethnic group. As Ronald Inden suggests, they are perhaps the first to make "sharp and essential distinctions between the different parts of Asia."[17] Schlegel tries to develop a scientific method for penetrating the mists of prehistory and discovering comparative linguistics. His historico-philosophical concept recognizes three stages in mankind's progression from an original unity via an interim period of chaos and fragmentation to a new unity and harmony for which one must strive. He perceives the first stage in India and the European Middle Ages, seeing the Indians as "refugees from paradise."[18] Contemporaneous India shows only "traces" of an original revelation in religion and poesy in its oldest writings. Sanskrit is not the language of the childhood of mankind but merely the original language of a branch of "mankind" that arose somewhere in Asia and spread over parts of Asia and the whole of Europe.

> [I]f we are to assume, therefore, that they were led northwards not merely on account of the outward pressure of necessity, but because of some wonderful conception of the high worth and splendor of the North, traces of which we find everywhere in the Indian legends, then the path of the Germanic tribes from Turkhind along the Gihon up to the north side of the Caspian Sea and the Caucasus would be easy to prove; but whether from this point on they sought out the mountains and settled there or whether they followed the great rivers and again sought the same way of life on the banks of the Nile and the Euphrates, as the old Asiatic nations had done on the banks of the Ganges; it is not the place here to further investigate this very vital question pertaining to the *history of our fatherland*.[19] (Emphasis added)

He focuses on the "fatherland," on this branch of mankind currently located in Western Europe and fulfilling its glorious destiny. The Northern Aryans were, by his definition, a homogeneous group until they split into the Germanic races who retained the physical and intellectual vigor of their Aryan ancestors, and the ancient Indians, who remained on the subcontinent and degenerated into passivity and apathy.

In *Deutsches Museum* Schlegel compares Islam with Christianity, initially mentioning their commonalities: "Christianity came into being in the Orient as did Mohammedanism, but it has expressed its most essential and outstanding effects wholly in the Occident, as well as easily finding a home in the Orient and has maintained itself there in part to this day, although not as an energetic and evolving principle."[20] Christianity has developed on Occidental soil, whereas any of its remnants in the Orient has degenerated into apathy. The simplicity characteristic of Christianity is lost in the hands of the Orientals who burden it with "the wildest rampant offshoots." The Occident, however, comprehends and interprets with sobriety, thus developing an effectiveness that permeates more deeply: "As proof one can also state that Christianity in its simple form was not sufficient for the needs of its Oriental followers, that it led to the wildest rampant offshoots there in the acts of penance of the Egyptian Anchorites and the teachings of the Gnosticians, and since then it sank into ignominy."[21] Moreover, although both Christianity and Islam are monotheistic, the Mohammedan God lacks his Christian counterpart's spirituality.

Schlegel never doubts the supremacy of Christianity:

One finds … individual traces of divine truth everywhere, especially in the oldest Oriental systems; but it is doubtful that anybody will find the context of the whole and the clear separation of the error mixed therein, unless it is through Christianity which is alone capable of providing the information about truth and realization that is higher than all knowledge of and reference to reason.[22]

Handwerk argues that Schlegel's *Über die Sprache und Weisheit der Indier* displaces both the Greek and the Christian traditions from their originary status.[23] However, the West claims the historically progressive continuity emanating from the Greek, Christian, and Indian traditions, denying it to the Indian. Handwerk's praise of Schlegel's cross-fertilization mistakenly attributes an element of intercultural exchange to his discourse.

In the fifth lecture, published in 1814–15 in *Geschichte der alten und neuen Literatur* (History of Old and New Literature), Schlegel says of the British colonizers in India:

The domination of the English in India is based solely on their ability to rule over the Indians only in accordance with the latter's habits, customs, and native laws. By doing this they have become … the benefactors of the Indians … in that they freed these same people from the persecution of the intolerant Mohammedans. The more extensive the rule of the English, the greater the necessity on the part of the government there

to protect Indian customs seems to have become, particularly because
a slight offence against Indian customs by the army … caused a terrible
mutiny to break out amongst them. Thus one can comprehend how the
protection "of the old customs of the country" can be extended to a
reprehensible toleration of those burnings and sacrificial killings.[24]

This is not an expression of humanitarian concern for and identification with what the British were undergoing. Theirs was a mounting
frustration at having to infiltrate the Indian psyche and simplify the
difficult job of administering a recalcitrant people.

Schlegel's unqualified praise for British wisdom in allowing the colonized people their customs serves a similar purpose. He also believes
in an "oriental mind-set" that can be used in a comparative analysis
of mythologies. He adopts not a synchronic, but rather a diachronic
approach, within a linear theory of historical progression. Consequently the Oriental mind-set depicts an earlier stage in the development of "man" (European) that is an interesting historical artifact, but
an artifact nonetheless. In his discussion of astrology and "wild nature
worship" Schlegel mentions what continues to be part of popular
Western ideas about Hinduism, that is the notion of fatalism: "Fatalism has developed to an artificially very widespread system among the
Oriental peoples."[25] The Oriental mind *is* fatalistic, *is* superstitious.
He ends the chapter with a strong criticism of the worship of Shiva
and Durga as bacchanalian, providing us with yet another Orientalist
strategy, that of seeing in "the Orient" all kinds of excesses, especially
sexual:

> What makes this nature service and materialism so dreadful and still
> differentiates it from the mere sensuality of some peoples who are in a
> state of simple wildness, might be that the idea of the eternal is added
> and woven into it which points back to a better origin; for it is precisely
> the highest and most noble that becomes a dreadful misshapen figure
> when it is unkempt and decadent.[26]

This then is the Orient that emerges from Schlegel's writings: fatalistic, apathetic, passive, excessive (with insatiable sexual appetites that
are licentious to the European and therefore all the more titillating),
without structure, yet perversely contained within a rigid system that
does not allow for progress.[27]

"Sensuality, promise, terror, sublimity, idyllic pleasure, intense
energy: the Orient as a figure in the pre-Romantic, pre-technical
Orientalist imagination of late eighteenth-century Europe was really

a chameleon-like quality called (adjectivally) 'Oriental,' " says Said of the Orientalist's imagined Orient.[28] Novalis (the pseudonym adopted by Friedrich von Hardenberg), another Romanticist, constructs such an Orient in his novel fragment *Heinrich von Ofterdingen* (1802). Schwab's words resonate in this context: "[Novalis] had another reason for linking Sophie's (Novalis's fiancee: KPM) death as a child at the age of fifteen and the India which his milieu considered the childhood of humanity."[29] The fragment opens with a description of what becomes the pivotal experience of the protagonist Heinrich:

> What attracted him with all its might . . . was a tall light-blue flower that initially stood at the source and touched him with its broad shining leaves. . . . He saw nought but the flower and gazed at it for a long time with inexpressible tenderness. Finally he wanted to near it when it suddenly began to move and transform itself; . . . the flower leaned towards him and the petals revealed a wide blue collar in which a tender face was suspended.[30]

The text narrates the life of the legendary minnesinger Heinrich whose encounter with the blue flower, the German Romantic symbol *par excellence*, leads him to discover the nature and function of Romantic poetry. Heinrich's poetic imagination is a reaction to a reality that Novalis detests as prosaic. In his search for a higher state of being Heinrich discovers in a cave a book containing a strange language that resembles Latin. It could be Sanskrit, since Novalis borrows Friedrich Schlegel's idea of an originary language for his novel. This discovery reflects one of the most crucial components in the German Romantics' search for origins as part of their self-definition. Although he cannot read a word of the language, Heinrich feels an "instinctual" acquaintance with it. On leafing through the book he "discovered his own form quite recognizably amongst the figures."[31] He belongs to this group of figures who are presumably the Northern Aryans and who possessed "traces of divine truth" (Schlegel), which were then lost to the ancient Hindus.[32] It is Heinrich's return to the origin, that is to the East of the Aryans, which enables him to discover his true vocation, that of an Oriental prophet. The book that the Oriental cannot interpret anymore contains all the wisdom that Heinrich already always possesses. As the "chosen" interpreter of knowledge he uses it to reconstruct the Oriental world in Occidental terms.

The Oriental woman Zulima is part of the perception of "India as feminine [. . .] a familiar practice of the literary imagination."[33] She is struck by Heinrich's resemblance to her own brother who was killed in the Crusades, allowing Heinrich to assume the garb of Oriental prophet. The contrast between the mythical Orient that Heinrich creates and his participation in the Crusades confirms his place within this discourse. Heinrich selects as wife the daughter of yet another Orientalist, Klingsohr the magician, who is a "universal" priest. Klingsohr has already revealed himself to Heinrich in the book with the strange language. Heinrich is a prophet to whom in a moment of Christian grace the blue flower (i.e., the blue lotus of India) appears. The lotus as the female principle, the *yoni*, conjures the image of an insatiably penetrable Orient, and Heinrich in his role as high priest interpreting the unknowable world of the Orient for his readers in Germany uses this flower to evoke increasingly potent sexual imagery. When his mother wakes him from his dream of the blue flower, his father remarks, "Cleverly have you chosen the teaching profession—in support of which we stay awake and work. But I have been told that a good scholar must also use nights to study the works of the wise ancestors."[34] This quotation shows the necessity of allowing the scholar (Orientalist) to recharge his energies through Oriental fantasizing. It also emphasizes the significance of the Orientalist's studies of the "wise ancestors," that is the Northern Aryans as enabled by Schlegel.

Another eminent contributor to Orientalist discourse is the German philosopher Hegel. As I have argued elsewhere, Schlegel and Novalis show enthusiasm for an India that was anchored in an immutable, monumental past that did not participate in the unfolding of a dynamic history. Hegel is less idealistic in his imaging of India. He acts as a counterpoint to the German Romantics' nostalgic dreams about India, as Balachandra Rajan shows in his insightful analysis of Hegel's India:

> The site that is India in Hegel's ultimate geography has been visited many times by the Western mind. It is the land of the lotus-eaters, Dido's Carthage, Cleopatra's Egypt, and Spenser's Bower of Bliss, with its reminder that Asia is part of the spelling of incontinence. ... Hegel forgets his book in writing of India because India is another traditional name for forgetfulness. It is the place where the will to move on is challenged because moving on is irrelevant to the dream state. This dream state, moreover, is not simply a pastoral hibernation. In its progress from absolute East to absolute West, history has passed through it and willed itself out of its snare. It remains vulnerable to its residual blandishments.[35]

Hegel himself declares: "The Indian people lack the principle of freedom, the ability of the *Geist* to retreat into itself; one cannot therefore talk about a state in this connection."[36] Consequently, the Indians have now relinquished to the Westerner "the true intuition of language," that they once enjoyed.[37]

Hegel's *Die orientalische Welt* shows the kind of intertextuality that reinforced the image of the Orient congruent to nineteenth-century European colonialism's agenda and lent authority to all these writings. In the second volume of *Vorlesungen über die Philosophie der Weltgeschichte* (Lectures on the Philosophy of World History) Hegel expounds on the Oriental world and its "essential" character.[38] He declares: "Es ist in China wie in Indien kein Fortgang zu anderem" [In China as in India, there is no movement forward], adding,

> [T]he English have shown themselves to be the people most capable of ruling over the land ... The English, or rather the East India Company, are the masters of the land; for it is the *necessary* fate of the Asian empires to be subjugated by the Europeans.[39] (Emphasis added)

Such a portrayal feeds directly into the conceptual building blocks that Aryanism has provided, and validates other discourses, including the one generated by missionaries. James Mill's (1773–1836) moral condemnation of Hinduism echoes Hegel's, as Inden rightly maintains:

> Mill was prepared to concede that he and the orientalists, Jones and Colebrooke, might disagree in their evaluation of Hindu thought. But, asserted Mill, "there is an universal agreement respecting the meanness, the absurdity, the folly, of the endless ceremonies, in which the practical part of the Hindu religion consists."[40]

About Hegel's construction of the Hindu mind, Inden says: "Hegel classed the religion of the Hindus ... as a 'natural' religion' and distinguished it from the 'later' religions of 'freedom' (among which were those of the Jews and Greeks, and, of course, Christianity."[41] For Hegel, religion has developed in three stages, the first being "nature religion," "i.e., religion defined as the unity of the spiritual and the natural, where the spirit still is in unity with nature. In being this way, spirit is not yet free, is not yet actual as spirit."[42] Eastern religions belong to this stage. Western man is nostalgic for the lost primal unity between spirit and nature contained in these religions, but he can regain this unity only after setting his spirit free: "In India there is perhaps a progress that shows the connections between the languages; but it is a subterranean, merely natural progress, not commensurate with consciousness; that which belongs to culture, to consciousness is another form of progress that is not based on a natural expansion."[43]

Self-consciousness is the highest form of consciousness for Hegel. However, the movement that he sees in India cannot match the progress that consciousness stimulates. The Indian is incapable of distinguishing between subject and object. Consequently, spirit (*Geist*) remains fettered below the level of consciousness required for self-awareness. The Hegelian consciousness has, however, reached this stage of self-reflectivity, of a consciously acquired "Natur." Hegel's dialectical conceptual structure requires that consciousness be recognized by another consciousness in order to attain self-consciousness: "It is a self-consciousness for another self-consciousness, unmediated for the moment as an other for an other. I see my own self in it, but [I also see] an unmediated existing [other] in it, as an independent 'I' object that is absolutely against me."[44] However, this reciprocal formation of self-consciousness is possible only between two Occidental minds. The Oriental, on the other hand, is an already always negative consciousness, one that can be used *ad infinitum* to help reinforce the hierarchically structured dichotomy of colonizer and colonized. This fits neatly into the structure of Hegelian dialectical thought, since linear progress requires an antithetical position. Ironically, the Oriental can never free him-/herself from this position, leading to the "master–slave" dichotomy crucial to colonialism that is defined by such a positioning of the Orient. As Rajan remarks,

> In Hegel's case, the acknowledgment and emphatic disavowal of the other in himself on the site that is India is deeply revelatory and, once recognized, can be seen as the driving force behind the otherwise inexplicable vehemence of his rhetoric. The scene and its consequences become an almost exemplary display of self-and-other dependencies. . . . So also is the insistence on withholding the opennesses of dialectical thought from relationships between cultures and confining those opennesses to the chosen culture of the historical moment.[45]

Rajan observes that immanence is a privilege of the West. "Hegel's setting apart of a West capable of progress by gradation and an Orient for which transcendence is necessary but impossible entrenches Western superiority in a manner difficult to overturn."[46] Hegel's use of the caste system to demonstrate India's inability to progress is instructive. Unlike China where the emperor's laws have disenfranchised the people, Indians were initially capable of differentiating their modes of existence. However, Hegel says, they carried this capacity to an extreme form whereby differences have become immutable and the system incapable of progress.[47] The passive voice in "Indien [ist] immer gesucht worden [India has always been sought]" needs no comment.

> Hegel denies India any claim to intellectual advancement:
> The grammatical system of Sanskrit undoubtedly reveals itself...as being very developed...People have thus wanted to conclude from this that the Indians already possessed in earliest times a high degree of education. This conclusion is, however, quite baseless; in empirical terms it is rather the opposite, since we see in Europe highly educated peoples with very simple grammatical systems. An excess of words, if it is merely sensual, reveals in fact barbarism; equally insignificant is mere training in grammatical forms.[48]

"Simplicity" as a measure of intellectual superiority surfaces here as it does in Schlegel's discussion of Christianity and Islam. The complex structures of Sanskrit grammar are indicative of a decadent mind busying itself with unimportant details. "Empirical" as the prerogative of the European mind suggests the careful compilation of irrefutable proof against such an Oriental mind.

India belongs to prehistory, since the spread of all things Indian does not possess a "geistige Realität [spiritual reality]," but rather a natural one through language that is "ein Geistloses, Inhaltloses [something dull, emptied of content]."[49] The Indian is inextricably caught in a dreamlike state of being. For both Schlegel and Hegel, India's "natural" religion thus remains "the product of a mind that was dominated by the imagination."[50]

Hegel employs Orientalism's strategy of feminizing in order to render inferior. "The curious beauty of things Indian can only be compared with the beauty of the women which is pure, mild, and soft in all its features."[51] Such beauty, however, betrays a "Nervenschwäche" (weakness of the nerves). Consequently, the Indian is incapable of manifesting the power of reason needed to counter the vicissitudes of life and the state.[52] "And thus of necessity it is confirmed that in reality a life that feels this way will plunge into the most ignominious slavery and degradation and will manifest itself in [this state of being]."[53] Once a people have fallen into servitude and debasement, they are not only vulnerable to oppression but are predestined for it.

This line of reasoning leads Hegel to postulate that the Indian mentality vacillates between extreme sensual pleasure and total abstraction of inwardness without ever achieving the synthesis that would result in morality, reason, and subjectivity.[54] "Der Verstand fehlt in Indien [The [faculty of] reasoning is lacking in India]."[55] The possession of reason presupposes a stable subject position. On the one hand, Hegel insists that the Indian lives in a dreamlike state without separating subject from object. Consequently, the Indian does not possess any consciousness of morality by which he could recognize and condemn tyranny. If there is any rule at all, it consists of lawless despotism. Religion, Hegel states, is available, but there is not enough religiosity. In every reasonable society differences between the various professions have to be maintained, classes and individuals identifiable. But the whole needs to be sustained by subjective freedom, morality, and the moral conscience of the individual. However, since Indians do not possess individual freedom, the castes they created have become rigid categories. A person belongs by birth to a caste. Hegel argues that in the European Middle Ages there was at least the possibility for an individual to progress toward higher classes. In contemporary Europe religion prevents discrimination, since each individual has an absolute value in the eyes of the Christian (universal) god. Religiosity leads to morality. However, the Indian's birth caste enslaves him. Hence apathy and resignation replace energy and the ambition to progress:

> [K]nowledge no longer requires application to reality; knowledge is what gets passed on silently, without comment, from one text to another. Ideas are propagated and disseminated anonymously, they are repeated without attribution; they have literally become *idées reçues*: what matters is that they are there, to be repeated, echoed, and re-echoed uncritically.[56]

Hegel's "truths" about India can thus be safely cited everywhere, gaining in authority with each reference. The myth of the lazy, lying native has one of its central sources in Hegel:

> Artfulness and slyness make up the basic character of the Indian; betrayal, theft, robbery, murder are part of his customs; he shows himself to the conqueror and master as humbly crawling and despicable, and towards the conquered and subordinate he is totally ruthless and cruel.[57]

The Indian male's excessive sexuality is a sign, not of virility, but rather of a decadent homoeroticism. As Suleri points out, "[T]his discourse of effeminacy provides an obvious but nonetheless useful method of ungendering imperial topologies, since it makes evident that the colonial gaze is not directed to the inscrutability of an Eastern bride but to the greater sexual ambivalence of the effeminate groom."[58] A homoerotic relationship introduces the aspect of complicity into the whole discourse of colonialism, thereby countering accusations of aggression and violence on the colonized body. Its similarity to patriarchal discourse on rape is enlightening. Such a multilayered sexual relationship between colonizer and colonized offers many more points of penetration into the Oriental consciousness than is otherwise acknowledged.

The general conceptual framework within which all these discourses work, be they religious, philosophical, or literary, always contains the claim of objectivity, of disinterested scholarship. Yet the scholarship is anything but disinterested. Despite its dissensions and diversities (which contribute to the aura of a search for understanding), its effect is uniform in reinforcing silently the supremacy of the strong, progressive, advanced West over the weak, primitive, degenerate East.

Notes

1. Raymond Schwab, *The Oriental Renaissance: Europe's Rediscovery of India and the East, 1680–1880*, trans. Gene Patterson-Black and Victor Reinking (New York: Columbia University Press, 1984), ix.
2. Ibid., 53.
3. Sheldon Pollock, "Deep Orientalism? Notes on Sanskrit and Power Beyond the Raj," in *Orientalism and the Postcolonial Predicament— Perspectives on South Asia* ed. Carol A. Breckenridge and Peter van der Veer (Philadelphia: University of Pennsylvania Press, 1993), 80.
4. Schwab, *The Oriental Renaissance*, 13.
5. Edward Said, *Orientalism* (New York: Random House, 1974), 19.
6. Suzanne Zantop, *Colonial Fantasies: Conquest, Family, and Nation in Precolonial Germany, 1770–1870* (Durham: Duke University Press, 1997), 6.
7. Ibid., 9.
8. Pollock, "Deep Orientalism?" 77.
9. Gary Handwerk, "Envisioning India: Friedrich Schlegel's Sanskrit Studies and the Emergence of Romantic Historiography," *European Romantic Review* 9.2 (1998): 235.
10. Friedrich Schlegel, *Studien zur Philosophie und Theologie*, Eingeleitet und herausgegeben von Ernst Behler und Ursula Struc-Oppenberg (München/Paderborn/Wien: Verlag Ferdinand Schöningh, 1975; Zürich: Thomas-Verlag, 1975; originally publ. in Heidelberg: Mohr und Zimmer, 1808), 111. All translations are mine unless otherwise stated.
11. Schwab, *The Oriental Renaissance*, 76.

12. Said, *Orientalism*, xv.

13. Handwerk, "Envisioning India," 235.

14. Ibid., 235.

15. Ibid., 235.

16. Ibid., 237.

17. Ronald Inden, *Imagining India* (Oxford: Blackwell Publishers, 1992), 50.

18. Schlegel, *Kritische Ausgabe*, 35 Bde. Hg. v. Ernst Behler unter Mitwirkung v. Jean-Jacques Anstett u. Hans Eichner u.a. (Paderborn-Muenchen-Wien-Zuerich-Darmstadt, 1958–), 192, 788.

19. Schlegel, *Deutsches Museum*, ed. Ernst Behler (Darmstadt: Wissenschaftliche Buchgesellschaft Darmstadt, 1975), 293.

20. Ibid., 293.

21. Ibid., 293.

22. Schlegel, *Studien*, 313.

23. Handwerk, "Envisioning India," 238.

24. Schlegel, *Kritische Ausgabe*, 126–27.

25. Schlegel, *Studien*, 217.

26. Ibid., 293.

27. For an excellent discussion of Mill, Hegel, and Schlegel, see Ronald Inden, *Imagining India*, especially 45 ff. and chap. 2 entitled "India in Asia: The Caste Society."

28. Said, *Orientalism*, 178.

29. Schwab, *The Oriental Renaissance*, 207.

30. Novalis, *Heinrich von Ofterdingen* (Stuttgart: Reclam, 1965), 11.

31. Schlegel, *Studien*, 92.

32. Schlegel, *Studien*, 217.

33. Balachandra Rajan, *Under Western Eyes: India from Milton to Macaulay* (Durham: Duke University Press, 1999) 120.

34. Schlegel, *Deutsches Museum*, 12.

35. Rajan, 101.

36. Georg W. F. Hegel, *Die orientalische Welt* (Leipzig: Verlag von Felix Meiner, 1919), 320.

37. In *Heinrich von Ofterdingen*, Novalis claims such an intuitive access to language (and thought) for his protagonist Heinrich, the true "Oriental" prophet.

38. Hegel, *Vorlesungen über die Philosophie der Weltgeschichte* (Stuttgart, Germany: Reclam, 1961), written between 1822 and 1825.

39. Ibid., 275, 365.

40. Ibid., 274–75; Inden, *Imagining India*, 92.

41. Inden, *Imagining India*, 94.

42. Hegel, *Lectures on the Philosophy of Religion. Vol. II, Determinate Religion*, ed. Peter C. Hodgson (Berkeley: University of California Press, 1987), 519.

43. Hegel, *Die orientalische Welt*, 275.

44. Hegel, *Enzyklopaedie der philosophischen Wissenschaften. Theorie Werkausgabe* (Frankfurt/Main: Suhrkamp Verlag), 1970, 430.
45. Rajan, 117.
46. Ibid., 109.
47. Hegel, *Die orientalische Welt*, 343.
48. Ibid., 348.
49. Ibid., 348.
50. Inden, *Imagining India*, 94.
51. Hegel, *Die orientalische Welt*, 350.
52. Ibid., 351.
53. Ibid., 351.
54. Ibid., 351.
55. Ibid., 353.
56. Said, *Orientalism*, 116.
57. Hegel, *Die orientalische Welt*, 391.
58. Sara Suleri, *The Rhetoric of English India* (Chicago: University of Chicago Press, 1992), 16.

The Colonial Pedagogy of Imperial Germany: Self-Denial in the Interest of the Nation

Sabine Wilke

In memory of Susanne Zantop

In this volume of essays on differing models of imperialism, different scholars engage in comparative studies of empires and imperial ideologies across various nations with British imperialism—and, to a limited extent, French imperialism—as the central point of reference. The main issue is the variety of dominance. To what extent is it true that imperialisms compete with each other? We all examine varieties of imperialism based on individual components in each case. The editors and authors of this volume argue that imperialisms fashion themselves in relation to their forms of nationhood, in relation to other imperialisms from which they discriminate themselves, and in relation to territories for which they compete. While it can be argued that the subvariety of British imperialism was distinguished by its prolonged and complex involvement with India, German imperialist discourse emerged in the Romantic era as a philosophical and scholarly discourse that is also sufficiently distinctive and cohesive to be taken into account. Susanne Zantop argued in a pioneering study of German precolonial fantasies that precolonial German letters from 1770 to 1870 saw the emergence of "stories of sexual conquest and surrender, love and blissful domestic relations between colonizer and colonized, set in colonial territory, stories that made the strange familiar, and the familiar 'familial.'"[1] These stories connect sexual desire with the desire for control and construct a patriarchal race-gender model. But, more importantly, through the narration of excess committed by others they facilitated the so-called German "colonial legend" (*Koloniallegende*) in the early twentieth century that rehabilitated the Germans as the better colonizers and became the centerpiece of colonial propaganda after 1919. These precolonial fantasies, in other words, had an enormous power over later German colonial practice by creating a sense of moral superiority and a sense of specialty in the German colonizer and pre-scripted the colonial encounter as a cross-cultural, cross-racial, and cross-gender romance.[2] The German model, therefore, differed from the British and French models of imperialism precisely because it was largely grounded in fantasy and the lack of a national colonial practice at first. Very little is known about the varieties of domination and cultural encounters in this early period and, although that would be a fascinating subject, it is beyond the confines of this investigation. I am dwelling on this early history of German colonialism simply to uncover the seeds for the later emergence of the specifically German encounter with colonial cultures.

Although the German colonial empire was officially sanctioned by Bismarck only in a telegram of April 24, 1884 to the German consul at Cape Town regarding German Southwest Africa (now Namibia) individual colonial ventures that included Germans date back "to the fifteenth and sixteenth centuries, when thousands of Germans took part in the conquest and colonization of the 'New World'—as adventurers or mercenaries in Spanish expeditions, as merchants outfitting ships or trading in slaves, as scientists, explorers, or interpreters."[3] German colonies were founded in South America, merchant societies were established, scientists including Georg Forster and Alexander von Humboldt explored Africa, South America, China, Australia, and New Zealand. Woddruff Smith and Horst Gründer have shown how beginning in 1499 the rich merchant houses of the Fuggers and Welsers financed expeditions and were responsible for bringing German miners and African slaves to South America and how the colonial experiments of Prussia, although short-lived and unsuccessful, set the stage for later colonial endeavors.[4] State-sponsored colonialism, on the other hand, only began after unification in 1871. While it is true, as Edward W. Said claimed, that the tradition of German Orientalism is largely academic in nature, German colonial fantasizing—academic as well as literary—has nevertheless had an enormous impact on German colonial discourse in the later nineteenth and early twentieth centuries.[5] It has also helped shape a distinctly German self-fashioning in the process of identity formation of German imperialism vis-à-vis competing imperialisms.

What Said referred to as the scholarly tradition of German Orientalism is, in fact, firmly rooted in a philosophical imperialism that culminated in Hegelian dialectics. Dialectical thought, as the German philosopher Georg Friedrich Wilhelm Hegel has shown in the famous passages referring to the intricate relationship between master and slave in his lectures on the *Phenomenology of Spirit*, excludes in order to articulate itself and then seeks inclusiveness to amend that articulation. Hegel conceives of the process of world history in a similar fashion. World history, according to Hegel, advances from childhood to maturity via the same processes of exclusion and inclusion, erasure and recycling. In his classification of historic data Hegel claims that the history of the world travels from East to West, with Europe as the absolute end of history, Asia the beginning.[6] Hegel considers the Oriental world as the childhood of history where unreflected consciousness constitutes the edifices of Oriental empires. "Unreflected consciousness—substantial, objective, spiritual existence—forms the basis, to which the subjective will first sustains a relation in the form of faith, confidence, obedience."[7] Hegel continues unfolding his philosophy of history by discussing China, India, and Persia as paradigmatic empires in the Oriental world with China as possessing the most ancient tradition of statehood, India serving as the land of imaginative aspiration and the region of fantasy and sensibility, and Persia as the cradle of Greek culture. Black Africa and parts of Asia with nomadic populations, however, do not appear in Hegel's scheme since no states have been formed there. Africa and nomadic Asia are, therefore, regarded by Hegel as trapped in a perpetual state of being that even predates childhood. These notions can be considered as the philosophical roots of German colonial pedagogy and the interesting question arises whether there is a relationship between this Hegelian philosophical construction of prehistorical existence for Africa and nomadic Asia and the later pedagogical belief that denies African students the possibility of growing up.

Russell Berman argued that German colonialism has to a certain extent paralleled the idiosyncratic history of the formation of the German nation-state in the nineteenth century. In sifting through the documents pertaining to the discourse of German colonialism Berman concedes that he "was struck by the extent of the capacity to attempt to appreciate the local cultures on their own terms, at times even to identify with them and, on occasion, to express articulately anti-colonial sentiments."[8] The following three parameters may have produced this strain of German colonialism, which all refer to the specific relation German culture had to its colonial project: (1) German belatedness in nation-building and hence its late official entry into the league of colonizers; (2) the early conclusion of the German colonial era precluding violent struggles of de-colonization in the post–World War II period; and (3) what Berman calls "a hermeneutic predisposition to grant at least relative legitimacy to local cultures."[9] As a consequence, Berman claims that German colonial discourse was less dismissive of local cultures than the discourse of other European colonizers. This empathy in German colonial discourse left considerably more room for identification with the colonized than, say, British or even French colonial discourse.[10] Berman claims furthermore that this specific discursive tradition makes possible the experience of alterity that in the colonial context translated as the possibility of exploring the world and experiencing something new. He claims "that a strand of German culture was quite curious about difference, and this interest produced a particular openness (perhaps less characteristic of the colonialisms of those nations with more rigidly defined identities)."[11] Georg Forster and the Enlightenment travelogue, for example, stand "for a capacity within the Enlightenment to recognize and appreciate other cultures," and Gerhard Rohlfs upholds the experience of alterity in geographic writing whereas "alterity may become the object of heterophile desire rather than the object of heterophobic displacement by the British 'white man's burden' or a francophone mission of civilization."[12] This complex reality of colonialisms leaves its marks in the intricacies of colonial discourse.

My essay examines the nature and the extent of a distinct form of German imperialism in relation to British imperialism on the example of the analysis of the discourse and the practice of German colonial pedagogy during and after the German colonial period. It offers, therefore, an afterthought on the rest of the essays collected in this volume that investigate varieties of domination in the colonial practice of a much earlier period. In pedagogy, discourse and practice are merged in unique ways and one can study simultaneously the rhetoric of German claims against rival imperialisms as well as the practice of subjecting others through dominance and constructions of otherness. The rhetoric is one of self-denial and we will find that it frequently serves as a cover for exploitative practices. As opposed to the British colonial administrator, however, who had to endure the pangs of a long exile but was frequently more than adequately recompensed for that hardship and enjoyed enormous power of an almost Olympian status, or the French administrator who spend some time in colonial "departments" as part of a normal career path, the German settler engaged in a far more masochistic enterprise in which the roles of the cruel woman and the masochistic male were pre-scripted to a large extent. German colonial pedagogy, I argue, reveals a conflicting picture of German imperialism. While self-denial as it will become the center piece of my argument has an ancient and diverse lineage including many religious traditions that call for self-discipline and even sacrifice today in exchange for the promise of paradise tomorrow, or many secularisms that require the individual to subordinate him- or herself to a cause, a mission, the state or the greater good and even argue that the individual finds his or her real self by subordinating his or her superficial self in this manner, German colonial pedagogy is rooted in a very specific Central European tradition of masochism as well as in the German hermeneutic predisposition toward alterity identified by Berman.

John K. Noyes has defined masochism as the "staged acting out of aggression, a strategy of recodification."[13] I would like to underline the importance of the theatrical context for the practice of masochism that I would like to understand as a social practice of masking and unmasking where the effects are built into the practices themselves. Read against the backdrop of the history of European nation-building and the emergence of the new woman in the late nineteenth and early twentieth centuries, masochism is made up of and, at the same time, examines culturally coded stereotypes (the cruel white woman, the week European male, the attractive Black female, etc.). The crisis of liberal masculinity is, therefore, staged as a masochistic scenario with the woman embodying the projected role of the cruel woman and the man reassuming power over her by dictating the terms of the spectacle. The displacement of the primordial scene of European male masochism into the colonies results in an enhancement of the sexual connotation of that scene. Noyes argues that "in the context of colonialism, the problem of masochism acquires dimensions that resist the standard models of conflict. ... Instead, it focuses on the eroticisation of social relations and of cultural stereotypes."[14] In the colonial text elaborate scenes of self-sacrifice are staged while at the same time the project of conquest and settlement is collapsing. The staging of the masochistic fantasy becomes a way of acting out the ambivalences inherent in the social and political project of colonialism. Masochism, as I understand it in the context of German colonialism, is a theatrical appropriation of cultural stereotypes with the effect of restaging the sexual tensions inherent in the scene. German colonial pedagogy is built on this economy of cultural production.

British colonial pedagogy is subject to fierce debate in historical research. A. J. Loveridge, for example, claims that "the British official attitude towards changing the minds of 'subject' people was one of remarkable diffidence" and that "British 'colonialism' was not established for the purpose of changing men's minds."[15] In fact, Loveridge cites government reports on education in Africa that show that until World War I the British African governments left some ninety-five percent of education in the hands of the missions that had begun to supply it before governments were established.[16] Contrary to this idea, in the essay on "Milton and Education," Gauri Viswanathan argues that British imperialism's attitude toward colonial education was primarily defined by the needs of the colonizers to amply supplement their commercial ambitions and secure a stronger empire by extending trade into programs of cultural influence.[17] Colonial subjects were treated as morally debased and intellectually deficient, and colonial pedagogy was to transform moral depravity into forms of civic usefulness. This line of argument was radicalized by Kilemi Mwiria who claimed that colonial education (at least in colonial Kenya) was essentially an education for subordination.[18] Clive Whitehead responded with the claim that British colonial policy was essentially an exercise in pragmatism and not a deliberately designed scheme to subjugate Africans.[19] He shows that "broadly speaking, colonies were treated as separate and economic entities" and that "they were expected to shape their own social, political and economic destinies."[20]

France had entered the race for African territories rather late and, unlike Britain, never had to look at colonization as a matter of economic life and death. As opposed to Britain—and similar to Germany—France did not possess many colonies in temperate regions (only in Northern Africa) and therefore never looked toward its colonies in terms of major settlements. "France's attitude on this matter was exactly that of the Japanese,—to have the spheres of influence outside the metropolis provide the necessary food, raw materials, and markets, and to offer safety and employment even to an increasing home population. This is diametrically opposed to the British idea of forming new societies overseas, and even to the German theory which confused the two aspects of emigration and raw materials, as the position of Germany demanded both outlets."[21] France always looked toward the motherland as a machine and toward the colonies as feeders of that machine. Several insights relating to French colonial pedagogy can be drawn from this brief comparison: French colonialism was governed by the principle of centralism according to which all regions, regardless of its distance from Paris, were administered like mainland *départments* from Paris; that meant that life in the colonies—including schooling—replicated life in a French province. French colonialism also displayed a much more lenient attitude toward miscegenation.[22] French colonial subjects were citizens of the grand nation and served in the national army.

With the growth and increasing bureaucratization of the colonial empire the need arose to educate not only the colonial subjects and make them into citizens of the state but also to train the British, French, and German imperial administrator. In the case of England, this new program followed a "course for producing the ideal Englishman, well-read, experienced, and knowledgeable of the world, yet able to adapt to it even as he shapes it according to the dictates of his will."[23] This meant the institution of a curriculum that included the liberal arts, the study of languages, religion, and a controlled and disciplined curriculum of literary instruction. German colonial pedagogy likewise can be divided into these two aspects of educating the German colonial administrator and settler for their specific tasks in the colonies as well as educating the indigenous natives and I examine these aspects in two separate subsections of my essay. They both, however, come together in a common discourse on pedagogical principles that is built around the notion of masochistic pleasure in the postponement of immediate physical gratification.

I

The education of German colonizers (administrators, missionaries, settlers) is part of a larger "educational program" geared toward the entire population of the new empire after it had joined the other European nations in the colonization of Africa and the South Pacific in the mid-1880s. In contrast to its competitors, especially England, which could look back to an extended involvement in India before it explored its options in Africa, Germany—not unlike France—grabbed what was left of the "dark continent" and established so-called protectorates (*Schutzgebiete*) in Southwest Africa, Cameroon, Togo, and East Africa in the 1880s, and in the South Pacific and China in the 1890s. The German population had never before been confronted with state-sponsored colonization and was not well educated as the English and French about the supposed goals and benefits of possessing colonies. A huge campaign was undertaken to mobilize the Germans for the colonial cause from the turn of the century until the beginning of the 1940s lasting until colonial propaganda collapsed in the increasing complications of World War II. The so-called colonial schools were part of this effort to produce colonial supporters.

But so were frequent and elaborate state-sponsored and commercial colonial exhibits (forty-one altogether between 1896 and 1939 inside Germany and several exhibits in Dar es Salam), colonial museums founded in Berlin, Bremen, Leipzig, and other major German cities with dioramas realistically reconstructing the colonial landscape, animal and plant life, as well as indigenous cultural practices, scientific and propaganda meetings of various colonial societies, annual colonial days in the port cities, countless books, films, and musicals with colonial themes and colonial settings, colonial magazines showcasing life and adventure in the colonies such as the monthly *Deutsche Kolonial-Zeitung*, the weekly *Kolonie und Heimat*, and the more scholarly *Koloniale Rundschau*, as well as a colonial direction in the German youth movement.[24] A number of painters painted a Romantic tropical Africa bar of native people who, if present at all, were shown in servile positions offering tropical fruits, and the like. These paintings were shown in museums and exhibits throughout Imperial Germany into the 1930s and featured stereotypes like erotic women, servile boys, and primitive warriors. They also showed German colonialism utilizing the native population to transform foreign landscapes into German plantations. The emphasis on a servile attitude, certain practical skills, and subservience toward leaders determines the canon of colonial education. This canon is displayed in Bernhard Dernburg's educational program and in Matthias Erzberger's guide for colonial professions. Both men were members of the *Reichstag* and actively engaged in promoting the colonial cause. Dernburg, who in 1906 became colonial director of the German Foreign Office, campaigned with the idea of a crusade for colonial education built on the principle of denial, adaptation, and special skills.[25] In January 1906 he gave a speech in Munich demanding special schooling of colonial administrators including the building of a firm character, the denial of domestic luxuries, and the psychological study of the African tribes, as well as a knowledge of local trade practices and the study of indigenous languages and religions.[26] In Dernburg's program, masochism and hermeneutics came together in a conflicting image of the colonial administrator; he is supposed to be very hard on himself while treating others with knowledge and respect. In a related fashion, Erzberger links service to sacrifice for the fatherland not to sexual fantasies and exotic adventures.[27]

At the beginning of the twentieth century several scholarly programs had been designed for the training of higher colonial administrators, including the Seminar for Oriental Languages at the University in Berlin and the Colonial Institute in Hamburg. Colonial geography was established as a discipline in Leipzig in 1915. In 1898 the first colonial school was founded in Witzenhausen near Kassel to train middle-class boys and young men as settlers in the colonies. The pedagogical principles are of great interest since colonial schools of this nature were pioneered in Germany and are one of the trademarks of German imperialism. Witzenhausen was an elite boarding school with a regimented schedule that resembled more a military drill than an educational institute, including rigorous punishment for transgression. Every year several students had to be removed from the school because of discipline problems.[28] The mornings were devoted to lectures and instruction in ethnology, history of religion, chemistry for tropical planters, plant physiology, the study of drugs, mineralogy, veterinary skills, as well as tropical health care and colonial agrarian policy. The afternoons were filled with practical instruction in laboratories, the study of different indigenous languages, and riding lessons. In addition, students had to work in the fields, tend to the school's garden, and clean the riding stables. The emphasis was on teaching practical skills, but also on forming a disciplined character. The future settler was considered to be a "teacher" of indigenous people who were likened to children. Director Fabarius, who himself was responsible for instruction in ethnology, writes in his report that the study of native peoples is an important lesson in applied pedagogy for the future "cultural pioneer" since the settler will have to function not only as the native's foreman and superior on the job but also as the educator of his servants and workers into reliable, clean, and punctual subjects.[29] In keeping with the hermeneutic tradition of respect for encountering the other, Fabarius promotes a middle way to his students by recommending that they not be too harsh with their "children" but not be too lenient either.[30] Although the natives may seem "like children" to the cultural pioneer, he nevertheless should be treating them "the right way," by which Fabarius means "according to their rightful customs and aware of their needs."[31]

The Colonial School in Witzenhausen was the first but certainly not the only venture in Germany to train future colonizers. There were also more specialized schools such as the Colonial and Agrarian Academy in Miltenberg, which opened in 1914, or, even abroad, the Biological-Agrarian Institute in Amani (East Africa), which was founded as early as 1902. But what is most interesting in the context of a study of German colonial pedagogy is to compare the teaching missions of these colonial schools that were open only to boys and young men to the colonial institutes that young women could attend. In fact, the training of women for service in the colonies in order to provide the settler with the cozy atmosphere of a German household and keep him from fraternizing with native women is another centerpiece of German colonialism. It is intimately tied to the strict prohibition of miscegenation and the projected image of the African primitive as possessing an excess of erotic energies and thus being able to provide the White male an experience of heightened eroticism.

The establishment of colonial training institutes for women goes back to the beginning of German colonialism when the Franciscan nuns of Nonnenwerth near Trier founded a school for the education of young women who have expressed the wish to seek a professional existence in the oversees colonies. What is interesting here is the willingness to look at the training of women to oversee a colonial household. Similar to the schooling for men, these women were trained in practical skills and received instruction—in the case of women: religious instruction—geared at building and maintaining a firm character that holds up even under the worst of all circumstances. Although women may have received more training in practical household and gardening skills, in providing basic health care, and in educating their children and domestic servants, and the like, men received more instruction in theoretical subjects, administering a plantation, overseeing a large number of native workers, repairing farming equipment. But the overall curriculum and the pedagogical principles applied were remarkably similar. Both men and women received an all-round education in practical matters pertaining to the life in the colonies and were told that only a steadfast character that can forego European luxuries and is willing to engage in the respectful education of indigenous workers will survive in the bush. In 1911 the Colonial Women's School in Bad Weilbach was founded as a school for young women from the higher middle classes for the goal of preparing them to become heads of colonial households. This is in itself quite a remarkable undertaking and speaks to the increasing acceptance of the fact that it became a woman's professional option to assume the role of head of a colonial household. The Colonial School in Rendsburg even taught young women to safely handle a rifle, ride a horse, and drive cars.[32] In other words, the educational options available for young women who expressed a desire to go into the colonies were frequently a lot broader than what would have been considered proper for them to learn at home and it seems little wonder that many chose that option.

The function of the colonial schools in Germany changed somewhat after 1919 when the German colonies were placed into mandates and the settlers were frequently subjected to discrimination in the various new mandate administrations. The colonial schools in Germany, however, still continued training future settlers. In fact, they turned into hotbeds of colonial propaganda and considered it their mission to continue to train people in the "colonial struggle" for the preservation of an ethnically pure German race in the former colonies. The students who attended that school in the 1930s were expected to conform to a political profile that embraced colonialism at all cost. During the postcolonial period the German Colonial School in Witzenhausen also turned into an institute of higher learning with a new archive and an agricultural laboratory for testing different plant species. Its graduates who could no longer go into the former colonies now swarmed out into the world in order to found new German settlements in South America, the Dutch Indies, South Africa, and so on, and were considered among the best-trained colonists in the world. In other words, the "colonial legend" of the Germans as the "better" colonizers also informs the discourse of colonial propaganda relating to colonial pedagogy after World War I. Director Fabarius writes proudly in 1925: "even among the richly equipped American agricultural colleges is none which could measure up to the German Colonial School in that respect and even less so the French and Belgian Ecoles coloniales. The British Colonial College had already folded before the war and the Italian and Japanese colonial schools never made it beyond their initial plans."[33] The pedagogy practiced in these schools became the centerpiece around which the identity of postcolonial Germany was built: its graduates were better skilled, more masochistically inclined to meet the various hardships, and proved superior in their knowledge about the indigenous people they encountered abroad vis-à-vis their imperialist competitors who meanwhile had assumed the administration of the former colonies.

II

In his article on "Creating Germans Abroad: White Education in German Southwest Africa, 1894–1914," Daniel Walther explores the measures "pursued by members of the propertied and educated classes in Germany and Southwest Africa between 1894 and 1914 to 'create' German citizens in the colony as well as the efficacy of such efforts."[34] These measures included a program that was geared toward turning the colony's White youth into productive members of the nation at home that was far more rigorous and earlier in effort than peers in Kenya and Southern Rhodesia. In fact, "in both Kenya and Southern Rhodesia officials did not institute comprehensive educational programs until the late 1920s, and even then they tended not to match the scale of degree of German efforts in Southwest Africa."[35] By 1908 many local communities had built elementary schools and a secondary school in Windhoek was opened with a curriculum that resembled that of a Prussian "Realschule." Walther also notes that—as opposed to German East Africa, which was not a settler colony—Southwest relegated instruction of the native population to the missionaries in a conscious attempt to segregate White settlers and Africans in order to protect White children from influence of the Africans and create a diligent and obedient workforce.[36]

In order to analyze fully the pedagogical principles adopted by the schools for indigenous people and put them into proper context we need to look at the popular discourse about educating indigenous people in general that circulated in Germany starting in the 1890s. The colonial military officer Hermann Wißmann, for example, published a pamphlet in 1895 "About the Treatment of the Negroes," which sets the parameters of this discussion by emphasizing the necessity and model of military training for those who will be teaching Africans: the same patience and respect for individual differences is necessary for training recruits as for training Africans who, in Wißmann's assessment, are a race that is only at the beginning of human development.[37] The image of "the African as child" runs through this entire discussion and is a cornerstone of the pedagogy practiced in all German colonial schools. But Wißmann also insists—at least in theory—on the hermeneutic element of respect for otherness. The treatment that he recommends to colonial educators in Africa is one of justice and strictness, but also one of mutual respect for each other's cultural differences. The respect for indigenous religions and customs and for the individuality of the other in the colonial encounter is, according to Wißmann, a prerequisite for teaching indigenous people good work habits.

The "education for work" is the second topic that continues to circulate through this popular discussion. The problem, as Hans Zache saw it, is that the African native, when judged from a European perspective, is lazy and unfamiliar with the concepts of surplus production, accumulation, expenditure, and savings (in an economic as well as psychological sense) and prefers to work only as much as is necessary to have enough food and shelter for the moment.[38] The native worker, in other words, will need to be accustomed to the European economy of masochism with its characteristic traits of denial and postponement of wish fulfillment, transcending physical gratification, and redirecting his sexual/psychic energies into material production.

But this "program" of educating the native population to become more efficient workers not only relies on the economy of masochistic postponement of gratification. It also creates consumers for the products that were now in circulation. With the introduction of taxation the largely barter economy was gradually replaced with circulating bills and coins. Africans with surplus funds could now buy various goods from merchants (especially goods they depended on now such as textiles, cigarettes, brandy, etc.) and were gradually introduced to certain consumer needs. The pedagogy that resulted from this popular discourse is full of conflicting attitudes toward the supposed nature and predisposition of the students and their capacities as learners of European knowledge and culture. As "children" in a developmental sense they are subject to drives that 2,000 years of Western civilization have (successfully?) contained in European men and women.[39] As workers they are not reliable, indolent, resistant to European concepts of order, and not trustworthy.[40]

Educational practice in government and missionary schools differed to some extent from colony to colony. Southwest had a long tradition in educating a small African elite where the Rhenish Mission had founded the *Augustineum* in 1866 to train teachers for their missionary schools. The *Augustineum* was even allowed to continue under the new South African mandate administration with a revised curriculum, which included religion, reading and writing in the indigenous language, arithmetic, and handicrafts for the boys and needlework for the girls.[41] The missionary schools in Southwest operated with a similarly conflicting attitude toward the training of the native population. By 1932 three denominations ran almost all the schools in the former colony. The curriculum in the missionary schools was primarily designed to produce suitable servants for the colonial household. As opposed to the government schools, which were single-sex institutions, the missionary schools trained both genders in the basics of reading and writing, and in useful household skills such as doing the laundry, cleaning rooms, mending clothing, and helping in the garden.

The educational successes of the German colonial project that the French tried to emulate in their model of imperialism seem to be greatest in schools that had a decidedly practical orientation, such as the government school in Tanga, East Africa. Established by Baron von Soden in the 1890s, the school was "designed to inculcate virtues of loyalty, industry and punctuality to be deployed in official German service."[42] From a comparative perspective it is interesting to note that "while there were in 1910 3,494 elementary and 681 middle or upper students in the state secular schools [in East Africa], and approximately 1,196 students in mission schools following the standard Swahili curriculum, neighboring Kenya admitted no official responsibility for a native education policy. Nor for that matter did Uganda or Nyasaland."[43] In fact, the colonial neighbor England, who had left the instruction of the natives entirely to the missions up to the beginning of the twentieth century, eventually began implementing government schools in Zanzibar after the model of the German government school in Tanga. This school, which was founded in 1892 by the *Deutsche Kolonial-Gesellschaft*, not only taught reading, writing, and arithmetic, but also the practical skills that are related to book binding as well as carpentry, and forgery. The "Usambara-Post," a German-language newspaper for the northern districts of East Africa, was printed here as well as the monthly "Pflanzer," a journal for tropical agriculture, and "Kiongozi," a Swahili newspaper for the indigenous population (printed in Latin script) with contributions exclusively written by Africans (who had been to missionary schools and learned to read and write the Latin script).[44]

The "images from the middle school in Bonaberi" in Cameroon transmitted by a former German teacher support the pedagogy of masochism that we saw at work in the example of the school in Tanga, East Africa. The first assumption is always that the local students are lazy, and "used to the *dolce far niente* from their home in the bush."[45] On the example of this school we can study the connection between the pedagogy of masochism and the instruction in Christian mores, which is filtered through the pattern of the renunciation of bodily pleasures: "With awe they experience the unfathomable, i.e., that there is a world where not the question of the stomach, female chattering, or naked, cruel selfishness is key, but a selfless, sacrificial love which has its roots in God and in the person of the savior."[46] The Christian instruction in bodily self-denial is meant to result in the adoption of a more productive attitude toward work.

This systematic and exemplary discussion of the most important issues confronting schools in the German colonies (as opposed to the schools in the British and French colonies) points to the following picture regarding the principle patterns of German colonial pedagogy:

1. Thousands of indigenous people of the German colonies sent their children into the missionary schools that provided for elementary and religious instruction. The pedagogical purposes of these schools were, besides the obvious one of creating Christian followers, teaching them rudimentary arithmetic, reading and writing

in their own language, basic training in European household and plantation duties, the introduction of a European work ethic, and a daily regimented work schedule. Broad and thorough instruction in the basic knowledge of European academic disciplines comparable to the elementary schools in Germany was not intended. As opposed to French imperialism, German imperialism did not leave a legacy of an attempt at "Germanization" of its territories and the content of the instruction differed greatly at the local levels.

2. Only a small number of native people, primarily the sons of tribal chiefs and sultans, attended government schools in the German colonies and received more advanced instruction in the basic subjects as well as in selected crafts. The graduates of these schools became teachers themselves or aided in other ways in the efficient administration of the colonies as officials, translators, scribes, or office assistants. The prohibition of miscegenation prevented the circulation of colonial subjects through the schools and universities of the home country. As opposed to Britain and France the talented native student in a German colony was not expected to continue his education at a German institution of higher learning.

3. The popular discourse on colonial education that surrounded the establishment of colonial schools was conflicting, to say the least. The indigenous people were constructed as children, as unfit for work in a European sense, or even as unteachable in the truly Hegelian sense. They had to be trained rigorously to become more reliable, punctual, predictable, and willingly denounce immediate physical gratifications.

German colonial pedagogy in the training schools for German colonizers and in the schools in the colonies, therefore, comes together in a common project of teaching denial of physical pleasures in the interest of redirecting that energy into work. It radicalizes general trends in Prussian pedagogy in the interest of building and strengthening the German nation as a competitive colonial power among its European neighbors and it links up this tradition of self-denial in the interest of the greater good with the specific tradition of European masochism, which stages cultural stereotypes and investigates their erotic functioning. Hegel's prehistorical nomad that did not even appear in world history mutates into the pedagogical object in the hermeneutic encounter with alterity that is refashioned in the pedagogical manuals as the elements of a masochistic staging of desire and control.

NOTES

1. Susanne Zantop, *Colonial Fantasies: Conquest, Family, and Nation in Precolonial Germany, 1770–1870* (Durham: Duke University Press, 1997), 2.
2. Ibid., 13.
3. Sara Friedrichsmeyer, Sara Lennox, and Susanne Zantop, eds., *The Imperialist Imagination: German Colonialism and Its Legacy* (Ann Arbor: University of Michigan Press, 1998), 8.
4. Ibid., 9.
5. See Edward W. Said, *Orientalism* (New York: Vintage, 1978), 19.
6. Georg Wilhelm Friedrich Hegel, *The Philosophy of History*, trans. J. Sibree (New York: Dover, 1956), 104.
7. Ibid., 105.
8. Russell A. Berman, "German Colonialism: Another *Sonderweg?*" *European Studies Journal* 16 (1999): 30.
9. Ibid., 33.
10. Russell A. Berman, *Enlightenment or Empire: Colonial Discourse in German Culture* (Lincoln: University of Nebraska Press, 1998), 10.
11. Ibid., 18.
12. Ibid., 64, 135.
13. John K. Noyes, *The Mastery of Submission: Inventions of Masochism* (Ithaca: Cornell University Press, 1997), 30.
14. Ibid., 114.
15. A. J. Loveridge, *British Colonial Experience in Educational Development: A Survey of Non-Formal Education for Rural and Agricultural Development* (Cardiff: University College Cardiff Press, 1978), 15.
16. Ibid., 18.
17. Gauri Viswanathan, "Milton and Education," in *Milton and the Imperial Vision*, ed. Balachandra Rajan and Elizabeth Sauer (Pittsburgh: Duquesne University Press, 1999), 289.
18. Cited in Clive Whitehead, "Education for Subordination? Some Reflections on Kilemi Mwiria's Account of African Education in Colonial Kenya," *History of Education* 22 (1993): 85.
19. Ibid., 87; for a similar argument regarding the situation in Nigeria see Chuka E. Okonkwo, "The Language Medium of the School and the Curriculum: The Case of Colonial Nigeria," *Journal of African Studies* 9, 4 (1982–3): 194–200.
20. Whitehead, "Education for Subordination?," 87.
21. Stephen H. Roberts, *History of French Colonial Policy (1870–1925)* (London: P. S. King & Son, LTD, 1929), 636.
22. Ibid., 653.
23. Viswanathan, "Milton and Education," 299.
24. See Sibylle Benninghoff-Lühl, *Deutsche Kolonialromane 1884–1914 in ihrem Entstehungs- und Wirkungszusammenhang* (Bremen: Übersee-Museum, 1983), 16–52 for an overview of some of these activities to promote colonial education of the German population.

25. Werner Schiefel, *Bernhard Dernburg: 1865–1937, Kolonialpolitiker und Bankier im wilhelminischen Deutschland* (Zurich: Atlantis, 1974), 60.

26. Benninghoff-Lühl, *Deutsche Kolonialromane*, 33.

27. Matthias Erzberger, *Kolonial-Berufe* (Berlin: Verlag der Germania, 1912), 5.

28. Direktor Fabarius, *Der deutsche Kulturpionier: Nachrichten aus der deutschen Kolonialschule* (Witzenhausen: Eigenverlag, 1900), 5.

29. Ibid., 46–47.

30. Ibid., 45.

31. Ibid., 46.

32. J. A. Onnen, "Die kolonialen Bildungsstätten Deutschlands," *Deutsche Kolonial-Zeitung* 50.1 (1938): 50.

33. Direktor Fabarius, "Aufgabe und Arbeit der Deutschen Kolonialschule nach dem 'Vertrage' von Versaille," *Koloniale Rundschau* 15.1 (1925): 13.

34. Daniel Walther, "Creating Germans Abroad: White Education in German Southwest Africa, 1894–1914," *German Studies Review* 24 (2001): 325.

35. Ibid., 328.

36. Ibid., 329.

37. Hermann von Wißmann, "Zur Behandlung des Negers," *Das Deutsche Kolonialbuch*, ed. Hans Zache (Berlin: Wilhelm Andermann, 1925), 39.

38. Hans Zache, "Deutschlands koloniale Eingeborenenpolitik," *Das Deutsche Kolonialbuch* (Berlin: Wilhelm Andermann, 1925), 69.

39. Hauptmann Leue, "Unsere Eingeborenen," *Koloniale Monatsblätter* 9 (1913): 363.

40. See Hans Meyer, *Das deutsche Kolonialreich: Eine Länderkunde der deutschen Schutzgebiete*, 2 vols. (Leipzig, Vienna: Bibliographisches Institut, 1910).

41. See Missionar H. Vedder, "Eingeborenenerziehung im heutigen Südwest-Afrika," *Koloniale Rundschau* 15. 6 (1925): 183.

42. Marcia Wright, "Local Roots of Policy in German East Africa," *Journal of African History* 9. 4 (1968): 625.

43. Ibid., 629.

44. Anon., "Die Regierungsschule in Tanga," *Kolonie und Heimat* 1.23 (1908): 6.

45. Pfarrer E. Dinkelacker, "Bilder aus der Mittelschule in Bonaberi," *Jambo watu! Das Kolonialbuch der Deutschen*, ed. Willy Bolsinger and Hans Rauschnabel (Stuttgart: Steffen, 1927), 46.

46. Ibid., 48.

Afterword: From Empire to Federation

Anthony Pagden

"Empire" and "Imperialism," which since the end of the First World War have been topics in steady decline, are back. What had been portrayed in the work of such global theorists as Schumpeter and Hobson, not to mention several generations of historians of the various national empires, as an important but now superceded phase in the history of the evolution of the peoples of Europe, their overseas settler population, and of some parts of Asia, has returned—often thinly disguised as other kinds of international politics but recognizably part of a long historical legacy. The diverse essays in this book are all attempts to describe parts of that legacy. Much of this interest, which has reached well beyond the Academy, has been triggered by recent events: the latest Afghan war and the invasion of Iraq and their continuing, deleterious consequences. We now have a concept of "Empire Lite"—to go with Marlboro or Coca Cola Lite—a dusted off version of the older "informal empire" thesis but in a new tone of moral urgency. We have the claims made stridently by Niall Ferguson and more mutedly by Michael Ignatieff that empires can be forces for good in the world, that peace stability and a civilized order could only be sustained by the imposition of massive and extensive state power. The "liberal imperialism" of Alexis de Tocqueville and John Stuart Mill is not only beginning to be thinkable once again; it is even, with a number of important qualifications, beginning to seem attractive—and not merely to the State Department.

All of this contrasts sharply with the earlier historical, literary, and anthropological approaches to empire, which, for many years were undertaken by "postcolonial" studies. Postcolonialism has unquestionably changed the entire perception of the rise and fall of the modern European empires. The problem with the postcolonial movement—though much of the work that has been done in its name is indubitably distinguished—is that it was precisely *post* and *colonial*. It has been overwhelming concerned with what took place after empire. And it has tended to assume that empires, imperialism, colonies, and colonials were much the same kind of thing. It also assumed, without exception (and generally without argument), that all of these things were, *eo ipso*, bad. By addressing only these issues and by blurring the distinction between empires and colonies, and finally by almost entirely eliminating any account of the possible interaction between colonizer and colonized, between colonial subjects and the metropolis, and between the various European powers in any given region, it has had the effect of assuming that there was only one basic kind of empire—and that a European one—which imposed its rule in one kind of way, and that all of the subject peoples of all empires were subject in very much the same way.[1] It seems at best an irony that if the commonplace that the "negative construction of non-European others" always had a certain kind of inevitability—for it "is finally what founds and sustains European identity"—is true (see Paul Stevens on Antonio Negri and Michael Hardt), then European identity could not fail to be at some level the outcome of that construction. Yet the assumption seems always to be not only that the construction itself had been arrived at *ex nihilo* and then imposed on whatever "other" happens to be available, but that, notwithstanding the use of such devices, the European concept of self has always been static and unchanging wherever and whenever it might be found. But of course it never has been. Europeans are as varied as Asians or Africans or as any generalized cultural political or geographical group. And the European empires were different not only from one another but different within their own spheres of influence. American Indians were not regarded in the same ways as African or Indians or—in the British and French cases—as Greeks or Arabs. All empires are, and have been since Rome, conglomerates, closer in form to modern multinational companies than the mega-states as they have often been portrayed. As Jonathan Hart says here, "The meetings of cultures and 'multiculturalism' in the Grand Banks, slavery in the West Indies, French efforts in 'Florida' and alliances with, and representations of Native and other groups all qualify notions of monological empires." The same could be said of just about any intercultural contact on any imperial frontier anywhere.

Since this book is precisely an attempt to bring together differing views of the imperial process it might useful to ask what an "empire" is or, at least, how the concept has been understood over the centuries in which "imperialism" of one kind or another was perhaps the dominant force in European political social and cultural thinking.

It is possible to speak of a tribute distribution system of the kind that flourished in Central and South America, and in what is today Nigeria, in the late fifteenth century, as an empire. The term also applies to the union of semi-independent states held together by dynastic alliances of the kind that existed in southern and central Europe in the sixteenth century. Empire designates, furthermore, a metropolis and a bewildering array of overseas dependencies, colonies, dominions, protectorates, and the like, of the kind that described Britain in the nineteenth and early twentieth centuries, together with the kind of network of economic clientage that characterizes the relation of the First to the Third World. The multiple usages of the term certainly pose some difficulty.

Empires have always assumed the existence of a polity with some kind of center and one or more dependencies. In this limited sense, all the situations I have described are clearly "empires." But most, if not all, of the empires discussed in this book also have something else in common: they were largely brought about by conquest. For this reason, Benjamin Constant, writing in 1813, relegated all such projects to an earlier phase in human history, one he described as dominated by the "savage impulse" of war. Like many of the liberals of his generation, he believed or at least hoped that "pleasure and utility" had "opposed irony to every real or feigned enthusiasm"[2] of the kind on which most recently the Napoleonic empire had been built and thus had finally made such archaic impulses obsolete. Writing as the German empire was in the process of disintegration, Schumpeter in 1918 made much the same kind of observation in his celebrated book *Zur Soziologie der Imperialismen* when he described territorial expansion as "the purely instinctual inclination towards war and conquest" and, like Constant, relegated this to an earlier atavistic period of human history.[3]

Like Constant, Schumpeter also looked to some kind of economic determinism as the next phase of human evolution. In many ways too, both Constant's and Schumpeter's theses are reworkings in the language of post-Smithian economics of a very powerful Smithian claim: namely that in the modern world the relationships between peoples are those that Adam Smith, in common with most eighteenth-century economic theorists called broadly, "the commercial society." True commercial relations were incompatible with conquest and indeed with any kind of political restraints upon economic activity. As Smith had seen in 1776, a successful—from the British point of view—outcome of the American war would have been a long-term disaster for all those concerned. A system of independent friendly nations engaged in commercial relations was always to be preferred to any other kind of international relations. Above all it is to be preferred to the condition of reciprocal hostility and dependence that had characterized the relations between metropolis and colony in all the modern European empires. What Benjamin Disraeli was to call as late as 1852 "those wretched colonies" would inevitably, as Smith had intuited in 1766, become in Disraeli's words "a millstone around the neck of the mother country."[4]

On this account, rational calculation follows institutionalized violence as aristocratic, kin-based societies give way to bourgeois meritocracies. (The same could be said *mutatis mutandis* of the traditional Eurasian empires.) The final stage in this progress might possibly be one in which the political orders, which had underpinned both the ages of conquest and those of commerce as well as their respective imperial forms, are replaced by something else. The replacement might take the form of global order in which the notions of sovereignty, as it has been conceived since the eighteenth century, is displaced away from the individual, political, cultural unit—the modern nation-state—to something rather more amorphous: a modern—or postmodern—global society not unlike Immanuel Kant's *ius cosmopoliticum*. This might I suppose still come about. But if it does, it will not be for a while yet.

It is obvious that once a state acquires territories beyond the limits to which it has been traditionally confined—and in particular when it acquires territories that are a long way beyond those limits—it will inevitably become a different kind of state, a different culture to the one it was, and, in important ways, its peoples will cease to be the people they were or might have been. Empire is inescapably a process of exchange—however unequal it might be—by which no group can remain unaffected for long.

The history of Europe's empires might be summarized as follows: with the collapse of the Carolingian Empire in the early tenth century, any serious attempt to recreate the Roman *civitas* came effectively to an end. The nearest approximation, the empire of Charles V, although it deployed the language of Roman imperialism, was—at least before the conquests of America—in effect a conglomeration of territories, secured by dynastic marriage. The discovery of America, of searoutes to Asia, and of the profits to be had from the African slave trade, however, created the possibility of a new kind of empire, seagoing rather than land-based. (It is noteworthy that the only non-European empires discussed in this book, including Mughal, Ottoman, and Chinese, were all unlike their modern European counterparts in being land based—the extensive Ottoman use of seapower aside—as had been the empire of the ancient world.)

Despite the obvious Roman imperial trappings, which all the European overseas empires would finally acquire, their origins were not imperial in the classical sense. Until well into the seventeenth century, the word "empire" was used exclusively to describe either the Holy Roman Empire or territorial sovereignty within individual nation states themselves, not what Edmund Burke in 1776 would come to describe as "extended and detached empire." Neither the Spanish nor the Portuguese, nor even the French, ever spoke of "empire," in this sense and the British only began doing so consistently after the loss of America. When the term is used earlier, it most commonly refers to the union of the various kingdom of the British Isles. America, declared Adam Smith in 1776, was "a sort of splendid and showy equipage of the empire," which in his view Britain could not longer afford. "The rulers of Great Britain," he concluded, "have for more than a century past, amused the people with the imagination that they possessed a great empire on the west side of the Atlantic. This empire, however, has hitherto existed in imagination only. It has hitherto been not an empire but the project of an empire."[5]

As Smith was aware, in the political and social thought of Britain—in contrast to say France or Spain—there seemed to have been very little serious attempt to come to terms with what the possession of overseas colonies implied politically, economically, or morally. As Sir Robert Seeley famously remarked, as late as 1883 the relative paucity of discussion about the nature and the objective of empire in English contrived to give the impression that England had "conquered and peopled half the world in a fit of absence of mind."[6] It might be true, as Daniel Goffman and Christopher Stroop complain of modern historians, that they tend to see the British Empire as some kind of norm, but it certainly did not look that way to most contemporaries. "I know of no example of it either in ancient or modern history," wrote Disraeli in 1878, "No Caesar or Charlemagne ever presided over a dominion so peculiar."

What both Seeley and Disraeli were looking for was a constitutional definition of empire and both were in a sense looking in the wrong place. But it certainly was the case that before the late nineteenth century any sustained or coherent attempt to understand the imperial project was hindered in part by the inescapable supposition that whatever else an "empire" might be, it could only be a political order brought about by conquest. And most Europeans were unhappy with the idea of conquest either as a source of legitimation or as an adequate legal description of the delicate relationship between the settlers, the indigenous populations (where there were thought to be any), and the metropolis. The French hardly even employ the term in Canada, nor do the Dutch in Asia. Despite the fact that all their colonies in America were legally held to be "lands of conquest" and had been so ever since Henry VII's letters patent to John Cabot of 1496, the English tended to agree with John Locke's condemnation of conquest as a "far from setting up any government, as demolishing an House is from building a new one in the place."[7] Since the oceans could not in any obvious sense be conquered, only the seas were exempt from this distrust. "The Sea," as Andrew Fletcher declared in 1698, "is the only Empire which can naturally belong to us. Conquest is not our Interest."[8] Similarly, the Portuguese described their overseas possessions as *nossas Conquitas* in *terras e mares da Guiné e Indias* (Brazil was an exception) in reference not to peoples but to the seas and to those areas over which they claimed exclusive trading rights. Even the Spanish whose America empire was so obviously based on conquest banned all official use of the term in 1680.[9]

Despite this conceptual squeamishness, the fact remained, however, that by the beginning of the eighteenth century, the English, French, Dutch, Spanish, and Portuguese had extensive territorial possessions outside Europe—most acquired in one way or another by force. If these and their settler populations were to be incorporated into the "mother country" in some way that would obviate or obscure the obvious implications of their having been conquered territories, then some alternative description of them had to be found.

The move from "conquest" to "commerce" performed this function if, in the long run, it did little else. Called by Isaac de Pinto, the "craze of the century," commerce became a kind of universal panacea, a moralizing balm that could revive the older increasingly discredited image of "empire" and offer a new set of guidelines for its possible future development.[10] Commerce, however, suggested a different kind of relationship between peoples, one that did not necessarily involve dependency of any kind. The highly optimistic vision of the future offered by Diderot in his contributions to the abbé Raynal's *Histoire des deux Indes* in 1780 imagined a kind of universal trade federation in which the different peoples of the world would swap new technologies and basic scientific and cultural skills as readily as they would their foodstuffs.[11] By then of course the perception of the folly and the archaicness of empire had been reinforced by the loss of one major imperial possession—British North America—and the apparently impending loss of another: Spanish South America. By the end of the century even the Spanish—most particularly perhaps the

Spanish—were lamenting that "conquest" had been their undoing. If the message needed any further reenforcement, it was provided in ample detail by the short-lived Napoleonic Empire. As Constant hoped, this had demonstrated once and for all that no future imperial project was possible in a world in which societies were large, with varied and complex economic structures. As much for Constant as for Diderot, the future seemed, as we have seen, to lie in a world governed through the unintended but inescapably beneficial consequences of economic self-interest. "It may be stated as beyond controversy," declared Schumpeter in much the same vein, "that where free trade prevails no class has an interest in forcible expansion as such."[12]

Behind all of these different projects lurked the problem of how to reconcile the fact of extended rule over diverse peoples with a single conception of political power. To a greater or lesser degree, all the European imperial powers during the initial phase of European empire-building preserved at least the legal fiction that the inhabitants, both indigenous and European, of the overseas dominions were equally subjects of the same ruler. Fighting the American Indians, as the great sixteenth-century theologian Francisco de Vitoria observed, was no different from warring against the population of Seville. In practice, even legal practice, this may frequently not have been the case. But the legitimacy of empire rested on the assumption that it was. Unlike sovereignty within Europe, sovereignty beyond Europe was, as Hugo Grotius had insisted in 1631, very much a divisible notion and was to remain so within all subsequent conceptions of international relations in which non-European powers were involved. As Henry Maine, Law Member of the Viceroy of India's Council, declared in 1887, sovereignty "has always been regarded as divisible in international law."[13]

Divisible sovereignty implied that empire was, in law, a relationship. It had, therefore, to involve at least two parties. If it did not, as so often was the case, then like slavery on which it frequently relied, it could be as corrupting for the conqueror as it could for the conquered. Britain in the late eighteenth century—and in fact until the end of its empire in the mid-twentieth—faced this problem in a particularly acute manner. In the first place it had never been very clear about just what the relationship between mother country and the colony was. Indeed it had been willfully vague and contradictory on the subject. Until the late nineteenth century, the Portuguese had ruled their overseas dependencies as military camps, as, in effect, had the Dutch. The Spanish had maintained since at least the late sixteenth century that the Americas were kingdoms in the same sense as Aragon or Naples, of an extended and composite monarchy. Ever since Colbert's "Etablissement de la Compagnie des Indes Occidentales" of 1664, the French had simply incorporated the colonies into the Metropolis to the degree that the residue of that empire—the "Dom-Tom"—is still a constitute part of metropolitan France.

Britain, on the other hand, had done almost nothing to clarify what its empire was supposed to be about and was still struggling with the problem in the late 1960s. Britain was also unlike its European rivals in another way. The language in which the debates over Empire had been framed in Spain, France, or Portugal had been frequently religious, sometimes—as in Canada—feudal, sometimes economic, sometimes, as in the Spanish case, dependent upon the project of a universal sovereignty, and frequently all of these at once. By contrast, almost every British discussion of empire was driven by the belief that theirs was and had always been a constitution dedicated to the pursuit of "liberty."

Yet the British insistence that their empire was essentially dedicated to improving the condition, the "liberty," both political and economic, of all with whom it came into contact, was not a mere sentimental reflection nor a simple ideological camouflage—although it also served both those functions. It was an essential component of English and later, with still greater emphasis, British identity. But the rhetoric of liberty inevitably involved the paradox—as Arnaldo Momigliano observed with regard to Herodotus's conception of Greek freedom versus Persian tyranny—to which (it should be said) the British notion was heavily indebted—that "freedom required power, because power is a condition of freedom, but power proved, in fact unobtainable without ruling others."[14] The whole "civilizing" project, which became such a central feature of every aspect of imperial policy until the end, ultimately foundered on this paradox. There were two moments, however, when what it fully implied became most obvious. One was the American Revolution, the other the attempt to impeach for corruption and for having acted like an Oriental despot, Warren Hastings governor of Bengal. Both involved Edmund Burke, and no one in the eighteenth century had understood the paradoxes of empire and its discontents quite like Burke.

Like Adam Smith, Burke speaks freely and frequently of the "British Empire." Like Smith, his conception of "Empire" was one that rested upon the ancient perception of an extended *civitas*—a single polity that embraced both the mother country and its colonies, however remote. It was this that allowed him to speak of "our distressed fellow-citizens in India."[15] Like Smith, Burke too thought of this empire as incomplete, as a polity that had singularly failed to integrate the various parts of which it was composed. The evil was twofold. It threatened the lives and well-being of the Indians. Less obviously, but quite as significantly, it also threatened to undermine Britain itself, or what the British constitution had always stood for. "I am certain," he wrote, "that every means effectual to preserve India from oppression is a guard to preserve the British Constitution from its worst corruption."[16]

The status of India was highly ambiguous, ruled as it was by a private trading company, but there could be no doubt that the Indians were beholden to His Majesty just like the Americans, and any illiberal or tyrannous act against them was *eo ipso* a menace to the stability of the constitution itself. The government of India was not the means to personal aggrandisement Hastings had made of it. It was a sacred trust, "given," as Burke insisted, "by an incomprehensible dispensation of Divine providence into our hands." As he must have been aware, Burke was echoing an vision of the possibilities and duties inherent in imperial rule, which went back at least as far as the Roman Republic. As long as "the empire of the Roman People maintained itself by acts of service, not of oppression," Cicero had written, "our government could be called more accurately a protectorate (*patrocinium*) of the world than a dominion (*imperium*)."[17] To abuse this sacred trust, to descend as Sulla had done, and Hastings after him, to bullying belligerency, threatened the very existence of what Burke thought of as "the civilization of Europe," and it threatened it in very much the same way as the French Revolution was to do some years later.[18]

"Our Government and our Laws," Burke wrote to Lord Loughborough in 1796," are beset by two different enemies, which are sapping its foundations, Indianism and Jacobinism. In some cases they act separately, in some they act in conjunction: But of this I am sure; that the first is the worse by far."[19] Knowing what Burke thought about the Revolution, this was damning indeed.

For Burke, "Indianism"—the peculiar brand of imperial pillage practiced by the East India Company—derived as did Jacobinism from conquest: the one external the other internal. A conquest was always in Burke's view an act of dismantlement, as it had been for John Locke. It involved the annihilation of the existing customs, laws, traditions, and the like of which all societies are composed. In Burke's view—and it has been shared, *mutatis mutandis*, by many later antirevolutionaries from Joseph de Maistre, Johann Georg Hamann, and Johann Gottfried von Herder all the way to Hans Gadamer and Charles Taylor—what his enlightened (French) contemporaries condemned as prejudices were in fact the materials from which all our knowledge of the world and hence the communities we built for ourselves to inhabit are composed. They could—indeed should—be subject to criticism and refinement. But they should never be swept away unexamined in favor of some other, necessarily abstract and alien, set of beliefs. This was why, unlike the overhasty French, the English, or so Burke wished to believe, "instead of exploding general prejudices," employ their sagacity to discover the latent wisdom that prevails in them. "If they find what they seek, and they seldom fail, they think it more wise to continue the prejudice, with the reason involved, than to cast away the coat of prejudice and leave nothing but the naked reason."[20] Conquest, revolution, and the "exploding of general principles," which, in Burke's narrative had led inexorably to the Revolution, were alike in seeking to replace all of these things with a single abstraction. Some years later, Benjamin Constant, who had of course witnessed the smooth transition from Revolution to Empire, which even Burke could not have predicted, made precisely the same observation. "It is somewhat remarkable," he wrote,

> that uniformity should never have encountered greater favour than in a revolution made in the name of the rights and liberty of men ... While patriotism exists only by a vivid attachment to the interests, the way of life, the customs of some locality, our so-called patriots have declared war on all of these. They have dried up this natural source of patriotism and have sought to replace it by a factitious passion for an abstract being, a general idea stripped of all that can engage the imagination and speak to the memory.[21]

In the end, Burke's and Constant's objection to modern empires was oddly much like Herder's. Although neither shared Herder's quasi-mystical attachment to nature, both held that societies—nations—were human creations, which in time came to resemble natural types. Their "goodness" or "badness" could not be assessed by some universal calculus. They were only good or bad in terms of what they were able to provide for their peoples. Thus we see why Burke was so adamant in his support of what must have seemed indefensible to most of his contemporaries, namely the *Shari' a*, which he went so far as to describe as "the wisest, the most learned, and the most enlightened jurisprudence that perhaps ever existed in the world."[22] Any attempt to interfere with such complex organisms by human agency could only lead to their elimination. And their elimination could only result in tyranny—intellectual, moral, and ultimately political. Burke, however, shared none of Herder's belief in the power of nature to undo what man had done. It was not nature that would in the end dissolve what Herder called "those inflated bladders," that is, the European overseas empires. Only human action could achieve that.

"Indianism" threatened to destroy the "Greater Britain"—to use Charles Dilke's term—which for Burke constituted the British *imperium*. It was the reason—or at least one of the reasons—for Burke's defense of the American revolutionaries. In his view, they at least had not been conquerors. They had settled *terrae nullius*, developed untended lands, built communities in accordance with ancient British practices, and in so doing had earned themselves the right of self-determination. This was not a "revolution" as Jacobinism had been. It was precisely as its leaders insisted: an attempt to preserve the "polity, laws, and manners" against a mother country, which had itself become a would-be conqueror. And in so doing the British were once again threatening to destroy their own constitution.

For both Burke and Adam Smith, the British Americans were like children come of age. A freed, but in some sense tethered, America would constitute the basis for a truly Greater Britain, something that could never be achieved within the confines of the older imperial thinking. Indeed, as many had observed, what was wrong with eighteenth-century imperialism was that it had tried to introduce the new while stubbornly refusing to abandon the old. "The present policy of Europe with respect to America," wrote the marquis de Mirabeau in 1758 in his great treatise on universal commerce, *L'Ami des hommes*, was a perpetual struggle to combine three entirely incompatible "esprits"—that of domination, that of commerce, and that of "population" (that is, settlement) into "a new ... monstrous system."[23] Ultimately it could only fail, and fail it duly did.

Very few of the critics of empire in the eighteenth century, not even Mirabeau and certainly not Burke, were abolitionists. If they had pursued the logic of their own arguments they could not have failed to be. But they also knew that the realities of power politics—the need to maintain prestige in the international arena—would always overcome any calculation of benefits, however obvious. Even Smith, who clearly did believe—if only for simple economic reasons—that Britain would have done well to abandon all its colonies, return Florida to Spain and, far more contentiously, Canada to France, recognized that no monarchy could appear to be making concessions to those officially classified as "rebellious subject."

The belief in the possibility of transforming the European empires into some other more just and ultimately economically more rational kind of polity came to nothing, however, and not only because the conditions necessary for their fulfillment remained, as Kant had warned, conditions of future time—and a future international political order. They also came to grief on the rock of the one historical development that even Burke, much less Kant, could not have adequately predicted: the modern nation state.

Nationalism has traditionally been seen as an instrument of liberation from colonial rule. And in many areas from late nineteenth-century Italy and Ireland to mid twentieth-century Egypt or Angola, it was. But it is often forgotten that in deploying the concept of the indivisibility and sanctity of the "nation" to tear down the older Empires, the insurgents and the dependent and colonized peoples were in fact appropriating to themselves a creed that their conquers had themselves created in very different circumstances.

The rise of the nation state within Europe in the years after the Congress of Vienna transformed the nature of empire by making the acquisition of overseas possessions a source of national pride and a potential instrument of national cohesion in times of crisis. It some sense, of course, it had always been that. The Roman general Scipio Africanus could evade charges of corruption by appealing to the Roman people in the name of what he had achieved for *their* empire. Empire was always a competitive business, and as Barbara Fuchs describes in her essay, the languages of empire tend to replicate themselves across different polities. The scramble in the seventeenth century by the English and French for possessions in the Atlantic had been driven overwhelmingly by the desire to "catch up" with Spain, as one commentator phrased it. But the modern nation was dependent to a far greater degree than the early modern European monarchies had been by the need to satisfy public opinion, without the support of which, as Constant had seen, no future, post-Revolutionary society could hope to survive for long. It was for instance, the main ground on which Tocqueville supported the French invasion of Algeria in 1830. As Linda Hutcheon and Michael Hutcheon rightly say in their essay, "the real motive for empire after Napoleon was not commerce or conquest, but rather a matter of restoring prestige." The French occupation of North Africa might have any number of benefits for both the settlers and the Arab population. Above all it would bring "civilization" in which Tocqueville, like Constant, like John Stuart Mill, was as firm a believer as his Enlightened predecessors had been. But the immediate motive was to reestablish the image of France still tarnished by the defeat of Napoleon, and the hope—unfulfilled as it turned out—that a quick victory might allow the unpopular government of Charles X victory at the polls. The same is broadly true of the concept of the

"British Empire," which was largely a fabrication of Disraeli intent on shoring up the image of a widely unpopular monarchy. Disreali's "British Empire" was, however, some distance from Smith's or Burke's. No sacred trust was involved. In Joseph Conrad's famous description, it was "only the taking away [of the earth] from those who have a different complexion or slightly flatter noses than ourselves." In the new nationalist calculus, the more of this earth you could take away, the greater you became. "C is for colonies," declared the *ABC for Baby Patriots* published in 1899: "Rightly we boast, / That of all the great nations/ Great Britain has the most." As Lord Curzon remarked the year before, imperialism had indeed now become "the faith of a nation."[24]

In some respects the second phase of European empire-building, which began in the second half of the nineteenth century, seems to have been a return to an earlier world. Only now, with enormously enhanced and superior technology, the maxim gun and the steam ship, the European powers were able to overrun most of the non-European world in a remarkably short time. (It has been calculated that in 1800 the major European powers, Russia and the United States, between them occupied or controlled some thirty-five percent of the surface of the planet; by 1878 they had taken sixty-seven percent and by 1914 over eighty-four percent.)[25] These figures are, of course, highly suspect. "Controlled" can mean anything from Algeria or Ireland to the Chinese customs service or the Mandate of Palestine. But they do convey at least a sense of the immense speed and range of their hegemony.

Yet for all that, the new European conquistadors could sometimes look depressingly like the old, the forms of government that they helped to create and above all the conception of "empire" that they fostered were, in certain significant respects, very different. One thing at least that had emerged from both the periods of intense introspection, which had followed the imperial political and economic crises of the second half of the eighteenth century and the rearranging of the balance of power between the various European states after the end of the Seven Years' War, was that any new imperial venture could not long remain the kind of run-and-grab operation that had characterized much of the old.

At the back of the eighteenth- and early-nineteenth-century confrontation with empire had been the conviction that empires were wholes that had to include, at least to some degree, all those caught up in them. Empire was a contract that somehow had to bring well-being to all its peoples without at the same time seriously damaging their previous ways of life. Burke had conceived this to be a moral and political objective. So had Constant and in a sense Tocqueville. Smith had very largely conceived it as an economic necessity. It could also be refigured as an anthropological principle: Bronislaw Malinowski, for instance, declared F. D. Lugard's conception of "indirect Rule" to be "a complete surrender to the functional point of view" that African society should not be tampered with since their ways of life were "functionally" the best suited to the conditions in which they had evolved.[26] Although the older enlightenment vision of a global order of trading nations had vanished with the French Revolution and the Napoleonic Wars, the idea of empire as extended protectorate had survived, and with it the project for transforming empire into some kind of federation. Burke, Smith, and Lord Kames had all proposed some kind of federal solution to the British–American crisis, as had both Turgot and the Count of Aranda for Spanish America.[27] All of these, however, had remained shadowy projects that, as Smith lamented, would always run foul of the need to maintain power and dignity which any concession to the colonists would greatly diminish both in the eyes of potential enemies and "in the eyes of our own people who would probably impute mal-administration."[28] They also stopped short of a fully federated state since, at least in the British case, the effect of distance was generally held to have rendered the various peoples to the empire "strangers" to one another, no matter their origins.

By the time Robert Seeley came to write *The Expansion of England* in 1883, however, modern technologies of communication had shrunk the Atlantic Ocean, which for Burke had seemed an insuperable obstacle to federation, until "it seems scarcely broader than the sea between Greece and Sicily."[29] It was now possible to envisage a true "Greater Britain," which would constitute a global state. Like most imperial federalists, Seeley is not very precise about what form this would take. Like most he assumes that it will be one in which the settler populations will have the upper hand. Like most, however, he is still haunted by Burke's concern that even if the various indigenous peoples of the empire were to be absorbed only slowly into the administrative fabric of the empire, Greater Britain must ultimately become some kind of multicultural community, even if many of the Empire's present subjects—the Maoris, the Australian Aborigines, the "Hottentots," and the American Indians—those "dying nations" singled out for extinction by Lord Salisbury in 1898, would in the process probably vanish altogether.

What has changed between Smith and Burke and Seeley is that whereas the enlightened vision of the future of empire involved the final withering away of the imperial state—the final undoing of the process of conquest that had created empire in the first place—federation envisaged precisely the transformation of that state. Imperial federalism has indeed much in common with the kind of federalizing solutions that began to emerge after the collapse of Napoleon and the Congress of Vienna as a solution to the difficulties facing Europe itself—from the kind of pan-European federation that both Constant's companion Madame de Stael and intermittently Constant himself enthusiastically endorsed, to Pierre-Joseph Proudhon's *Du principe fédératif,* all the way to the Monet Plan. (I do not want to get involved here in discussion over whether or not the Europe Union is an "empire." But that it owes a very considerable intellectual debt to the several attempts to transform the older Europe empire during the nineteenth century is obvious.)

Like its enlightened predecessors, imperial federalism itself came to nothing—unless we consider the British Commonwealth to be something. But it served to revive some lingering notion of Burke's "sacred trust." Casting his eye over Britain and its soon-to be-liberated colonies in the late 1940s, the British prime minister and architect of the Welfare State, Clement Attlee, remarked prophetically, "We cannot create a heaven inside and leave a hell outside and expect to survive." Since then, of course, the heaven has come to seem more like purgatory and the hell has become, if anything, yet more hellish. Today the former European imperial powers are still struggling with the problems that Burke had seen so clearly, but in ways that Burke could never have envisaged. For as the colonies have one by one been reduced to a few embattled settler communities, Monserrat, Gibraltar, the Malvinas/Falkland Islands, or heavily subsidized protectorates—Tahiti, Martinique—or fortress garrisons—Ceuta, Melilla—the populations of the old empires have come flooding into Europe in a reverse migration. And it is now Europe itself that is well on its way to becoming a federation. How it will adapt itself in the long run to the fact that most of its major constituent parts have been formed though the experience of empire, and that many of them—Britain, France, and Spain most obviously—are still inescapably attached to former colonies, remains to be seen.

NOTES

1. There are, of course, some distinguished exceptions. See, for instance, Catherine Hall, *Civilizing Subjects. Metropole and Colony in the English Imagination 1830–1867* (Cambridge: Polity Press, 2002).

2. *The Spirit of Conquest and Usurpation and Their Relation to European Civilization*, in *The Political Writings of Benjamin Constant*, ed. B. Fontana (Cambridge: Cambridge University Press, 1988), 53, 55.

3. Joseph A. Schumpeter, *Imperialism and Social Classes* [Zur Soziologie der Imperialismen], trans. Heinz Norden, ed. Paul M. Sweezy (New York: Augustus M. Kelley, Inc., 1951), 7, 8.

4. Quoted in ibid., 12.

5. *An Inquiry into the Nature and Causes of the Wealth of Nations*, 2 vols., *The Glasgow Edition of the Works and Correspondence of Adam Smith*, ed. R. H. Campbell and A. S. Skinner, (Oxford: Oxford University Press), 2: 946–47.

6. Robert Seeley, *The Expansion of England* (London: Macmillan, 1883), 12.

7. John Locke, *Second Treatise*, 2.175 in *Locke's Two Treatises of Government*. A Critical Edition with Introduction and Notes by Peter Laslett, second ed. (Cambridge: Cambridge University Press, 1967), 403.

8. Andrew Fletcher, "A Discourse on Government with Relation to Militias," in *The Political Works of Andrew Fletcher* (London, 1737), 66.

9. *Nueva Recopilacion de leyes de los reynos de las Indias*, Bk. 4 Tit. I Ley 6, 1791, II, 4.

10. "Lettre sur la jalousie du commerce," in *Traité de la circulation et du credit* (Amsterdam, 1771), 234.

11. See Anthony Pagden, *Lords of All the World: Ideologies of Empire in Spain, Britain and France c.1500–c.1800* (New Haven and London: Yale University Press, 1995), 178–87.

12. Schumpeter, *Imperialism*, 99.

13. Quoted in Edward Keene, *Beyond the Anarchical Society Grotius, Colonialism and Order in World Politics* (Cambridge: Cambridge University Press, 2002), 63.

14. "Persian Empire and Greek Freedom," in *The Idea of Freedom: Essays in Hour of Isaiah Berlin*, ed. Alan Ryan (Oxford: Oxford University Press, 1979), 139–51 at 149.

15. "Speech on the Nabob of Arcot's Debts," quoted in Uday Singh Mehta, *Liberalism and Empire. A Study in Nineteenth-Century British Liberal Thought* (Chicago: University of Chicago Press, 1999), 157.

16. See P. J. Marshall, *The Impeachment of Warren Hastings* (London: Oxford University Press, 1965).

17. Cicero, *On Duties*, trans. and ed. M.T. Griffin and E.M. Atkins Cambridge: (Cambridge University Press, 1991), 72.

18. David Bromwich, ed., *On Empire, Liberty and Reform. Speeches and Letters of Edmund Burke* (New Haven: Yale University Press, 2000), 15–16.

19. Quoted in Mehta, *Liberalism and Empire*, 166.

20. Edmund Burke, *Reflections on the Revolution in France*, ed. J. G. A. Pocock (Indianapolis: Hackett Pub. Co., 1987), 76–77.

21. *The Spirit of Conquest and Usurpation and Their Relation to European Civilization, The Political Writings of Benjamin Constant*, ed. B. Fontana (Cambridge: Cambridge University Press, 1988) 73–74.

22. Quoted in Mehta, *Liberalism and Empire*, 185–86.

23. Quoted in Pagden, *Lords of All the World*, 186.

24. Quoted in Harold Nicolson, *Curzon: The Last Phase 1919–1925* (New York: Harcourt Bruce and Company, 1939), 13.

25. Paul Kennedy, *The Rise and Fall of the Great Powers: Economic Change and Military Conflict from 1500 to 2000* (New York: Random House, 1987), 148–49.

26. Bronislaw Malinowski, "Practical Anthropology," *Africa* 2 (1929): 22–38.

27. Adam Smith, "Thoughts on the State of the Contest with America," in *The Correspondence of Adam Smith*, ed. E. G Mossner and J. S. Ross, *The Glasgow Edition of the Works and Correspondence of Adam Smith* (Oxford: Oxford University Press, 1977), 6: 382–83; Kames, *Sketches of the History of Man*, 2 vols. (Edinburgh, 1774), 2: iv.

28. Smith, "Thoughts on the State," 6: 383.

29. Seeley, *The Expansion of England*, 297.

Notes on Contributors

Florence D'Souza is the author of *Quand la France découvrit l'Inde*, Editions de l'Harmattan, Paris (1995). She is Lecturer in English at the University of Lille 3 and has been researching the presence of the British in India in the eighteenth century.

Dorothy Figueira is Professor and Head of Comparative Literature at the University of Georgia. She is author of *Translating the Orient* (1991), *The Exotic: A Decadent Quest* (1994), and *Aryans, Jews and Brahmins: Theorizing Authority through Myths of Identity* (2002).

Barbara Fuchs is Associate Professor of Romance Languages at the University of Pennsylvania. She is the author of *Mimesis and Empire: The New World, Islam and European Identities* (2001), *Passing for Spain: Cervantes and the Fictions of Identity* (2003), *and Romance* (2004).

Daniel Goffman is Professor of History at DePaul University, Chicago. He is the author of many books, including *Izmir and the Levantine World, 1550–1650* (1990), *Britons in the Ottoman Empire, 1642–1660* (1998), *The Ottoman City Between East and West: Istanbul, Izmir, and Aleppo*, with Edhem Eldem and Bruce Masters (1999), and *The Ottoman Empire and Early Modern Europe* (2002).

Jonathan Hart, Visiting Professor and Fellow (Princeton), is the author of numerous books and collections, including *Representing the New World* (2001), *By Speech or Signs: Columbus, Shakespeare and the Interpretation of the New World* (2002), *Comparing Empires: European Colonialism from Portuguese Expansion to the Spanish-American War* (2003), and *Contesting Empires: Promotion, Opposition, and Slavery*, (2004).

Linda Hutcheon, Professor of English and Comparative Literature at the University of Toronto, is the author of numerous books, including *Narcissistic Narrative* (1980), *Formalism and the Freudian Aesthetic* (1984), *A Theory of Parody* (1985), *A Poetics of Postmodernism* (1988), *The Canadian Postmodern* (1989), *Leonard Cohen and His Writing* (1989), *The Politics of Postmodernism* (1989), *Splitting Images: Contemporary Canadian Ironies* (1991), *Irony's Edge: The Theory and Politics of Irony* (1994), and most recently, two books on opera, coauthored with Michael Hutcheon. Among her numerous other achievements is her election to the position of President of the Modern Languages Association in 1999.

Robert Markley is Professor of English at the University of Illinois and Editor of *The Eighteenth Century: Theory and Interpretation*. He has authored several books, including *Fallen Languages: Crises of Representation in Newtonian England, 1660–1740* (1993), *Dying Planet: Mars and the Anxieties of Ecology from the Canals to Terraformation* (Duke University Press, forthcoming), and *Fictions of Eurocentrism: The Far East and the English Imagination 1600–1800* (Cambridge University Press, forthcoming).

Nabil I. Matar, Professor of English and Head of the Humanities and Communication Department, Florida Institute of Technology, is the author of over fifty articles and five books, including *Islam in Britain, 1558–1685* (1998) and *Turks, Moors, and Englishmen in the Age of Discovery* (1999). He has produced the introduction for *Piracy, Slavery, and Redemption: Barbary Captivity Narratives from Early Modern England* by Daniel J. Vitkus (2001); *Renaissance Europe through Arab Eyes* is in progress.

Kamakshi P. Murti is Professor and Chair of the Department of German, Middlebury College. Her most recent book is *India: The Seductive and Seduced Other of German Orientalism*.

Anthony Pagden, Professor in the Department of Political Science at UCLA, is the author of numerous books and editions, including *Peoples and Empires* (2001), *Lords of All the World: Ideologies of Empire in Spain, Britain and France c.1500–c.1800* (1995), and *European Encounters with the New World: From Renaissance to Romanticism* (1993). His most recent book, *The Idea of Europe, from Antiquity to the Union*, is forthcoming from Cambridge University Press.

Patricia M. Pelley, Assistant Professor of History at Texas Tech University, is author of articles on Asian historiography and a book, *Postcolonial Vietnam: Visions of the Present and Past* (Duke, 2002) in the series "Asia-Pacific: Culture, Politics, and Society." Her new research focuses on Chinese immigration to Vietnam in the nineteenth and twentieth centuries.

Balachandra Rajan, Professor Emeritus at the University of Western Ontario, Canada, has written six books on Milton, Yeats, Eliot, the unfinished poem, and the representation of India in imperial discourse. These include *"Paradise Lost" and the Seventeenth Century Reader* (1947, 1967), *W.B. Yeats, a Critical Introduction* (1965), *The Lofty Rhyme: A Study of Milton's Major Poetry* (1970), *The Overwhelming Question: A Study of Poetry of T. S. Eliot* (1976), *The Form of the Unfinished: English Poetics from Spenser to Pound* (1985), *Under Western Eyes: India from Milton to Macaulay* (1999). Professor Rajan is an Honoured Scholar of the Milton Society and a Fellow and medallist of the Royal Society of Canada.

Shankar Raman is Associate Professor in the Literature Faculty at the Massachusetts Institute of Technology. His first book, *Framing "India":*

The Colonial Imaginary in Early Modern Culture, was published in 2001 by Stanford University Press. *Untimely Meditations: Early Modern Crises of Representation* is in progress.

Elizabeth Sauer, Professor of English holds a Chancellor's Research Chair at Brock University, Canada. She is author of *Barbarous Dissonance and Images of Voice in Milton's Epics* (1996) and *"Paper-contestations" and Textual Communities in England 1640–1675* (2005), and is coeditor of *Agonistes: Arenas of Creative Contest* (1997), *Milton and the Imperial Vision* (1999), winner of the Milton Society of America Irene Samuel Memorial Award, *Books and Readers in Early Modern England: Material Studies* (2002), *Reading Early Modern Women* (2004), and *Literature and Religion in Early Modern England: Case Studies* (2003).

Paul Stevens holds a Canada Research Chair in English and Comparative Literature at the University of Toronto. He is the author of *Imagination and the Presence of Shakespeare in "Paradise Lost"* (1985), and coeditor of *Discontinuities: New Essays on Renaissance Literature and Criticism* (1998) and *Early Modern Nationalism and Milton's England* (in progress). He has twice been awarded the Milton Society of America's Hanford Prize for most distinguished article.

Christopher Stroop holds a B.A. in History and German from Ball State University. He is currently studying Russian and teaching English in Vladimir, Russia, and is beginning his Ph.D. in Russian history at Standford in 2004.

Sabine Wilke is Professor of German and Chair of the Department of Germanics at the University of Washington. She has published many books and articles on theory, intellectual history, feminism, and twentieth-century German literature and culture, including most recently *Ambiguous Embodiment: Construction and Destruction of Bodies in Modern German Literature and Culture* (2000).

INDEX